W9-CUJ-310

A
COMMUNITY
IN LIMBO

A COMMUNITY IN LIMBO

AN ANTHROPOLOGICAL
STUDY OF AN AMERICAN
COMMUNITY ABROAD

Dennison Nash

INDIANA UNIVERSITY PRESS
Bloomington & London

COPYRIGHT © 1970 BY INDIANA UNIVERSITY PRESS
All rights reserved
No part of this book may be reproduced or utilized in any
form or by any means, electronic or mechanical, including
photocopying and recording, or by any information storage
and retrieval system, without permission in writing from
the publisher. The Association of American University
Presses' Resolution on Permissions constitutes the only
exception to this prohibition.

Library of Congress catalog card number: 72–98985
SBN: 253–11285–0
Published in Canada by Fitzhenry & Whiteside Limited,
Don Mills, Ontario
Manufactured in the United States of America

*To the Memory of
Nancy Cugat*

For more than twenty Years I had been almost continually engaged in Journeys and Voyages and had often undergone severe Tryals, as I thought; great hardships, cold, rain, Snow, heat, fatigue, bad rest, indifferent nourishment, want of Sleep &c. &c. &c. But I had never experienced any Thing like this Journey. If it were now left to my Choice to perform my first Voyage to Europe with all its horrors or this Journey through Spain, I should prefer the former. . . .

JOHN ADAMS, *Autobiography*

CONTENTS

PREFACE

W HAT HAPPENS TO AMERICANS WHEN THEY GO abroad? The practical aspects of this question seem to be particularly pressing at a time when upwards of two million Americans are living overseas and the number visiting foreign places (voluntarily or involuntarily) is increasing each year. However, reliable knowledge about the fate of these people is hard to find. We have a number of impressionistic accounts in which the concepts of "culture shock" and "acculturation" stand out, but systematic research organized by appropriate theory has only begun to throw light on this subject. This book, in reporting on the adaptation of a small group of American expatriates in a large city in northeast Spain, takes a small step in this direction.

The problem of Americans' adaptation abroad may be fitted into a broad area of theoretical concern which has animated sociologists and anthropologists over the years, i.e., the psychology of social or cultural change. Sociological interest in this problem has been expressed by the study of people in the process of moving from one group to another or of becoming assimilated into a new group; sociologists have conducted numerous studies of immigrants to the United States and to American cities,[1] people in the grip of vertical mobility,[2] and American soldiers at various stages of their odyssey during World War II.[3] Anthropological interest has been demonstrated in acculturation studies which detail the psychological consequences for primitive peoples of contact between primitive and modern cultures.[4] Both anthropologists and sociologists appear to have been struck by the dramatic changes being effected in and by modern Western culture, but they have approached the study of the individual's side of these changes from different perspectives.

The anthropological effort, which has been carried on mainly by

members of the so-called culture and personality school, has been
heavily dependent on psychoanalytic and, to a lesser extent, learning theory. Perhaps less sophisticated psychologically, the sociological approach has been strongly influenced by W. I. Thomas' social
psychology and by subsequent developments in symbolic interaction
and reference group theory. As Wallace [5] has demonstrated, the
different approaches to the problem are not mutually exclusive, but
may be considered within the same theoretical framework.

One promising approach to the psychology of culture change—
one which applies especially to the study of mobile individuals—
has not received the attention which it appears to deserve. We refer
to the theoretical leads provided by Georg Simmel [6] and Alfred
Schutz [7] in pointing to the stranger as an object (or subject) of
sociological and psychological concern. Until quite recently, the
latent possibilities of the stranger concept for theoretical development and empirical research had not been tapped. Now, however, a
small but growing literature has demonstrated the viability of this
concept in different situations and its potential for generating test-
able hypotheses. One interesting line of research in this area has
dealt with the adaptation of the stranger and factors which are related to this adaptation. From the results of a series of controlled
experiments, it now is possible to piece together a fairly coherent
picture of individual and collective reactions to taking the role of
stranger.[8] This book, in part, represents an attempt to test this picture against the relatively uncontrolled conditions of the real world.
We will be concerned here with a group of expatriates who were
something more than travelers and something less than immigrants.
Our principal interest is in the adaptation of a group of American
residents in a Spanish setting; but as far as the theoretical justification for this study is concerned, we might as well be studying the
adaptation of Americans in Ethiopia or Eskimos in Timbuktu.

Other things being equal, a preliminary study in any field ought
to generate hypotheses of broad rather than narrow significance. It
is more likely to accomplish this end if it deals with the typical
rather than the atypical case. The bulk of resident expatriates in the
real world appear to live in overseas communities which mediate

their adaptation to foreign places. Unfortunately for our theoretical interest, a very large number of Americans overseas live in more or less complete "Little Americas," i.e., large communities with prefabricated, externally supported American institutions. Because such communities tend to screen most of their members from significant contact with the foreign, they could not be used in a study which concerns itself with the adaptation of the individual to a changed situation. There are, however, some American communities abroad which do not possess such effective institutional screens. The members of such communities could be considered more or less bona fide strangers who face the problem of adaptation to a changed situation. One of these smaller overseas communities could serve as an appropriate arena in which to carry out a preliminary investigation of American adaptation abroad.

Not all of these communities would serve, however. Even without their own institutional screen, a group of expatriates may be protected from the problem of adapting to the foreign by certain situational factors. If the culture into which they have moved is highly compatible, or if they are very powerful, problems of adaptation could be minimized to the point where they would be difficult to observe. Certainly any complete study of American adaptation abroad would have to consider powerful Americans in highly compatible cultures, but a preliminary study could not afford the luxury of dealing with such expatriates. Therefore it was important to select for investigation a less powerful community located in a comparatively incompatible foreign culture. Of these, I ruled out those in which I had no cultural facility because the study had to be completed in a comparatively short space of time (eight months or less). If I were to have encountered the same problems of adaptation as my American subjects, there would have been insufficient time to function effectively as a field worker. Because of my previous experience in Hispanic culture, judged to be comparatively incompatible for Americans,[9] I sought to locate an American overseas community in one of the Hispanic areas of the world.

In order to ensure the "typicality" of my American subjects, I began looking for a community which conformed to the strictures mentioned above and was comprised largely of average Americans engaged in ordinary overseas pursuits such as business, diplomacy, military missions, and missionary work. These people were more likely to reflect central tendencies in American culture than would a group of American bohemians. Since it was not possible to conduct a longitudinal study, and since some reference to the home culture of the sojourners would have to be made, it was considered advisable to come as close to the ordinary American as one can get in an overseas location.

Finally, because it was to be a pioneer study, it was important to cover the problematic ground both thoroughly and deeply. With the limited amount of time available, the community to be studied would have to be small. Once the significant parameters of the problem had been discovered and defined, it would be possible to turn loose hordes of interviewers armed with schedules on both small and large communities in various overseas locations.[10] In a preliminary study, however, it is especially important to allow the situation and the problem to reveal itself and to suggest the line of inquiry and the method of study. I felt that at this stage of our knowledge of American adaptation abroad, it would be more valuable to look at and listen well to a few people rather than a great many. Accordingly, this study does not employ rigorous, standardized methods of survey research, but rather the traditional anthropological technique of participant observer.

THE APPROACH

Although no study of an American community abroad had been attempted by the time the present investigation was begun, the subject of Americans overseas had been of some interest to novelists and scholars. In my approach to the problem of American adaptation abroad and to the community in which the field work would be carried out, I was especially influenced by two books: *The Overseas Americans* by Cleveland, Mangone, and Adams[11] and *The Ugly American* by Lederer and Burdick.[12] Almost totally devoid of theory and lacking methodological sophistication, *The Overseas Americans* nevertheless remains the definitive work on Americans abroad. Besides presenting many facts about Americans overseas, it offers a number of stimulating hypotheses which call for investigation. Any student of Americans in foreign settings can refer to it with profit. It has proved indispensable in orienting, guiding, and reporting on this particular investigation.

The Ugly American, though not a scholarly work, was significant for the present study because of the effect which it had had on people. The social scientist must deal with people who can either smooth his path or put obstacles in his way. In this study I had to contend with many who had read or heard about *The Ugly American.* This book had brought into the foreground of the nation's consciousness the subject of Americans overseas. Lederer and Burdick tended to portray the Americans in Southeast Asia, especially, as a sorry crew who were actively contributing to defeat abroad. The wrecking operation carried on in the book was greeted with enthusiasm and consternation. On the whole, the reaction in Washington probably turned out to be constructive. However, among people overseas who had been singed by the Lederer and Burdick prose, an attitude of fear and suspicion began to develop toward people who were concerned with them. It was felt by many that any study in this area would end up by casting the worst possible light on overseas Americans. It is difficult to say how much *The Ugly American* helped and how much it hindered this study. Some Americans (mostly civilian government people and their satellites) did not cooperate because they feared the study would become another sensational exposé of their alleged foibles and ineptitude. Others were pleased to be in the study and used the label *Ugly American* as a kind of badge of significance.

In order to select a community which conformed to the strictures listed above and to secure some cooperation in advance, I enlisted the aid of overseas experts and officials in large overseas organizations. Almost all of them turned out to be both knowledgeable and helpful. People in high places, especially, seemed to have learned the lesson of *The Ugly American.* Because they were interested in improving the posture of their representatives abroad, they **were** able to grasp immediately the practical value of a study of Americans overseas. None of these people were reluctant to put me in contact with their representatives and to provide the necessary pressure to secure their cooperation.

When one first visits the headquarters of government overseas organizations in Washington, it is easy to be overwhelmed by the sheer size and intricate organization of the American overseas establishment: the Department of State, the Defense Department, the Agency for International Development, the Department of Commerce, the United States Information Service, the Peace Corps, the Central Intelligence Agency. All of them have more or less extensive overseas interests which require the expenditure of vast personal and material resources. In watching the people at work in these bureaucracies and in talking with them, one begins to share their taken-for-granted attitude about the American presence abroad, a presence which is in considerable part generated and directed from Washington. One also learns that there is such a thing as "the national interest" and that a part of this interest is served by clandestine operations which cannot be adequately scrutinized by an ordinary anthropologist. This meant that some overseas Americans at the ends of chains of command emanating from Washington might not be available as subjects in this study.

Of all the American organizations contacted, the Department of State proved to be most helpful in locating a proper overseas community. By talking to State Department and A.I.D. officials in Washington, who work in parallel organizations in the same building, and by contacting other officials in overseas locations, it was possible to narrow down the number of possible field locations for this study. The American community in Ciudad Condal finally was selected for the primary field study on the basis of information provided by the Consulate General there and the subsequent offer of cooperation extended to me by the consul general. In order to secure comparative data about Americans in other overseas situations, I arranged a secondary field trip to an American community in Scandinavia and a brief visit to one in Madrid.

On the whole, the technique which I used for making preliminary contacts for this study involved working from the top of organizations at home down to their representatives abroad. By the time of my departure overseas, I had worked up a list of Americans in the Condal city who would be available to me from the beginning of my sojourn there. After contacting these people, I planned to work out by means of their recommendations to others in the community. Considering that Americans are supposed to be non-authoritarian in character, the technique of making contacts through "orders" from headquarters proved to be very effective. However, unlike the Japanese overseas community in Cuba where I had worked previously,[13] the American community in Ciudad Condal had no powerful "headman" or leader who could "command" cooperation with a visiting anthropologist. Indeed, the consul general's offer of cooperation (as I was to learn later) did not necessarily extend to the other consuls or even to his wife. My penetration of the American community depended in large part on personal initiative and acceptability. In retrospect, it appears that my acceptability was promoted by my institutional connections.[14] The prestige of a grant from the National Institutes of Health and an affiliation with an established American university seemed to carry occasional weight with people who were uncertain about participating in the study. On the other hand, my connection with the National Institutes of Health sometimes heightened suspicions about the purposes of the study.

METHOD

The basic method which was employed in this investigation of an American overseas community has become traditional in social anthropology. The anthropologist immerses himself in the life of a people and attempts to strike that precarious balance between involvement and detachment which is necessary to give an empathic but objective account of their culture. In this case, in addition to participating in American community life, I also entered the host world and, to a lesser extent, that of some foreign nationals. After a period of familiarization in which I interviewed primary and secondary contacts, worked on a rough census of Americans in the city, and participated in various American and host functions, I constructed a standard schedule-interview, oriented in terms of the problem of adaptation, which was to be used on a cross-section of informants. My early experience with the Condal Americans enabled me to include questions and phrase them in terms which were more meaningful to them. This kind of interviewing, begun about a month after my arrival, continued to the end of my sojourn (eight months) in the city. Although the cross-section of people does not constitute a representative sample (the nature and extent of the universe was never satisfactorily defined), it does include adults from all known sectors of the American community. A copy of the questions raised in the schedule-interview is included in the Appendix.

In order to obtain information about specialized sectors of American life in the city, I turned to expert informants who possessed intimate knowledge about these areas. The following method was used to draw conclusions about areas such as the Chamber of Commerce, the Consulate General, the schools, the Cultural Institute, and the American Women's Club: Information obtained from a first informant was checked against that provided by a second. Discrepancies were resolved by questioning a third informant and by personal observation. Generalizations about each area, therefore, are based on the majority testimony of special informants. In addition, I interviewed a number of hosts and foreign nationals to find out their views about Americans in the city.

By living in the American community and by daily participation in events involving its members, I was able to gather a great deal of other information which could be added to and checked against the interview material. The files on individuals and groups which were built up in this way permitted me to make more accurate assessments of their typical natures than would have been possible on the basis of a single interview. Also, although a longitudinal study of lines of adaptation was not contemplated, it was possible to trace these Americans' progress as strangers over a short duration. This kind of observation proved to be useful for checking conclusions about adaptation presented especially in Chapter 8. Finally, my constant and increasingly intimate association with these Americans enabled me to "steal" their impressions of each other to be checked against my own. Thus daily contacts provided information which could be used to fill out and correct the picture of these Americans which was emerging from the various interviews. Unlike field work in many primitive societies where the anthropologist can keep an eye on people and events without straying too far from his living quarters, an adequate range of daily contacts in Ciudad Condal required considerable activity and mobility among the spread-out Americans. It was not sufficient to lurk about the Cultural Institute and Consulate General, the two principal American institutions in the city. One had to check on current events in various sectors, e.g., the missionaries, the consuls, the businessmen, the teachers, and participate in occasions which sometimes conflicted with each other in time. Where I could not attend an event myself, I sought to locate reliable informants who would be willing to tell me what had happened.

In primitive societies there are no written documents to assist the anthropologist in his study. Although documents pertaining to Americans in the city were comparatively scarce, those that did exist proved to be helpful. There were, for example, various lists, none complete or up-to-date, of Americans in and around the city, which could be used in taking a census and selecting interviewees. The *Condal Courier,* a small, rather crude newspaper devoted primarily, but not exclusively, to American affairs, contained information about American events, some gossip about individual Americans, and "portraits" of successful Americans and their enterprises in the city. A content analysis of the *Courier* provided one important basis for the generalizations contained in Chapter 11 entitled "The World View of a Stranger Community." Finally, some American institutions in the city published information about themselves. The schools, for example, provided brochures, and the American Women's Club had a monthly circular.

In summary, the method employed in the preliminary study of an American community abroad was conceived to be appropriate to an investigation into a new, comparatively unstructured field. The rigid application of specialized research techniques might have defeated the purpose of the study which was to uncover hypotheses as well as to test them. Interviews, observation, and written documents provided information which inevitably generated further questions about the American community. The give-and-take between incoming information and the questioning researcher continued to the end of the field work and after.[15]

Personal Transactions in Field Work

An increasing body of literature attests to the fact that sociologists and anthropologists are becoming increasingly aware of themselves, as well as the people they study, as factors in their research.[16] In field work, the role of the investigator may be seen as the locus of personal transactions which affect not only the progress of the investigation but the nature and shape of reality which develops in the investigator's mind. In an earlier work I proposed that the anthropologist in the field be considered a stranger whose viewpoint reflects the nature of his adaptation to that role.[17] Such adaptation, or lack of it, proceeds through transactions between the investigator and his subjects, and between the investigator and himself. In the manner of a Chinese puzzle box, the present study involves the investigation of strangers by another stranger. The course of the investigation and the views which resulted from it were affected not only by the way in which I, a stranger, was received by my stranger subjects, but also by my reaction to stranger *anomie* encountered in this particular foreign situation.

If we measure adaptation (as in Chapter 8) in terms of the degree to which a person feels at home in a foreign place and assume that the effectiveness of the field worker is positively associated with this feeling,[18] then optimum effectiveness in this investigation probably was not attained until my fifth or sixth month in the field. Before that time I suffered through most of the difficulties encountered by other Americans in the city.[19] The host population of Ciudad Condal could not be taken lightly. They and their city excited the most extreme negative and positive feelings and, until the late stages of my sojourn, a constant undercurrent of stranger anxiety. I could readily empathize with the Americans and their problems of adaptation. However, unlike them, I could not try out social defenses which involved venting hostility or receiving nurturance. Americans could turn to their families or cliques for support or meet together to gripe about the hosts or gossip about each other; but I had no family, could commit myself to no clique, and certainly could not air my anxiety-ridden views about Americans or hosts. Any of these lines of defense might have jeopardized the study either by alienating individuals or undermining my ideal image as an impartial investigator. As a result, my own constriction in the face of *anomie* tended to lead in the direction of private symptoms such as apparent psychosomatic disturbances. The lack of an adequate social "safety valve" undoubtedly slowed down my penetration of American and host worlds and perhaps contributed to at least some of those early impressions which required laborious revision later on. The emphasis on the negative side of existence in Ciudad Condal which pervades this book, although dictated by theory, may in part be a result of my own difficulties of adaptation in this foreign setting.

The welcome which I received from the Condal Americans and the extent of their cooperation was more favorable than I had anticipated. Considering that I, an uninvited guest in their midst, could not offer these strangers any immediate tangible return for their participation, the rate of cooperation was very high. Of the approximately 90 people who were approached for interviews, no more than 5 refused to cooperate. The most important nest of resistance to the study consisted of a few government and business people who, when asked by others about their resistance, tended to refer to *The Ugly American*. In the face of my persistent, if occasionally forced, friendliness, some of these people eventually agreed to be interviewed and the others to speak with me in public. I encountered no problems with people on secret missions during the course of the investigation.[20]

From the beginning of my encounters with the Condal Ameri-

cans, I tried to be strictly honest about the purposes of the study. In
early interviews with community leaders, a talk at the Cultural
Institute, and an interview for the *Condal Courier,* I sought to
convey the image of a scholar who was concerned with the problem
of Americans' adaptation abroad. The article in the *Condal Courier*
referred to the study as follows: "Dr. Nash's work is mostly with
the [Condal] American Community. He is correlating [*sic*] information about the adjustment of individuals to this country, endeav-
oring to learn what adjustment problems there are and why they
exist. During his stay Dr. Nash will interview most of the Americans. . . . Later, the results of his conferences will be compiled. Dr.
Nash is working as a private citizen on a grant from the World
Health Organization [*sic*]."

My affiliation with the National Institutes of Health (not World
Health Organization) and my concern with the problem of adaptation probably contributed to the widespread belief that I was a
psychiatrist or psychologist bent on exploring the darker side of
American character in the city, but it is not possible to avoid the
conclusion that these people were projecting their own often considerable hostility onto the anthropologist-stranger. My reaction to the
imputation of base motives in myself took the form of privately
expressed anger which may have contributed to the rather unflattering picture of the community which is presented in this book. I tried
not to react in public and to remain noncommittal when asked my
opinion about people who fell under my purview.

Every field trip can be a journey toward self-understanding. The
anthropologist-stranger finds himself in situations where he can
re-evaluate himself and perhaps try out new roles. The sojourn in
Ciudad Condal functioned in this way for me. After an initial
period of distress, I began to find myself moving with some confidence in the foreign setting. I accepted the more aggressive interpersonal mode and, to some extent, the effusive emotionality. Unlike
some other Americans I never did become pro-Franco, but I certainly lost my liberal dogma in the light of the encounter with
modernizing Spain. In unearthing new aspects of my character and
trying them out successfully I acquired the kind of self-confidence

which is treated in Chapter 8. The city then may have functioned somewhat as a "magic helper" [21] in my process of self-development. One might argue that the anthropologists should not experience stranger anxiety and should not use the field trip for self-realization. But to argue that the field trip does not contribute importantly at any age to the development of character seems to me to be non-sense.

INDEBTEDNESS

No study in the social sciences can be undertaken without the cooperation of others. Why do people cooperate with the social scientist in his investigations? Whatever the reason, I find myself in their debt for such cooperation. In the present investigation, I received financial aid from the National Institutes of Mental Health (Grant number MH 08316), from the University of Connecticut Research Foundation, and from financial arrangements associated with a sabbatical leave from the University of Connecticut. A number of other organizations provided assistance in setting up and carrying out the study. As I mentioned earlier, the Department of State and its representatives were particularly helpful; I would like to thank especially Harlan Cleveland, then an Undersecretary of State, for his support and technical expertise during the early stages of the investigation. Louis Harris Associates, through the agency of a former associate in the survey for *The Overseas Americans,* Penn Townsend Kimball, also provided early technical assistance. Unfortunately, because of the guarantee of anonymity to all those who were affected by the study, I cannot list the many other organization which cooperated with me in the research.

In Ciudad Condal, where I took up residence as an uninvited guest, I eventually secured adequate cooperation. Most of the people in the American community had sufficient faith in my integrity to submit to my observations and questions. Because of the strictures on anonymity which govern the study, I cannot name those Americans who were generous with their time and tolerant of my prying. I wish to thank them all now and hope that they find this book a fair-minded appraisal of the way it was at that particular juncture of the community's history. It is not possible to predict how the publication of this book will affect the lives of those who participated. I have tried to protect them from prurient interests by keeping their names secret and by using fictitious names for individuals, places, and institutions. The inside dopester will know the correct names for many of them, but it is hoped that this procedure will save those who came under my purview from avoidable affronts to their dignity.

The inevitable clerical work associated with a study of this kind has been carried on by Tove Brus Jensen, Antoinette Iacovazzi Roy, Sharon Radom, and Betty Jean Hagen. Selma Wollman of the University of Connecticut Research Foundation and Betty Csiki typed the manuscript. I am grateful to these assistants and to the Research Foundation for making its typing facilities available to me. In addition, I would like to thank Carole Berman Murphy, John Sharkey, and my colleague Jerold Heiss for reading and commenting on portions of the manuscript. Finally, I am indebted to the students in my course at the University of Connecticut ("The American in Foreign Cultures") for the opportunity to work out my ideas in class with them. They and the others who have helped me may not know how much I have depended on them. Without their assistance I could not have made this book. If they ever read *A Community in Limbo,* I hope they will conclude that their participation in this research led to something of value.

Portions of this book have appeared earlier in professional journals as follows: "The Fate of Americans in a Spanish Setting," *Human Organization,* vol. 26, no. 3 (Fall 1967), pp. 157–163; "Cohesiveness in an American Community Abroad," *Pacific Sociological Review,* vol. 12, no. 1 (Spring 1969), pp. 40–48; and "The Domestic Side of a Foreign Existence," *Journal of Marriage and the Family,* vol. 31, no. 3 (August 1969), pp. 574–583.

D. N.

Storrs, Conn.
December 1968

A
COMMUNITY
IN LIMBO

I

AN OUTPOST OF
AMERICAN IMPERIALISM

> We will move forward to our work ... with
> gratitude ... and thanksgiving to Almighty
> God that He has marked us as His chosen
> people, henceforth to lead in the regeneration
> of the world. ...
>
> SENATOR ALBERT BEVERIDGE
> in the United States Senate

AS MAURICE STEIN HAS ARGUED IN *The Eclipse of Community* [1] every community study should be a case history of broader historical processes. The historical process we are concerned with here is modern—particularly American—imperialism, and the community chosen to illuminate this process is a small American overseas enclave in Spain.

It is tempting to think of imperialism in terms of organic growth. A country is born, grows in power, expands, declines or contracts, and dies. The rise and fall of the Roman empire is seen as an inevitable unfolding of its original potential. A period of vigorous growth and expansion is followed by decay from within and defeat from without—the entire process being governed by forces originating with the imperialistic country. Occasionally we permit ourselves a consideration of the other parties in this process, i.e., the foreign countries which have been invaded and who react by resisting, submitting, rebelling, and finally expelling the invader from their land. This reminds us that imperialism is not a one-way street in which traffic flows entirely from the imperialistic source, but rather a species of interaction between two or more parties marked by the flow and ebb of power or influence. [2]

The military-political conception of the extension of a country's authority into foreign areas has dictated much of our thinking about imperialism. Official decisions are seen to be made by a nation to

further certain interests, military power applied, and political do-
minion established or disestablished. This view is a limited one, and
it is perhaps the Marxists [3] with their concept of economic imperialism who have done the most to convince us that the strictly
military-political conception is too narrow. If imperialism refers to
the extension of a country's authority into foreign areas, we have to
conclude that there are various kinds of authority and, therefore,
various imperialisms. Entire ways of life may enter into imperialistic
transactions, and it is not necessarily military or political means and
ends which are most significant in a given instance.

Not only are there different kinds of imperialisms, but different
degrees as well. We might argue that *any* expansion of a country's
interests and authority into a foreign place would constitute an
imperialistic process. When such an expansion assumes large pro-
portions as, e.g., in the cases of the United States today or Britain
and France yesterday, we are entitled to call a country an imperial
power. Such a country may be extending its authority on many
fronts and in many areas of culture. Not all of its imperialistic
projects need to be in harmony with each other. As far as the
United States is concerned, for example, many different interests are
represented abroad and they compete and conflict there even as they
compete or conflict at home.[4] Most of the modern imperial powers
have had to contend with anti-imperialist sentiment at home,[5] even
as the United States has had to contend with criticis of its policies in
Southeast Asia. The assumption that an imperial power is a monolithic entity may obscure rather than clarify the imperialistic process.

Imperialism may be intentional or unintentional. Expatriates may
or may not know that they are extending a nation's interests abroad.
Nevertheless, they have the weight of the imperial power behind
them. Such expatriates have personal and organizational missions to
perform, but they must also face the problem of adaptation to a
more or less foreign situation. Using a dramatic analogy, we see
these people coming on to a strange stage bearing scripts which
have been written for them at home. Here they encounter foreign
actors with foreign scripts. It seems obvious that the outcome of the

scene with the foreign actors will be different from what the agent-actors and their script writer at home anticipated. We cannot know how the imperialistic process will work itself out without considering the foreign stage and the human actors on it. The foreign setting is not the only place where the process may be analysed fruitfully, but it is an important analytical point and one which appears to have been somewhat neglected to date.

When a number of people from the same country go abroad to the same location they display a tendency to clump together with their colleagues.[6] Many of the representatives of an imperial power abroad will be found in enclaves which have a distinctly home-like character. We have some excellent descriptions of such communities by novelists,[7] but it is only recently that scientific analyses have been undertaken.[8] In the present study we will be concerned with a small American enclave in a large industrial-port city in northeast Spain in the early 1960's. It is not likely that this community could be considered a first-line outpost for any American overseas interests, but it will show us how such interests are carried out. Similar case studies of a number of other American communities abroad at various times and places will be necessary before we can attempt to make generalizations about overseas representatives of American imperialism.

The general facts about modern imperialism are clear. The big industrial nations have, by a variety of means, expanded their spheres of influence into foreign territories around the world. In the early part of the twentieth century Britain and France were the foremost imperial powers. From the time of World War II, however, it became clear that the United States and Soviet Russia had attained the highest power and the largest spheres of authority. While Britain and France were withdrawing in the face of various struggles for independence, the United States and the Soviet Union were extending their hegemonies and testing each other's wills in the cold war. At the time of this study, however, even they had felt the effects of independence movements and were in retirement in several areas. The United States had suffered setbacks in China and the Caribbean and had entered inconclusive wars in Korea and

Vietnam. The Russians had been blocked in much of Africa and confronted with the increasing autonomy of their Eastern European satellites and of China which, itself, was emerging as a first-class power in opposition to both Russia and the United States.

Although the United States gave up many of the foreign bases which it had acquired during the war, it added some others in accordance with its strategic requirements vis-a-vis Russia and China. It continued to maintain a substantial military (or para-military) presence around the world. In 1960 there were approximately 600,000 American servicemen stationed overseas, a figure which was about double that of 1950.[9] A network of military and political alliances existed. In all of them the United States was the chief partner and chief donor of military and economic assistance—from 1945 to 1962 it amounted to nearly one hundred billion dollars, approximately one-third of which was in military supplies and services.[10] In addition, American assets and investments abroad were substantial, rising from approximately thirty-two billion dollars in 1950 to approximately eighty billion in 1962.[11]

Americans who went abroad were not only the agents of American power, but also conscious or unconscious prophets of what we can call modernization. They carried with them the products of an advanced technology and the value of rationality. They undermined parochialism and contributed to what has been called "the revolution of rising expectations." The people they encountered overseas wanted the benefits of the modern way of life, but they frequently did not have the means to attain them. In underdeveloped countries they often reacted to resulting frustrations by intense nationalism and rebellions.[12]

In Europe the United States and NATO maintained a large military establishment in direct confrontation with Russia and her satellites. The main share of this defensive enterprise was contributed by the United States. In an attempt to revive Western European economies which had suffered heavily during the war, the United States created the Marshall Plan, which is sometimes cited as the source of the recent "economic miracle" in Western Europe. Some Americans do not consider Europeans appreciative enough of this assistance. American tourists, for example, who have been going to Europe in rapidly increasing numbers [13] often complain about their treatment by the hosts. It is not likely that most of these travelers are aware of the huge American investments in Europe, which are larger than for any other major world area. Direct investments, which at the time of the study amounted to approximately nine billion dollars, were said to produce profits in excess of those which can be realized at home.[14] More advanced technically, more efficient, and with far greater capital resources, the United States at the time was on its way toward effective economic domination of Western Europe. It also provided goals for the new generation of European consumers. The "consumer revolution," so evident to anyone looking into European shop windows, was heavily influenced by American culture.

The saying that Africa begins at the Pyrenees probably was meant to indicate that Spain is not like the rest of Europe. As far as recent developments in American overseas interests are concerned, there appears to be some truth in this statement. The Spanish Civil War elicited much popular sympathy in the United States, but the official policy of the United States government was one of non-involvement. The triumph of the Nationalist forces of Franco was not welcomed in a nation with democratic ideals whose volunteers had gone to serve in the International Brigades.[15] Relations with Spain were not much improved during World War II. Franco, who had received support from Hitler and Mussolini during the Civil War, remained officially neutral during the conflict. The official attitude of the United States was correct, but distant. It was thought by many that this attitude could not possibly change as long as Franco remained in power.

But the Franco regime, profoundly anti-Communist in its orientation, proved to be long-lived. As America's Communist allies generally were transformed into enemies, the value of Spain's opposition to Communism began to be appreciated in official circles in Washington. Agreements were made with the Spanish government to establish a series of military bases in Spain and to provide Spanish armed forces with military matériel and services. During the period

1950–1964 the value of such assistance amounted to approximately half a billion dollars.[16] Non-military financial assistance was also extended. From 1951 to 1962 (when AID was concluded) this assistance amounted to a little over one billion dollars.[17] The extension of such aid to a totalitarian regime—even one serving American military interests—was not accomplished without reservations and popular opposition by Americans.

It seems possible to characterize Spain in the years immediately prior to 1959 as no more than a reluctant participant in the modernization of Europe. Up until that time the general economic picture—even with American aid—was not very promising. There was a conservative, even reactionary, attitude toward the kind of program which would have enabled Spain to follow the rest of Europe in its economic development. As a result, foreign investments in Spain were discouraged. American direct investments in 1950, for example, were only thirty-one million dollars.[18] In 1959, however, the Spanish government formulated and put into practice an economic development and stabilization program which created extremely attractive opportunities for foreign investment. The receptive attitude of the Spanish government has persisted to the present and seems to have been responsible for a dramatic rise in foreign investments, which, in turn, has been associated with a rapidly changing economic picture marked by a consistent year-by-year increase in the gross national product and standard of living. During the period 1959–1962 American direct investments in Spain (which amounted to about forty percent of all foreign investments) rose from fifty-three to eighty-five million dollars (about one percent of the American investment in Europe).[19] Since the United States also was Spain's principal trading partner, it seems to have been heavily involved in the Spanish economic resurgence.

Foreign economic and technical intervention meant the diffusion of modern European and American ways into the Spanish culture. The introduction of more rationalized procedures was not accomplished without major dislocations in the society and, as we shall see, personal frustrations for both Spaniards and foreigners; but apparently these obstacles were not enough to prevent the modernizing trend from continuing. One reason that it undoubtedly will keep on is the rising expectations of Spaniards who have become increasingly aware of what life can be like in Europe and America. Such an awareness comes through the less strictly controlled media, from Spaniards who have gone north to work, from foreigners on the job in Spain, and from tourists who have descended on the country in such numbers as to make tourism the leading source of foreign exchange.[20] The surge of tourism with its inevitable accompaniments of real estate speculation, building construction, and various kinds of tourist services is an authentic phenomenon which has transformed the major tourist meccas, particularly the coasts and islands of Spain. American participation in this "invasion" (which reached thirteen million people a year at the time of this study) was substantial, but exact figures are unknown.

The effects of economic expansion and modernization have not been felt evenly throughout Spain. The major scenes of Spanish development have taken place in the coastal areas and islands, rather than in the interior (with the exception of Madrid, the capital), and in the cities, rather than in the country. As far as cities are concerned, the capital and the industrial-port city in which this study was undertaken were the largest and most influential. They were also the principal points of foreign involvement. Both exhibited characteristics typical of European cities in the midst of the "economic miracle," i.e., large-scale immigration from rural areas, increasing population especially on the periphery, rapidly rising income and cost of living, and social problems such as housing shortages and traffic congestion.[21] At the time of the study nearly one-sixth of the Spanish population of about thirty million were pursuing their individual fates in the atmosphere of incessant change which dominated these two cities. In such an atmosphere it was at last possible for the average Spaniard to look ahead, rather than back to the agonies and triumphs of the Civil War.

Of the two communities Madrid was slightly larger. Because of Spain's totalitarian polity, a very considerable amount of power was concentrated in its palace and ministries. More particularly, it was concentrated in one man who, at the end of the Civil War, had made himself the leader of Spain. Although Madrid was an important industrial city in its own right, its paramount importance to Spaniards and foreigners was its decision-making function. This appears to be the reason that foreign activities in Spain were also centered there. It was the largest outpost of the United States in the country. The American Embassy, headed by an ambassador, maintained ultimate control over all American government operations in Spain. A large air base, jointly maintained by Spain and the United States on the outskirts of the capital, was one of three on Spanish soil utilized by the Strategic Air Command. The central—and in some cases only—offices of American business operations in the country were in the capital. In sum, the spearhead of American operations in Spain was located in Madrid.

On occasion, the large industrial port (hereinafter called Ciudad Condal [22]) in which our American outpost was located has been compared to Madrid as an arm to a head. Its industrial character was established at the beginning of the industrial revolution in Europe, and its many industries—principally textile, chemical, and metallurgical—did in fact make it the largest industrial city in Spain. As an important seaport, it was also a center of commercial activity. Its history as a maritime and commercial center went back at least to the eleventh century when, according to Chaytor, "its commerce was considerable and it was a point at which foreign influence could enter Spain by land and sea." [23] It is not surprising, therefore, that the people of Ciudad Condal were typified as businessmen, workers, or, especially in the past, sailors.

Although the general historical trend had been toward increased industrial and commercial activity, the Condal city had never experienced such a surge in economic development as was occurring at the time of the study. Because it was located in the heart of a famous tourist district and subject to tourist "invasions," the city experienced the effects of the tourist "explosion" as well as the consequences of industrial and commercial expansion. The increasing wealth resulting from these developments produced higher incomes and costs, and many tourists, bent on realizing a cheap vacation in Spain, were surprised and infuriated by the current economic facts of life.

It would be a mistake to assume that the modernization of Ciudad Condal kept pace with the economic developments we have described. Although the average citizen had come to want what other Europeans wanted, i.e., consumer goods and a higher standard of living, and although he pursued these goals in his peculiarly individualistic and aggressive manner, he was not always willing to adopt the highly rationalized way of life which, say, in the United States, had been necessary to attain them. Unlike most communities in the United States at the beginning of the twentieth century, the Condal city had a long tradition and a proud citizenry. Not only were its people not always willing to adopt the techniques of modernity, but they were unable or unwilling to cope with the many social problems resulting from drastic social change. Although new housing was urgently needed for the labor force, construction tended to concentrate on tourist facilities and upper-income dwellings. The constantly increasing traffic was impeded by an archaic network of streets and highways. Rail, port, and air facilities were proving to be inadequate for handling more passengers and cargo. Efforts had only begun to deal with a severe smog problem. Confronted with problems such as these, the governmental bureaucracies tended to continue exquisitely irrational methods which contributed too little to their solution.

In the Condal city, the American presence had been virtually wiped out by the end of the Civil War, and was slow in reestablishing itself. Until the 1950's only a few American businessmen had found their way back into the area. They and the American staff of the Consulate General (charged with handling American interests in the northeastern part of Spain) comprised the bulk of Americans there. However, during the 1950's the large-scale American military build-up in Spain brought many Americans to the city. The establishment of a joint Spanish-American air base at a nearby inland city and the decision to make Ciudad Condal a "home port" of the Nth Fleet in the Mediterranean required the development of sustaining operations and the location of Air Force and Navy personnel in the area. But the military "invasion" was of brief duration. By the time of the present study the city was no longer a "home port" of the fleet, and the air base inland, built to accommodate SAC bombers, was being maintained on a stand-by basis only. As a result, nearly all of a once sizeable military contingent had been moved away. Almost overnight the American community there was transformed from a largely military outpost to a civilian establishment. During the several years in which the military held sway there was a slow increase in the number of American civilians of various types so that, even with the departure of almost all of the military, the size of the community was larger than at the beginning of the military build-up. At the time of the study an estimated three hundred fifty Americans were residents of Ciudad Condal and its immediate environs.

As far as American overseas interests were concerned, what were the functions of the Americans in the city? Or, to put it another way, what were the missions of the various representatives of the United States in this particular foreign setting? Keeping in mind the conception of imperialism we developed at the beginning of this chapter, we will hold that *any* overseas representative of an imperial power such as the United States participates in the imperialistic process to the extent that his project is acceptable to his government. *Whether he knows it or not,* he bears the stamp of an imperial power, and by his very existence abroad, contributes to the expansion or maintenance of its authority. In Ciudad Condal there were a variety of such American representatives.

First, there were the tourists, bohemians, and servicemen on leave. We would be straining our definition to call all these people imperialists. In some cases their interests ran counter to those of the United States government. Tourist spending abroad was contributing to the balance-of-payment deficit, and bohemians and servicemen were alienating the hosts with exuberant and illegal actions. These people were transients who could not be considered part of the outpost we have chosen to analyse. Undoubtedly some of them, with their wealth and example, played a part in extending American influence, but they were not "working at" it. This largest category of American visitors in the city, then, will be of only peripheral concern to us here.

An estimated 35 percent of the adult American population were unemployed or dependents of unemployed and therefore not actively involved in overseas missions. The most respectable members of this group were those older people who had declared their retirement. They lived for the most part on a fixed income and anxiously watched the rising cost of living. The rest of the unemployed were trying to find a job, a fortune, or, in a few cases, a husband, but the chances for their success were not very great. Several of these people took ill-paying jobs teaching English at the American Cultural Institute, an information or propaganda outlet for the United States government. Although these jobs were strictly stop-gap operations which helped a person make ends meet, they were, ironically enough, among the more obvious imperialistic activities of Americans in Ciudad Condal.

From the number of people involved (an estimated 26 percent of the adult population), the amount of money invested, and the considerable government concern, it is obvious that the principal American mission in the city was business. There was substantial American participation in the annual trade fair. The American exhibition at the fair was designed to promote the small, but rising market for American techniques and products in Spain. The interest of the United States in this project was indicated by support from the Department of Commerce, the Consulate General, and the Embassy in Madrid, and by the annual official visit of the American Ambassador to open the American exhibition.

The American business operations in the city were of considerable variety. Unlike well-known American business outposts in, for example, Venezuela or Central America, no single company or type of operation dominated the scene; and unlike Madrid, where many major American corporations were represented, there were comparatively few adjuncts of first-line American business organizations in Ciudad Condal. The largest American firms were engaged in petroleum exploration; manufacturing of plastics, feed, and pharmaceuticals; business reporting; and air and sea transportation. The bulk of American businesses, though, were not major industrial powers; a substantial minority were individually owned, high-risk operations such as clothing manufacturing, newspaper publishing, advertising and public relations, insurance, stockbroking, running a bakery, innkeeping, and buying and selling of various kinds. Whether a business was large or small, there was usually no more than one American in it, and he tended to be of an individualistic entrepreneurial type which we often associate with an earlier era of capitalism.

The climate for foreign business activity in Spain improved drastically after 1959. At the time of the study there was a heady atmosphere of optimism about undiscovered and improving opportunities for American business in Spain. The expanding economy and political stability provided the American businessman and his counterparts from other countries, e.g., France, Germany, and Italy, an apparently ideal opportunity for economic intervention. A succession of American businessmen were coming to Ciudad Condal to sound out possibilities for establishing operations there. On these preliminary visits they usually consulted with the local office of the American Chamber of Commerce in Spain and/or the economic section of the Consulate General. If the visitor had the usual impracticable scheme with which he hoped to make a lot of money he was likely to receive a skeptical reception from both these agencies. If he had a sound plan which deserved encouragement, he still would have to contend with cautionary tales about the problem of political succession in Spain. In his talks with other Americans he would hear that as long as Franco remained alive the economic situation probably would remain favorable. But what would happen when Franco died? Here visions of another catastrophic civil war sometimes arose to haunt businessmen's thoughts.

The second largest group of Americans (an estimated 15 percent of the adult population) were those working more or less directly for the United States government: consuls, agents of propaganda or information, and military personnel in transportation and supply. The headquarters for government operations in and around Ciudad

Condal was the Consulate General. Its principal mission was economic, i.e., the promotion of American business interests; but it also analysed and reported home on the local political situation, supervised cultural exchanges, provided information, carried on the especially heavy load of consular duties (made necessary in part by the large number of American transients in the district), and maintained liaison with the Nth Fleet when it was in port. Since American sailors on leave were notorious for their brawling and transients for getting into trouble of one kind or another, the last two functions probably required the mobilization of more "diplomatic" skills than all the others.

The American Cultural Institute, an adjunct of the United States Information Service, cooperated closely with the Consulate General. According to its director it was trying to carry on a "sophisticated propaganda operation" which included the aforementioned English classes, cultural presentations, conferences, and social gatherings. A more politically delicate information or propaganda operation was carried on by a somewhat mysterious "private" radio station whose policies appeared to be loosely coordinated with those of the government. This station, which was part of a world-wide network, beamed broadcasts to Communist Europe from its transmitter to the north of Ciudad Condal.

Finally among government personnel, a very small group of army transportation men supervised the unloading of military supplies from ships and their transport to various bases in the interior. Even though all other American military had left the city and the air base inland was being maintained on a stand-by basis only, the handling of supplies at the port continued to be a substantial operation which paid out more than one hundred thousand dollars a year to the hosts. As in the diplomatic chain of command, the next higher power over this logistic unit was in Madrid.

In America it has become a tradition for certain kinds of artists and scholars to get inspiration and education in foreign lands. At one point the American writer or composer who had not visited Europe was considered less competent and perhaps less creative. Paris in the 1920's was a well-known mecca for American artists, and sagas of American expatriates on the Left Bank have become well-known.[24] A number of legitimate artists and scholars were at work in Ciudad Condal but it had not become an artistic culture center for foreigners. The islands off the coast were well-known as rendezvous of artists, and Madrid and Salamanca as places to study, but the Condal city had not acquired that charismatic quality which could attract many artists and intellectuals. We surmise that this may have been due to the emphasis on business in the city. This observation would be anathema to the hosts who were extremely proud of their cultural tradition and to those American Fulbrighters who were concerned with studying it, but there were enough complaints about the "cultural climate" of the city to justify such a hypothesis.

People on missions create missions. As in most American outposts abroad outside of war zones, the majority of working Americans in Ciudad Condal had their families with them.[25] The children required an education, and three schools had been founded to provide it. Although host children and children of other nationals were admitted, these schools addressed themselves to the needs of the American community. Two of the schools employed American personnel only, and the third, English. Since all the schools tended to follow American curricula and since host children were among those educated, the teachers, besides serving the needs of the American community, were agents for the diffusion of American culture as well. In all, American teachers, artists, scholars, and their dependents comprised an estimated 16 percent of the adult American population in the Condal city.

The last, but by no means least, significant group of American overseasmen (an estimated 3 percent of the adult population) in Ciudad Condal probably were the most active agents for the diffusion of American culture. They were the Protestant missionaries who represented denominations of a fundamentalist persuasion. Since religious freedom was officially non-existent in Spain and since proselytizing was against the law, the careers of these people took on a somewhat heroic cast. At the time of the study they had managed to achieve a more or less reluctant *de facto* tolerance for their activities and were making some inroads into the Spanish working class. Although these missionaries might argue that they were not in sympathy with many American secular values and would resent being called agents of the United States, the religious and non-religious culture which they were attempting to propagate in Spain had a recognizable American flavor.

We have been considering the various kinds of missions which Americans were carrying out in one American outpost abroad. What kind of people had been voluntarily or involuntarily selected for these missions? Those who are concerned with Americans abroad sometimes refer to the overseas realm as a frontier and the people who man American outposts there as frontiersmen. In its literature the Peace Corps emphasizes the challenge of life in the boondocks. Such an appeal seems to have found a sympathetic public in a nation which continues to idealize the frontier spirit. If we take this idea about an overseas frontier seriously, what kind of character would we expect to find among Americans abroad?

The most famous statement about the character of the American frontiersman is by Frederick Jackson Turner.[26] Without subscribing to his entire argument, we can accept his description as a legitimate hypothesis about American national character in the 19th century. Although we never will know how prevalent his "reckless, energetic, practical, optimistic individualist" was, it seems likely that he was heavily represented among the developers and expanders of America. What we know about Americans on the edge of the wilderness, the founders of industrial empires, and the men who began to extend American influence overseas suggests that they were of this type. As far as Americans on missions abroad are concerned, we can think of such men as Ben Franklin, Hiram Bingham, Jim Dole, Theodore Roosevelt, Townsend Harris, and Robert E. Peary as conforming more or less to this kind of character. The early agents of American imperialism appear to have been, like many other Americans, frontiersmen.

The work of David Riesman and William Whyte, Jr. has tended to popularize the hypothesis that American national character has changed drastically since the nineteenth century.[27] According to this hypothesis the typical American has changed from an individualistic entrepreneur to a consumer-bureaucrat living in the shadow of the large organization. Even with inadequate data and the serious challenges from certain quarters,[28] it is still difficult not to accept the general outline of this hypothesis. A new type of American—an "organization man"—seems to have emerged, and "other-directed" qualities now appear to be more widespread than in the nineteenth century.

If the national character of Americans has changed, does this mean that the character of Americans on the foreign frontier has changed too? The data for 1960 indicate that about six out of seven of the 1,400,000 Americans residing abroad were employees of the United States government and their dependents.[29] By far the largest single category, about 1,100,000, were the military and their dependents, but civilians working for the government also outnumbered any other category of non-military people. Thus, a very large part of Americans living overseas in 1960 were dependent on the biggest bureaucracy of all. If we consider any employee of a large organization to be an "organization man,"[30] it seems safe to say that this kind of person dominates the contemporary American scene abroad. Unfortunately, we lack adequate data to determine the prevalence of such Americans overseas in the past, but the literature gives one the impression that they are much more frequently encountered now than in the nineteenth century.

The scarcity of frontiersmen of high quality among Americans abroad is attacked by Lederer and Burdick in *The Ugly American*,[31] a savage criticism of the American overseas establishment. The authors argue that American failures abroad are in part due to the tendency to entrust overseas missions to second-rate, comfort-loving, security-conscious bureaucrats. They urge that we recruit able, old-fashioned frontiersmen of the type represented by their hero, the "Ugly American," before it is too late. However, if we have correctly described the trend in American national character, the number of these types in the population would appear to be dwindling. If this is so, then Lederer and Burdick are asking us to do the impossible. What has to be recognized is that institutional change at home appears to have been associated with the advance of a new type of character, i.e., the "organization man." Considering the nature of most American imperialistic missions overseas, the appropriate program would seem to be to seek out the most able representatives of this type and give them adequate institutional support in the overseas setting. Because the "organization man" is not a loner, and because he has learned to look to the group for direction, it is required that he have organizations around him. The growth of "Little Americas" on the American overseas frontier, therefore, would seem to contribute to the maintenance of the new breed of Americans there.[32]

But the day of the frontiersman or entrepreneur is not yet over either at home or abroad. In Ciudad Condal, for example, they were heavily represented. The majority of the American community were more or less able entrepreneurial types. Using our rough method for assessing character, we can say that slightly less than one-half of the resident adults were organization men. In order of numbers, these included the government employees, some of the business people, and possibly the missionaries. The percentage for this kind of person would be lower still if the businessmen were examined closely. A number of the larger firms were attempting to create a new business or explore the possibilities for doing so. They were represented by individualistic entrepreneurs who, like their counterparts in smaller enterprises, welcomed the freedom, variety, and challenge of opening up a new enterprise in a foreign land. Most of the Americans, like the hosts, valued individual enterprise and were seeking to practice it in Ciudad Condal. Semi-retired people looking for a job, retired people seeking to live cheaply but well, divorcees and unmarried girls looking for husbands, artists and bohemians seeking to find inspiration or diversion, businessmen seeking to work out their own personal "angle,"—all these people and their projects created a frontier-like atmosphere which tended to dominate a large part of the American community in the city.

At the beginning of this chapter we argued that understanding the imperialistic process requires that some attention be given to an analysis of the life and missions abroad of the representatives of the imperial power. In our brief survey of one small American outpost we have found a number of different interests and missions represented. Because the United States is not yet a totalitarian society, these interests were not always consistent with each other. From the vantage point of this overseas outpost it was very difficult to conceive of a monolithic American imperialism. Rather, there seemed to be a variety of American imperialisms being worked out through more or less effective individuals.

The effectiveness of such representatives abroad is dependent not only on their technical competence, but also on their adaptation to a foreign scene. Even as it is not possible to assume that a nation will be successful in realizing its imperialistic interests, it also is not possible to assume that its agents will surmount the problem of adaptation abroad successfully. Among the factors which affect an imperial nation's destiny are the adaptive qualities of its people. It has been said that Americans are "lousy imperialists," which might be interpreted to mean that they are lousy adaptors. This study of one American community abroad will attempt to evaluate this hypothesis for Americans in general and for different kinds of Americans in particular. Turner found that Americans developed a way of life and a kind of character which was adaptive to the frontier situation.[33] Will we, when our study is over, be able to conclude that the same degree of adaptation is occurring on the contemporary American overseas frontier?

2

ENTRANCE
OF THE GUESTS

In outward appearance it was a town in which
the wealthy classes had practically ceased to
exist. Except for a small number of women
and foreigners there were no "well-dressed"
people at all. Practically everyone wore rough
working-class clothes, or blue overalls, or some
variant of the militia uniform. All this was
queer and moving. . . .

GEORGE ORWELL
Homage to Catalonia

THE COAST AT CIUDAD CONDAL RUNS FROM NORTHEAST
to southwest. A coastal range of mountains rises abruptly
to the height of five hundred meters from a narrow
coastal plain on which the city is erected. The harbor lies midway
between the mouths of two rivers which cut through the mountains.
In recent years the harbor has been improved and extended by the
addition of a long breakwater-roadway. If you stop halfway along
this drive and face the docks and mountains, you will see rising
directly from the water a small height on which is situated an old
fortress. This height is the single significant eminence in the slowly
rising expanse bounded by the two rivers, the sea, and the mountains.

Archeological evidence tells us that Iberians lived here when the
Greeks came to colonize this coast. The first historical reference is to
a Carthaginian base established by Hamilcar Barca in the 3rd
century B.C.[1] His military campaigns had renewed the authority of
Carthage over the northeastern coastal regions and prepared the
way for a new Carthaginian invasion route to the Italian penin-
sula. Carthage then was engaged in a protracted conflict with Rome,
and Spanish territory was the scene for a part of the warfare
between the two powers. As Roman arms gradually prevailed in

21

this struggle and as Roman control was extended southward along the coast and into the interior of Spain, the site of the present city came under Roman domination and became one of the more important towns of Hither Spain. Parts of the wall constructed by the Romans to protect the place still remain.

Most Americans arriving on the scene today have little knowledge of the city's Roman past, or of the Visigothic, Moorish, and Frankish periods that followed. They do not know about the forces which molded the autonomy of the region called Cataluña nor of more recent events which excite Catalan pride. They are unlikely to know of the Catalan expedition in the fourteenth century which became, according to Chaytor, "the terror of Asia Minor, of Constantinople and of Greece," [2] or of the great military and commercial influence exerted by the city throughout the Mediterranean in the years that followed. Although some Americans might be acquainted with names such as El Cid, Columbus, Ferdinand, and Isabella, they probably would not know in what ways they were associated with the city. The names of local heroes such as Berenguer, Muntaner, de Lauria, and de Flor would mean nothing to them. More recent names might be more significant. An American artist might know Gaudí and his buildings; a writer, Margall's works; and a liberal or a leftist, Durruti and "La Pasionaria," or the PSUC, UGT, CNT, FAI, and POUM, those perplexing appellations for organizations on the Republican side of the Civil War. On the whole, however, Americans arriving in the city at the time of the study tended to display a vast ignorance of their host city, not only because they were strangers, but because Americans tend to lack the profound historical sense which one finds among Europeans. It does not mean that the Americans were not prepared to absorb history or to be impressed by it. Indeed, for some the foreign sojourn would turn into an enthusiastic—even fanatical—effort to add historical depth to their lives by associating with the age of Spain. For most, however, the lack of rationality, not the presence of tradition, would constitute the focus of obsessive concerns during their sojourn.

In order to find out what it meant to an American to arrive in Ciudad Condal let us see how the city appeared to several new arrivals.[3] The main entryways to the city are by road from up and down the coast and from the interior, by rail from France and from the interior, by sea into the harbor, and by air to the airport. The first of the American arrivals, a young secretary employed by the Department of State, took the highway, which was favored by most foreigners, including Americans. She had finished a tour of duty in another European country and was driving south to assume her next post at the Consulate General in Ciudad Condal. She passed along the French Mediterranean coast and crossed the border at the low pass in the Pyrenees, which once had served as the principal exit for nearly half a million Spaniards toward the end of the Spanish Civil War.

The secretary was a matter-of-fact girl who was despondent about leaving her post in northern Europe. She drove rapidly without noticing much of the Spanish countryside along the way. Unlike some other Americans, she did not attend to the castles on the hills nor stop to inspect old buildings in the towns. When she came to the sea at a point where a road branches off to the famous vacation coast she began to encounter heavy traffic. It was November and the annual tourist season was over, but it also was Sunday, a day when many Spanish vehicles are on the road. She was irritated by the increasing traffic and the poor condition of what according to the map was a first-class highway. She passed factories and housing developments on the outskirts, followed a winding route through streets incredibly full of people and vehicles, and entered the heart of Ciudad Condal at a point where a major road construction job was under way.

Because she tried to be self-sufficient and because she knew no Spanish, she had been relying on her map, but it proved to be of little value for fathoming the ways of the dusty detour. By following the rest of the traffic she came at length to the end of the road repairs, stopped, and looked around. To her it seemed that she was in an exceedingly barren, ugly, damp, and dirty city. A touch of desolation was added to her view by the dead leaves on the trees lining the street. But the crowds of people passing up and down the sidewalks and across the street seemed to belie their surroundings.

They were animated—even gay—and created an incongruous air of vitality amid lifeless surroundings. The secretary consulted her map, gritted her teeth, and eased her car into the flow of traffic. This maneuver, properly signalled and apparently perfectly timed, nearly caused her to collide with a motorcycle and its pair of riders who, quite unflinching in their brush with a car, swept on along what looked now like a rather dangerous thoroughfare.

It is not too much to say that the secretary was happy to arrive in the outer office of the Consulate General. A sympathetic receptionist there and the usual accouterments of American government offices overseas made her feel as if she had come home. She had been alone for a week in strange places. Now she was back in the hands of her government. She liked it.

The second American arrival was the wife of a young business executive, a Mrs. E. She and her two children arrived in the city aboard one of the ships of an Italian line. Her husband, following a recommended course for men with families,[4] had flown in earlier to prepare the way: he had secured hotel accommodations, located a home, and worked into the business. Because he had worked previously in Latin America, knew Spanish, and was assisted by Spanish representatives of his company, he came to know his way around rather quickly. When he arrived at the pier to meet his family, however, he had neglected to acquire from the Naval Ministry the necessary pass to board the ship.

As the vessel steamed along the breakwater into the harbor that hot summer afternoon, Mrs. E. was too busy to take more than a brief look at Ciudad Condal. She saw the fortress looming above and, in the background on top of the mountains, what looked like a splendid white cathedral. (She would later be able to look down on the city and the sea from that spot.) It was one of the infrequent smog-free days and her view was excellent, but last-minute preparations for departure and for locating her husband tended to occupy her mind. She took the children below again for a few minutes to attend to the last details.

When Mrs. E. and her children again emerged on deck the ship was drawn up to the dock and men were attempting to put the gangway into place. She could not find her husband on the pier immediately—there, a policeman in gray; there, members of the docking crew; and there, an excited crowd obviously waiting to meet people from the ship. The crowd were excitedly scanning the lines of passengers at the rail even as the passengers were scanning them. At last she saw her husband waving and smiling in his self-conscious manner. She moved toward the gangway with the children ahead of her.

Under normal circumstances we would be able to report the joyful reunion of Mr. E. and his family. But arrivals and departures in Spain do not always follow normal procedures. It is here that the foreigner meets the petty Spanish official, and it is out of this often hilarious encounter that great tales may be created. Events did not follow a normal course and the E. family was not immediately reunited; according to Mrs. E., "The children ran down to meet him; but he didn't have a permit. You have to have a permit to come aboard. The police took him and accused him of being a kidnapper. He was put inside a fenced-in place. And the captain of the ship went down and argued. He said, 'I'm the captain of the ship.' And the policeman said, 'I'm a Spanish policeman.' And they said this over and over again. Finally, I went down and cried that that was my husband. I threatened to have hysterics with the port director and he let him go."

What could adjudicate such a serious international incident but the wiles of a woman? On the one hand was the jealously guarded exercise of authority by the Spaniard; on the other, the habit of command of the sea captain, and in between, the innocent American who had neglected to get an official piece of paper (costing the equivalent of fifty cents plus a "contribution") from the Naval Ministry. From this event it may be understandable why a number of Americans in the city recommended that new arrivals bring with them a healthy sense of humor.

Later when the E. family left the ship and passed through customs Mrs. E. had a pleasant surprise. Living in Puritan New England she had forgotten that there were places in the world where men stared at women in open admiration. The looks of the customs officials and the feelings she experienced as a result reminded her of her time in South America. The manner in which the luggage was inspected (casually) and stamped (authoritatively) were familiar also. It seemed to her that the customs men were more in the business of admiring women than of inspecting luggage. She felt that glances were following her out into the late afternoon sunshine to the car. The air, cooled with the advance of evening, felt damp. She made a mental note to watch out for mildew.

Mr. E. drove down the pier to the *paseo* that fronts the city. To the left was the eminence with its fortress. Directly ahead in the distance were the mountains with the white cathedral on top. Between the mountains and the *paseo* there appeared to be nothing but city. A right turn at the Aduana (customs), a circle around a monument, and then up the famous tree-lined Ramblas which leads from the waterfront to the central plaza of Ciudad Condal—the E.'s were now in an area which once had been surrounded by Roman fortifications. To right and left are sections of the old city filled with historic landmarks; dwellings mostly of the poor; business establishments, including many devoted to prostitution; government buildings; and cafés and restaurants of various kinds. Mrs. E. could see that the streets off the boulevard were narrow and pleasantly mysterious. She made a mental note to visit this area as soon as she could.

The traffic on the Ramblas was intense. The car seemed to be assaulted by hurrying crowds of people. Formidable looking policemen in white helmets made imperious gestures to impatient motorists who gunned their motors as they waited to break away. The surging vehicles, intense faces, and movement of the crowds gave the scene an air of vital force which Mrs. E. had not known in New England. Even the people seated in the cafes or on the central walk under the trees gave an impression of exuberance which was, to her, altogether attractive.

Mr. E., handling the traffic with apparent equanimity, drove his family across the central plaza with its posters and signs, subway entrances, gardens and pigeons, and up another, quieter boulevard to the Castillo Cataluña, a large hotel of modern design. The E.'s thought that they would have to hurry to make the dinner hour. It was not until later that they learned that it was customary to have dinner at 10 P.M. They had arrived just in time for aperitifs.

The third American arrival was an anthropologist. Like the majority of the American residents in the city, his history (biography) included previous experience in a less rationalized culture such as is found in an "underdeveloped" or "primitive" society. For his first study of Americans abroad he had sought an enclave in which Americans were not shielded from a foreign environment by prefabricated American institutions such as one finds on a large military base abroad. The American community in Ciudad Condal appeared to meet this and other requirements. He had secured offers of cooperation from some Americans in the city, and as the plane touched down at the airport on a warm autumn morning he could not help feeling that a number of people were waiting impatiently for him to arrive.

The airport of Ciudad Condal is situated on low-lying land near the coast about six kilometers south of the city. It is difficult to sense the nature of a city from its airport, but the anthropologist gained an impression of primitive, inefficient facilities strained to the limit. The place reminded him of certain Latin American cities where airport facilities did not seem to fit or go together with the modern airliners parked outside. There was a great deal of construction under way, but it seemed to be going very slowly. A tall, rakish control tower was being erected, but it was far from completion. What the anthropologist did not know (perhaps it was better that he did not) was the symbolic significance of this new edifice. He learned later from confidential sources that the state of readiness of the tower at that time signified in a rough way the degee of advancement toward modern technical competence among host control tower personnel.

What kind of impressions does one gain on the airport bus which goes to the in-town airline terminal? In the quarter-hour trip along the coastal highway to the Plaza de España at the southwestern end of the city's Gran Via, it is possible to gather quite a variety:

lowlands and mountains to left and right, farmland and factories, a wide assortment of vehicles ranging from hand- and horse-drawn carts to tiny motorcars and heavy trucks. An American probably would notice the American cola bottling plant on the left just before the bus comes into the plaza and discharges its passengers. One senses now that the city is noisy and that the pace of life here may be rather hectic. From the way baggage is handled it appears that archaic, inefficient procedures prevail. For a traveler in a hurry the disorder and lack of expedition prove to be something less than entrancing.

The taxi ride along the Gran Via to his hotel took the anthropologist much of the way across the city. He learned then, that despite his knowledge of Spanish, he would have many difficult moments in communicating with the hosts. Both Catalan and Spanish are spoken, and local Spanish usage includes a number of colloquialisms. The hotel proved to be a welcome respite from the noise and turmoil of the street: the staff seemed friendly, the room was clean and comfortable, and there was warm water in the bathroom (which smelt only faintly of drains). He thought that he would be able to rest here. It was not until late that night when strains of music from a nearby dance hall penetrated his room that he realized that he had been given one of the least desirable rooms in the hotel.

The first impressions of three American guests, based on their own accounts, will serve to familiarize the reader with some of the grosser aspects of the environment in which these Americans would have to live. Like Ulysses' travels, their journeys through foreign territories would consist of a series of incidents; like the study of a foreign language, their penetrations of the alien world would move by plateaus, proceeding forward, and then stopping to rest.[5] The first point of rest in the strangers' progress was the hotel.

The hotel is part of the "front" which the city presents to the visitor. We have drifted into Goffmanesque terminology here because it seems to describe most aptly the rituals and play-acting which are designed to convince the guest that he is the center of the universe and that those who serve him are princes of good fellows.[6]

As a general rule, the larger the establishment the more likely it is that the visitor will be treated on his own terms. In a great international hotel one never has to feel that he is at a loss or that he must apologize for being a foreigner. In a small pension one probably will have to begin accepting host definitions immediately.

Most of the Americans who intended to reside in the city stopped first at one of two de luxe hotels: the Castillo Cataluña downtown (where Mr. E. and his family stayed) and the Hotel Cuadrado [7] at the beginning of the mountains (and the edge of the smog which tends to be confined to the lowest part of the city's air space). The Cuadrado, situated in the heart of the well-to-do district inhabited by most Americans, was the hotel favored by United States government agencies in Ciudad Condal. Because it provided housekeeping facilities, it occasionally became a permanent residence for single people or couples without children. At the time of the study several older people resided there.

In almost all cases the hotel was a temporary haven only, the length of stay being dictated almost entirely by success in finding a home. If a suitable house or apartment did not turn up soon the hotel could begin to acquire the qualities of a cage. One American wife, commenting on this phase of her sojourn, said, "We were at the Hotel Cuadrado. We were there for two months . . . I was here with two tiny children and needed help and nobody offered it. You don't know where to look for help in a new place. I was stuck twenty-four hours a day in the hotel. Nobody came to visit me and I couldn't get out." It is not clear why this woman and her family had so much difficulty locating a home. The E. family moved quickly into a home which had been located by Mr. E. prior to the arrival of his family. For the E.'s, therefore, the hotel could function as an enjoyable way-station and base of operations for making sorties into the foreign world.

During their stay at a hotel or pension it was customary for Americans to make an early trip to the Consulate General to register and acquire information. Many also spent time house-hunting, a not particularly rewarding activity in a city where the pressure on housing facilities was so great. Most managed to undertake exploring expeditions around the city and even beyond it to such places as the sacred mountain of Cataluña or, in season, to the beaches above and below the city. A necessary consequence of all of these ventures was the accumulation of new experiences which, in turn, posed greater problems of interpretation than were likely to occur at home. As Mrs. E. put it concerning this period of her life in the city, "It was confusing. I thought I'd never get to know my way around."

Schutz points out that "the stranger starts to interpret his new environment in terms of his thinking-as-usual." [8] He attempts to sort out his new experiences in terms of the repertoire of perceptual categories which he has brought with him. He makes comparisons: "There is a building; but unlike those modern ones in South America, this seems to be very old. Here is a street; but unlike the streets in that Turkish city it has shade trees and voluptuous fountains. Here comes a trolley car which looks just like those we used to have back home." If a person is a cosmopolite he probably will find his interpretive apparatus adequate for handling his new experiences. If not, he may soon begin to labor in his sorting operations and, as Schutz suggests, lose confidence in his habitual "thinking-as-usual." [9] Ingmar Bergman in some of his films has presented a macabre visual account of what it feels like to enter the extremes of such a condition. In these films we come into places which we literally cannot understand, and it surely is no accident that Bergman has associated the threat of death with such scenes (it is, perhaps, symbolic of the death of meaning). We are more vulnerable to this threat when we are strangers than when we move in our taken-for-granted world at home.

So much, for the moment, of dark existential corridors. Americans are not accustomed to prowling in them—certainly not at the very beginning of their foreign sojourn. Initial reactions of Americans to the city varied from favorable to unfavorable, but not even those who disliked the city on sight were likely to have begun experiencing significant stranger anxiety. It takes some time for new impressions to "sink in," and, too, Americans tend to be optimistic. As John Gillen,[10] in his comments about American culture, has said,

"Optimism, as contrasted with fatalism or melancholy, is valued. Any problem can be solved if suitable energy and ingenuity are applied to it." It seems reasonable to infer that such a belief would tend to sustain people in adversity and put off their recognition of problems likely to prove insurmountable. It usually was not until later in his sojourn that an American would begin to realize that the problems of strangerhood might be too much for him.[11]

The anthropologist's mission was the study of the American community in Ciudad Condal. As an American he exhibited what Parsons has called "instrumental activism," i.e., relentless activity in the direction of a goal. In order to begin he made his first appointment by telephone with the consul general. The Consulate General was the second stopping place or plateau for most American residents. It was usual for them to register there and, perhaps, to ask for information. The act of registration functioned to allay whatever anxiety one had begun to feel about being in a foreign place without a protector. In case of an emergency of a serious nature the Consulate General would be responsible for evacuating all Americans from northeast Spain. In times of crisis most Americans in the area tended to look on this office as a leader and protector.

At the Consulate General were the consuls,[12] laden with the responsibilities of their office. American consular or diplomatic officials abroad tend to be beset by people who want something from representatives of a powerful and wealthy nation. Also, because Americans appear to regard government officials as public servants who are required to concern themselves with the problems of ordinary people, a State Department outpost often gives the impression of a place under siege. The American tends to think about his diplomatic or consular representatives as a mixture of aristocrat and public servant. It may be the "public servant" image which makes American officials especially vulnerable to harassment. Diplomats from countries such as France or Britain, on the other hand, seem to be regarded by their own nationals as sacred personages who are above the affairs of ordinary men.[13]

In order to survive in the face of continual demands for their attention, American officials abroad have had to develop schemes for screening or separating petitions in terms of their significance and credibility. At the same time, an attempt is made to convey to the petitioner the impression that his case is being considerered with appropriate devotion. Having learned his lesson in Latin America, the anthropologist came armed with a grant, an institutional affiliation, and a powerful protector in the government. He was reasonably confident that his case would be given one of the higher priorities by American officials in the city.

The most direct way to the American Consulate General from the hotel on the Gran Via is along a busy, modern thoroughfare through the heart of the Old City (*Barrio Gotico*) to the waterfront. It is a street of business, and it is perhaps symbolic that an outpost devoted primarily to commercial affairs should be situated on it. The anthropologist made his way down the street with somewhat more than the usual difficulties. He had the impression that people were running into him and laying their hands on him in a way that one does not expect even in a large American city like New York. This physical intimacy (which he interpreted as aggression) was somewhat disturbing. If he had heard the famous lecture which is given to State Department employees about the "bubbles" which Americans carry around with them he might have understood these events better, but he probably would have been no less disturbed. Americans of all degrees of sophistication complained of the physical contact which they had to endure on the streets and public transportation of Ciudad Condal.

The anthropologist passed a number of banks (one of which served most Americans), a formidable looking police station, and a plaza which extended to the right into a very old sector and led to a magnificent cathedral. The Consulate General overlooked the plaza on one side and the street of business on the other. The elevator in the building usually worked, but on infrequent occasions when it failed one had to negotiate several flights of marble stairs to get to the reception room.

The Consulate General was not very imposing. It had the look of an ordinary business office. The reception room, which was a congregating place for Americans, often gave the appearance of the state of siege to which we have alluded above. The receptionist was one of the ill-paid host employees on the staff. She was an extremely efficient young woman who liked being associated with Americans. It was her custom to handle telephone calls, receive visitors, check lists, and carry on a variety of minor negotiations—often simultaneously. She was particularly adept at handling destitute Americans who dragged themselves into the office looking for money to get home (procedure: send a collect cable home for funds by return cable). Her dealings with representatives of the Nth Fleet, which visited the city periodically, were extensive.

The Consulate General had five working sections: consular, economic, political, administrative, and public affairs (including "culture"). At the time of the study the staff consisted of fourteen Americans (eleven officers and three secretaries) and twenty host employees, making it the second largest diplomatic outpost in Spain. All the officers spoke Spanish and one was an expert on Spanish affairs. The pictures of the President of the United States, the American flag, and the businesslike atmosphere in which these people worked tended to give the stranger a feeling of security which was not always reinforced by further contact with this office.

The "front" which the people of the Consulate General presented to the anthropologist that day was full of cordiality and willing assistance. The consul general received him and the public affairs officer was detailed to assist him. He was promised full cooperation. What the anthropologist could not know at the time was that what was being given to him on one level was beginning to be withheld on another. It was within the confines of the consular circle of diplomats and wives that the single significant focus of resistance to his project developed. The anthropologist had varying opinions of consulate personnel during his sojourn, but as he left the office that day his impression was entirely favorable.

Not all Americans were so favorably impressed by their initial contact with the consulate. Businessmen, in particular, were prone to complain about the economic section. Concerning one of the economic officers, one businessman said, "——— is worthless. He doesn't know anything. He can't remember anything." Another said, "——— is a washout. He didn't even know that our company existed."

The psychological kinship with one's fellow nationals, which may have been obscured in the day-to-day routine at home, tends to become clearer when abroad. One may love them or hate them, but as James Baldwin has suggested, one begins to realize that all of them (including oneself) come out of the same national mold.[14] One tends to expect things of colleagues that are not expected of others; and when the colleagues fail to meet expectations it may be difficult to forgive them. If the stranger abroad finds that he cannot count on other Americans, particularly representatives of his own government, his reactions may be extreme. Colleagues then are adding to his problems with meaninglessness, not helping to solve them.

The first encounter of an American in the city with a substantial group of his colleagues usually occurred at the Consulate General. To the extent that first impressions are important, this event would tend to influence the American's conception of himself and his relations with others. The American Consulate General was to become a reference point for American residents in the city. Whether it was a positive or negative reference point depended in part on the nature of the initial encounter with the office and its personnel. At the time of the study a substantial group of Americans had formed an aversion toward their government's headquarters in Ciudad Condal. Later in this narrative we will have an opportunity to consider why this was so. (Such widespread antipathy toward the diplomatic or consular outpost was not discovered by the author in two other American communities in Europe.)

Whatever the nature of American feelings about it, the Consulate General was one of the few public places in Ciudad Condal in which an American could feel at home. A bull, when he comes into the ring, is said to develop *querencias* or preferred localities,[15] places where he feels that he is on home ground, so to speak, and where he is especially confident. Strangers in a foreign setting seem to go through an analogous process. In the course of their exploration they find and tend to favor certain locales where it is easier to make preferred definitions prevail. For Americans the Consulate General was one of these.

A second American *querencia* was the Cultural Institute. It was situated in the region inhabited by most Americans. Because the Institute was located at some distance from hotels and from the Consulate General (the principal *querencias* during the early part of the sojourn), and because it was not concerned with the crucial details of beginning a life in the city, it was not usually "found" by Americans until later in their stay. Once a home had been established, one might begin to visit the building on the Via Viuda, participate in one or more of the educational, cultural, and social activities there, and savor the normal use of English in thinking and communicating with others.

Early or late, the American was to learn that there was very little home ground for him in the city. When we mention the Consulate General, the Cultural Institute, and the American schools we have exhausted the list of American territories. There were no American churches or graveyards, no American shopping centers, no "blocks" of American housing, no American hospitals, and no American restaurants. The impression of being in a foreign place, therefore, was for the American almost inescapable.

There were, however, more or less compatible sectors of the foreign scene. In the British *querencias* an American could function fairly effectively in terms of his thinking-as-usual. If he were a Protestant, he could attend the Anglican church which served both the American and British colonies. The Foreign Enclaves Hospital was oriented also toward Anglo-American requirements (though its standards were questioned by some). In addition, there were a number of internationalized or Americanized points in the city. Supermarkets (*supermercados*) had been inaugurated recently in Ciudad Condal and the one in the principal American sector was frequented by many Americans. Here one could shop for a wide variety of items without struggling to communicate with sales people. The better shops and restaurants, available to the average American because of his comparatively greater wealth, and the principal tourist facilities were thoroughly internationalized. An international bohemian culture (centered in the Plaza Vieja in the Old City) and student culture (centered at the university) attracted Americans with appropriate inclinations. Finally, the entire complex of fun and games which catered especially to the men of the Nth Fleet was located in the lower portion of the Old City close to the waterfront.

At the beginning of his sojourn, of course, the American did not possess a "topographical map" of cultural compatibilities. What he probably did possess was an ordinary map of the city marked with points of significance to the tourist. A good many of them were located in that portion of the Old City between the street of business and the Ramblas. To most Americans this area was the most interesting part of Ciudad Condal, and they spent a good deal of time wandering through the narrow, twisting streets which lent to this sector (in the American mind) an air of quaintness. The Old City could be considered a living museum which had no opening or closing hours. The many points of archeological and historical interest, magnificently maintained by the city, could be entered casually and considered at length. In such an atmosphere one tends to "sink into" history rather than continue to observe it from outside. The stranger, as Schutz has suggested, "does not partake of the vivid historical tradition by which the approached group has been formed." [16] The evidence indicates that wanderings through the Old City tended to make Americans more aware of this problem.

Our discussion of the entrance of American guests into the city has focused on territorial arrangements and the grosser aspects of the physical environment because these elements tended to preoccupy our American residents-to-be during the early part of their sojourn. They were concerned with geographic space and the inanimate objects in it. But they also had begun to have encounters with people *en masse* and as individuals. Early contacts with the hosts often made lasting impressions on lost wanderers. Appealing for aid from people who in most cases did not speak English, Americans sometimes found themselves overwhelmed by helpfulness. It was customary among the hosts to take a personal interest in problems of this nature and go out of their way to help. As one American put it, "The Spanish people are the most helpful and hospitable in Europe. . . . They are willing to show you where to go—to go out of their way to take you some place. Only yesterday a man turned around to show me where to go." If one had come from France where an extremely surly populace was supposed to exist,[17] the encounter with this kind of hospitality in a strange city was particularly gratifying.

We would be well advised, however, to suspend judgments about the hosts on the basis of encounters on the street. The quality of friendly helpfulness, so highly valued by most American strangers, was not always encountered in other areas of life. Transients who had experienced the friendly "front" of the city would be amazed to hear the sometimes vehement expressions of hostility toward the hosts by some American residents. The residents, for their part, used to say that the transient could not know what it was like to live in the city and deal with the hosts on a day-to-day basis. Sooner or later the American had to move into the hosts' *querencia,* and it was out of encounters there that significant attitudes were formed. The majority of American residents held mixed or unfavorable attitudes toward the people of their host city. The reasons for the development of such widespread antipathy will be considered in the pages that follow.

3

NESTING

My thoughts were now wholly employed about
securing myself against either savages ... or
wild beasts ... ; and I had many thoughts of
the method how to do this and what kind of
a dwelling to make....

ROBINSON CRUSOE

IN THE TAKEN-FOR-GRANTED WORLD OF THE TYPICAL
American, if there is such a person, there looms a
suburban dwelling with a garage and a place for the
children to play. Within this context the dominant theme of American suburbia, child-centered familism,[1] is enacted. Were this typical American to go abroad with his family we would expect that he would carry with him his suburban ideal and attempt to realize it in the foreign setting. Give this American a substantial purchasing power and multiply him by the thousands. It is possible, then, to envisage a very great pressure on certain kinds of housing in countries where the detached home may not be as frequently encountered. Considering the scarcity of this type of housing, if Americans who go abroad today are in any sense typical, we would expect many of them to be faced with more or less significant threats to their thinking-as-usual.

Although difficult to prove, we presume that the problems of Americans in obtaining suitable housing overseas have become more serious in recent years. The higher standard of living among Americans, coupled with the increasing tendency to marry and emphasize family life,[2] seems to have been associated with the greater demand for detached dwellings. If this historical trend were reflected among Americans overseas,[3] we would expect that increasing numbers of them would be unhappy in countries where detached housing is a scarce commodity. One American method of solving this housing problem is practiced at some American military bases abroad. In these locations crash building programs have produced American-style housing developments designed to meet the requirements of the military and their families.[4]

Most Americans in Ciudad Condal experienced the housing problem to which we have just alluded. An estimated 60 percent of the resident adult population were family people who had come abroad *en famille.* They sought to find dwellings in the city in which they could live a more or less typical American existence during the several years of their foreign sojourn. But substantial single-family dwellings were at a premium. One American said, "Finding a place to live is difficult because of the standards Americans have. We wanted a house with a yard. They are few and far between." Another said, "We wanted a house. There was the problem of upkeep, heating expense, etc., but we thought that it was worth the effort to have our own place and a place for the children to play. Houses are difficult to find here." The inevitable compromises evolving out of the house-hunting process included moving to the suburbs (where single-family dwellings were more readily available), into one part of a two- or three-family house, or into a furnished or unfurnished apartment. The poor and the unmarried rented rooms in Spanish homes or lived in pensions.

FINDING A HOME

If, in his initial wanderings about the city, an American were to arrive at the foot of the Ramblas at the waterfront and ascend to the top of the monument there, he would have a commanding view of Ciudad Condal. From this vantage point (a machine gun nest during the fratricidal strife on the Republican side during the Civil War) he could scan much of the territory in which Americans lived. Taking the Ramblas, which leads up to the central plaza as a clock hand pointing to twelve, and continuing this line of sight to the mountains, he would establish one "boundary" of American habitation. To the right of this line, i.e., in the entire northeastern half of the city, no more than two or three Americans lived. It was an area heavily dominated by the working class. It was not likely that an American would find a suitable home there. Nor was it likely (unless he were a bohemian) that he would settle in any part of the downtown region of the city below the Gran Via which crossed the "clock hand boundary" about half a kilometer away.

Many informants reported that Americans did not live in any one sector of the city. They presumably meant that there were no "blocks" of American homes as in, say, Madrid or Bonn. There was, however, an area of the city clearly favored by Americans. The chances were more than two out of three that the American at the top of the monument would finally locate in the distant upland sector between ten and twelve on our imaginary clock. Beyond this, on top of the mountains, the small village of Valldosta offered living possibilities (five American families had homes there). Extending beyond the American's range of vision along the imaginary line of ten o'clock was the suburb of San Gelardo (four families), and to the left on the coast at a distance of twenty kilometers, a resort community in which seven American families lived. The territorial possibilities for the American home-hunter seem to have been, in effect, rather circumscribed. Why was this so?

Most American homes were acquired through American contacts. Americans often moved into homes being vacated by other Americans. But why did Americans select certain territories in the first place? The favored areas simply offered more housing of the kind compatible with American expectations of a spacious, detached dwelling with modern facilities and a yard. American families in the city generally had enough money to "command" these comparatively scarce accommodations; but most of them were not entirely satisfied with the homes they finally found.

About half the Americans were able to move directly from their first stopping place in or around the city to a permanent home. The other half made one intermediate stop, usually in a furnished apartment, before establishing a permanent residence. The intermediate stopping place usually was used by those who found the hotel or pension an increasingly unbearable place in which to wait out the housing hunt. A move there could be accomplished rather easily because furnished apartments were much more numerous than the kind of dwellings Americans would accept as permanent residences.

In the process of locating a home, certain economic facts of life in the city became apparent. As a rule, Americans arriving in Ciudad Condal expected that life there would be inexpensive. Some even entertained visions of renting a castle or a mansion at a bargain rate. It was not unusual for American families to expect to spend no more than fifty dollars a month for a large apartment. It *was* possible to obtain an apartment at this price, but it would fail to meet so many American requirements that it was virtually ruled out as a possible home. At the time of the study, American families were finding it almost impossible to rent suitable accommodations for less than one hundred dollars a month plus utilities. From this minimum, rentals ranged upwards to around three hundred dollars plus utilities. Below this price spread was the cost of a room or pension (less than forty dollars per month) for a single person; above it, the cost of buying an apartment outright. The price of a luxury apartment owned by one American family was almost $25,000. Unless the American wanted to change his style of living drastically he would have had to pay almost as much for housing in Ciudad Condal as at home. In reaction to the realization that the cost of living in the city was considerably higher than expected, Americans tended to take the attitude that they were being cheated and that they had been deceived.

Some Americans claimed that rates had been raised when it became apparent to the agent or landlord that his prospective tenant was from the United States. It is difficult to gauge the extent of this claim or to substantiate it, but taking into consideration the character of the hosts, it seems reasonable to suppose that some clipping practices did, in fact, occur. This surmise is supported, first, by the widespread belief among the hosts that all Americans were wealthy (*"todos son millionarios"*). Second, the hosts idealized the businessman who could enter into, and succeed in, sharp business practices. A naive person with money ready to be taken was called a "big fish" (*pez grande*). Since at least some American strangers fell into this category, we should not be surprised that some of them had been subject to price-gouging. It would be a mistake, however, to assume that this practice (when it occurred) represented discrimination against the Americans, but Americans affected by it usually did not realize that as far as the hosts were concerned the nationality of the *pez grande* was of little importance.

The contract which was required to rent a house or an apartment introduced many Americans to the legal aspect of business transactions in the city. The contract, an impressive-looking document filled with high-sounding phrases, minute stipulations, and official seals, occasionally masked sub rosa practices such as a non-returnable opening payment (*entrada*) [5] or an expensive door key (to circumvent rent ceilings). The contract served to formalize a situation in which the American renter was at a distinct disadvantage. Suppose that the landlord did not fulfill his part of the bargain. Although he was legally liable, the task of instituting and carrying through the action necessary to secure a legal judgment against him was so forbidding that it rendered him, in effect, immune to prosecution. For most of the Americans, their sojourn in Ciudad Condal was to be brief (no more than four years). It was not likely that they would want to enter a labyrinthine legal tangle which could consume a good part of their existence there. Even with a local lawyer, the process was bound to be an extended one. Not only the legal situation, but also the seller's market in housing worked to the advantage of the landlord. His principal method of utilizing this advantage was to fail to provide services and the major or minor repairs which were always necessary. Most Americans were angry with landlords who, according to them, charged exorbitant rentals for defective dwellings and provided inadequately for their upkeep.

What did a typical American dwelling look like? The E. family moved into the second-floor apartment of a large two-family house located in the heart of the district favored by Americans. It was an impressive, castle-like edifice previously occupied by a single Catalan family. There was a yard surrounded by the usual impregnable fence. If this had been a Catalan home, a fierce shepherd dog probably would have lurked in the yard waiting to snap at passersby through the bars of the fence. If one had business in such a house, he pushed the bell at the gate and endured the raging beast until a maid came to admit him. The E.'s had no dog, and their gate was often left open—a nice American touch in this defensive-minded sector.

The rooms of the unfurnished building occupied by the E.'s had high ceilings, cement walls, and tile floors. There was no central heating; butane, kerosene, or electric space heaters would be required for the colder months. The six rooms in which the E.'s lived on the second floor were furnished with E. furniture shipped from home at company expense. Mr. E. had obtained transformers to provide the correct electric current for their American refrigerator and washing machine. A very small electric hot water heater served the bathroom and kitchen. Adjoining the kitchen was a room for a maid. Downstairs, inside the fence, was a space to park the E. car.

At first glance, this menage would seem to be more than acceptable for a typical American family with two children. The heating probably could be counted as a headache, but aside from Spanish-type bathroom and kitchen fixtures, there did not appear to be any significant barriers against establishing a home in the American fashion. However, the E.'s found that appearances can be deceiving.

MAINTENANCE

Commenting on their apartment, Mrs. E. said, "In the hotel it was easy. Here, nothing worked. . . . It took two months before we got the john to flush—which can drive you to distraction." Another American woman said, "There were rats and cockroaches in the apartment. . . . The hot water [heater] exploded. The floor fell in. There was flooding, and the walls were turning green from the humidity. . . . One thing leads to another. I have had some kind of workmen in my house repairing something almost every other day since I have been here."

In the United States one learns to rely on the various utility systems in the home. One assumes that the telephone, the electricity, the water, the heating, and the sewer will function and that immediate repairs will be made in rare cases of break-down. Such an assumption was at odds with the realities of life in a place where lower standards of reliability prevailed. It was customary for Americans in Ciudad Condal to have more or less serious difficulties with one or more of the utility systems in their home and to struggle through the transactions needed to get them repaired. The principal parties in the repair transactions were the landlord and the *lampista*.

Notified of the failure of, say, the hot water system in a house, the landlord would respond in one of two ways: (1) Sympathize and promise to get the *lampista* to take care of it immediately. (2) Sympathize, point out that the contract required that the tenant be responsible for repairs, and urge the tenant to contact the *lampista* immediately. In either case, the ultimate success of the appeal depended on the availability and response of the *lampista*.

The *lampista* is a neighborhood handyman who devotes himself primarily to plumbing and electrical work. Notified of the disaster in the house, he would respond with some sympathy and promise to attend to it directly. He might say that he would come "tomorrow" (*mañana*). Any American in a Spanish-speaking country [6] would learn that *mañana* is a quixotic expression meaning, in terms of performance, "sometime in the future." The *lampista* probably would not appear "tomorrow," and the American who may have been raised to believe that words must be matched by deeds, would experience one more disturbing jolt to his thinking-as-usual. In the face of repeated and possibly increasingly angry calls for help, the *lampista* was likely to remain unperturbed. The frustrated American then might begin to think of him as a liar, which was, of course, incorrect. The *lampista* simply attached a different meaning to the word *mañana*.

The transactional problems with the landlord and the *lampista* were not merely a matter of differences in meanings attributed to Spanish or Catalan words. The landlord and the *lampista* rarely spoke English; and the American, especially at the beginning of his sojourn, rarely possessed the technical vocabulary to make his meanings clear. Considerable time and effort, therefore, were necessary to make oneself understood. An American who started out to get his hot water system repaired might find that he had forgotten his original intention in the struggle to explain himself. In this way, means could be transformed into ends and subjective worlds reoriented to include the value of effective communication with the hosts.

In the first chapter we spoke of Americans as representatives of an imperial power and emphasized the two-sided nature of imperialistic transactions. This two-sidedness is illustrated by the relationship between the American tenant and the landlord and the *lampista*. Because of his wealth, the American could "command" a dwelling and maintenance services; however, the process of renting and the provision of such services were carried out very much in terms of host definitions and the American was often at the mercy of his hosts.

SERVANTS

For the American woman in the city, the most significant host figure was the maid. In the United States, the American woman usually did not have full-time servants. In Ciudad Condal she was likely to employ at least one full-time maid. The maid exercised a considerable fascination for American women in Ciudad Condal,[7] a fascination which seemed to be derived not only from her prestige and novelty value, but also from the number of problems that she created in the household.

In transactions with their servants, Americans, particularly the women, experienced the clash of cultures in its most direct form. It has been suggested that the lack of a well-developed serving tradition tends to make Americans unsure of themselves when handling servants,[8] but to judge from their reports, the American women found the servants of Ciudad Condal especially difficult. One woman, for example, who had been brought up in servant-laden situations and who had employed many servants throughout an overseas career, said that the Spanish servants were the worst she had ever encountered. Another commented, "The maid situation is absolutely impossible. . . . They are like animals. They are filthy. I should not be saying these things, but they don't know what the paper in the bathroom is for." Still another said, "When they do things they may conform to your way once, but then they will go back to their own way of doing things. They aren't going to conform to you."

These statements were made by people who were experiencing the problems of strangerhood. We should not expect them to evaluate their servants fairly. They could not, for example, be expected to make distinctions between local (Catalan) servants and immigrants from rural Andalucía, some of whom had previously lived in caves. Other Americans with fewer problems sometimes made such distinctions. They also were more likely to offer favorable comments about their servants. On the whole, however, Americans in the city tended to see servants as problem-generators rather than problem-solvers. Why was this so?

At the time of the study servants were becoming harder to obtain in the city. The relative scarcity of servants was created by the rapid improvement in the local economic situation. People who never had servants in their lives had begun to expect them. Others, who could have looked forward to nothing more than a servant life, were learning of alternatives. A maid, for example, could quit for a better paying job in a factory or on the vacation coast to the north. In such a seller's market the cost of servants and their degree of independence tended to increase. A good maid was in the enviable position of being very much in demand.

At the time of the study the wages for a live-in maid ranged from the equivalent of twenty-five to thirty-five dollars per month plus room, board, and uniforms. Host employers, feeling the pinch of the rising wage spiral, sometimes blamed Americans for creating it by paying exorbitant salaries. There may have been some justification for this claim, especially where the recently departed military contingents were concerned. However, it probably would be more accurate to say that the Americans tended to serve as scapegoats for the complex economic developments which had contributed to the rising expectations of what had once been an available and tractable serving class.

To the newly-arrived American, the servant in her home appeared to be a paradoxical mixture of obedience and impertinence. She seemed sloppy, sometimes dirty in her personal habits, and often unreliable. She had her own way of doing things which was generally not the American's way. As the American woman tended to see it, the problem was simply to get the servant to change her habits. Lacking insight into the technique of dealing with servants in this particular culture, the American's attempts to train the servant were fraught with difficulties. In addition to problems of communication, there was the sometimes infuriating tendency of servants to appear to acquire the new method, but then abruptly revert to the old. An American housewife might gain the impression that she was starting a new day with her maid at the point where they had begun the day before. As one frustrated woman said, "One has the feeling that one isn't getting anywhere with them."

In the hopeless struggle to turn the maid into an adjunct of the American way of life, most American women found it difficult to strike the correct authoritative posture and degree of familiarity which would be most effective for eliciting the servant's full cooperation. An extremely authoritarian line might wound the personal *dignidad* which is so important to any Spaniard. On the other hand, the friendly-democratic approach could cause the maid to lose respect for her employer and, as a result, to take liberties with her. Even if the American were lucky enough to hit upon the right proportion of familiarity and superiority in her transactions with servants, it was still not possible to bring about the degree of Americanization in her servants which would turn the home into a *de facto* American *querencia*. Once the American woman had decided that a servant was necessary, she could avoid a great deal of storm and stress by being prepared to compromise with some of her servant's ways. Eventually she had to capitulate in some degree to a lower level of individual responsibility, lower standards of cleanliness and order, sloppy workmanship, and, in some cases, petty theft.

Louise Winfield points out that the number of servants employed by American abroad (as well as the number available) varies from one foreign situation to another.[9] American families in Ciudad

Condal found that servants were "necessary" for at least two reasons. First, the lack of labor-saving appliances, defective utilities,
and tortuous shopping expeditions made it nearly impossible for the
American woman to run her house alone. Second, specialized baby
sitters seldom were to be found. A maid who accepted baby sitting
as part of her normal duties and who could assist with various other
household chores promised to help the American woman maintain
some semblance of the female role to which she was accustomed.
Additional servants might permit her a degree of freedom and
self-indulgence which had only been a dream in the United States.

The number of part- or full-time servants employed in American
households ranged from 0–5 with a mean between 1 and 2. The
most frequent serving roles were the maid (*chica*), cook (*coci-
nera*), and nursemaid (*niñera*). In the more modest establishments
one serving woman played all these roles. In the larger, three or
more servant-specialists constituted a host force to be reckoned with.
A serving staff was a source of continuing difficulties for their
employer. Not only did they create difficulties themselves, but they
frequently brought their problems with boyfriends (*novios*) and
relatives into the home.[10] Such problems could have endless ramifications and might be used by the servant to excuse poor performance. Knowledge of them on the American side tended to person-
alize the relationship between employer and servant and to increase
the American's penetration of the host culture. Since servants spoke
little English, the extent of American involvement was related to
American fluency in a host language, usually Spanish. Americans
who would not learn the language of their hosts would not get
involved in the host sphere; but lack of fluency in Spanish or
Catalan might have its price in difficulties with servants and others.

FOOD

In order to get food for her household the American woman had
to make direct or indirect contact with host tradespeople. In the
United States, contact with such people has been reduced and
impersonalized by the growth of the supermarket. In Ciudad Con-

dal, the bulk of marketing was done in traditional markets which contained stalls specializing in fruits and vegetables, meat, fish, poultry products, canned goods, etc. In each of these stalls a separate business transaction was required. Afterwards, one probably would stop at the *panadería* for bread, the *bodega* for wine or bottled water, and the *lechería* for milk. Among the hosts it was customary to make this shopping round *every* day. It seemed to most Americans that this kind of shopping consumed much too much time and effort.

Virtually all the American women made some use of a traditional Spanish market. There one encountered scenes reminiscent of S. Klein's in New York during a sale. In order to be served, one had to enter the crush of women and push and shove with the rest. Concerning host women in the market, one American woman said, "When a woman here goes into the market she has to begin to push. At the fish counter they have to get their noses up in the mouth of the fish." The kind of physical assertiveness which the hosts displayed in public places such as the market or on the street tended to provoke Americans. The more accustomed one had become to physical privacy at home the more threatening shopping expeditions tended to appear.

Allowing ourselves the use of an overworked term, we would suggest that the physical intimacy to which Americans were exposed in public provoked anxiety because it tended to break down physical alienation from others. The shopping expedition also threatened another form of personal alienation which prevails in modern America, i.e., alienation from one's body and its processes.[11] In the Spanish market one came into more direct contact with blood and guts than is customary in the American supermarket. Instead of neatly packaged or canned meats, fish and poultry, one encountered physical facts which could remind one of forbidden bodily organs and processes even as remnants of feces in the Spanish-style toilet bowl could remind one of disturbing anal facts of life.

Transactions with tradespeople in the market involved the ubiquitous problem of communication and trust. It was necessary, for example, to learn the technical vocabulary for the local cuts of meat. Having accomplished this, the buyer could only hope that she was getting the best of the desired cut at a fair price. Most American women had at least passing qualms about the honesty of tradespeople and, in time, developed techniques for reassuring themselves that they were being treated fairly. Some added up figures ostentatiously. Others relied on the personal relationships which they built up with individual tradespeople. The authority with which one carried off such attempts to control the situation depended—at least in part—on the ability to talk and figure in Spanish or Catalan.

It was possible to mitigate some of the problems which Americans encountered in their expeditions to the Spanish market by sending a maid in one's stead (as was customary among the hosts). Although it might be an appealing expedient, it could raise problems of the trustworthiness of the maid. Would she follow instructions to the letter? Would she be scrupulously honest, or would she arrange some form of kickback with the tradespeople? Some American women, unwilling to trust their maids completely, adopted the compromise procedure of doing their shopping with them, but it required a relatively great expenditure of time and effort.

A second means of mitigating the problems involved in shopping at a traditional Spanish market was to patronize one of the new supermarkets which had begun to appear in Ciudad Condal. Almost all the American women did at least some of their shopping there. In the supermarket one could select conspicuously priced items directly from the shelves. Contacts with tradespeople had to occur only in the few specialized sections with non-packaged goods and in the check-out line. Problems of trust and communication, therefore, were reduced. The supermarket offered items at or slightly below the prices of the traditional Spanish market, but most American women regarded the quality of non-packaged goods obtained at the supermarket as somewhat inferior. In addition, during peak periods there were crowd scenes and extended waits in the check-out line where (in the judgment of many Americans) impertinent young women operated the cash registers in desultory fashion.

Perhaps the most successful method of mitigating the problems posed by the traditional Spanish market was to do one's shopping in a United States government PX (Post Exchange). The privilege of shopping in one of these emporiums was limited to the military and non-military government people and one or two non-government families with special status. It was customary for those with PX privileges to form car pools and make one or two expeditions a month to one of two PX's at distances of 100 km or 200 km from the city. When the Nth Fleet was in port some Americans made use of a store on board ship which offered a limited number of items.

Americans without PX privileges tended to be envious of those who possessed them and the privileged ones often wore an apologetic air about their special shopping status and access to desirable consumer goods. The PX items coveted by Americans were frozen foods (especially meats cut in the American fashion), paper products (including softer American toilet tissue), soaps and detergents, cake mixes, and portable kerosene space heaters. This list suggests one kind of relative deprivation experienced by Americans (especially non-government Americans) in Ciudad Condal. Since this deprivation was not uniformly distributed among the Americans in the community, "have" and "have not" categories were created with regard to these important consumer items. The fact that these categories partly coincided with the two antagonistic subgroups within the community, i.e., government people and businessmen, tended to exacerbate intra-community conflict. In other American overseas communities where PX privileges were either entirely absent or available to all, this kind of unequal relative deprivation would not exist.

In Spain at the time of the study, refrigeration and freezing of foods for mass home consumption had not advanced as far as it had in America. Spanish refrigerators tended to be smaller and to contain (by American standards) inadequate freezing compartments. Castillo Puche, in observing Americans and their way of life in a famous apartment block in Madrid, thinks that Americans have turned the refrigerator into a sacred idol. He says, "La nevera para los americanos, mas que un objecto domestico, es una especie de ídolo sagrado." [12]

In Ciudad Condal it was extremely rare for an American house or apartment to be without this sacred machine. The kind of refrigerator possessed was an indication of life style in this foreign setting. If a family had a large American model with a capacious freezing compartment to match their PX card, they could store up American foods and maintain more American food habits. The smaller Spanish machine with its insignificant freezing compartment and ice cube trays would not permit this. It was, however, adequate for those who did not have access to a PX. The freezing and packaging of goods for sale in Spanish stores had not advanced beyond the limited capacity of the Spanish home refrigerator.

The Americans who possessed American refrigerators stocked with American foods were the government people who had brought their machines with them and who managed, with the appropriate transformer, to keep them operating in the face of precarious electric current and inadequate maintenance facilities. Stocked with PX items, these refrigerators enabled the government types to preserve more American food customs than could their non-government colleagues.

It may seem that our discussion of the refrigerators of Americans in the city has been making too much of what, after all, was an insignificant factor in their lives. Of course, the degree of dependence on the refrigerator and American foods varied from one American family to another, but the importance attached to these facets of American culture by American expatriates cannot be overlooked. In the city it was the military families whose concern with and dependence on American foods was most extreme. For these families the value of American, and fear of foreign food products was great enough to suggest the working out of an emotional factor. According to a host doctor who treated Americans, the fears of local food were almost entirely unjustified. Aside from brief bouts of diarrhea which may have been partly or wholly caused by local food and drink, they suffered no other significant food-related diseases. Why, then, were the American military so anxious about food?

There is some evidence that American military men tend to be more dependent.[13] We would suggest that part of this dependence exists in the oral realm. If you meet a military man on a new post it is likely that he will make some comment to you about the chow. If the food is good he may tend to think well of his situation and feel that his military organization is taking good care of him. In a foreign area where one may be subject to stranger anxiety (expressed, perhaps, in fears of foreign foods), the valuation of American food provided by the organization could constitute a particular kind of oral defense reaction. In the military home abroad, therefore, the refrigerator could indeed be considered a kind of sacred idol serving to exorcise the demons of a foreign existence.

HEATING

The typical American arrived in Ciudad Condal in the late summer or early fall, well before the advent of cold weather. It would not be until mid-November when the temperature began to edge down toward the freezing mark that he would become aware of what were for him inadequate heating facilities in his home. Host families might sit around in apparent comfort with their breaths steaming in the air, but the typical American, accustomed to an indoor temperature of approximately 70 degrees Fahrenheit, began to be concerned about keeping himself and his family warm. Of 35 adult informants who gave adequate information, 20 said that their concern about being cold had increased since coming to the city, while only one said that it had decreased. Fourteen said that it had neither increased nor decreased.

Efforts to keep the cold out of the family *querencia* involved the use of various heating appliances. Some American households were warmed by more or less primitive central heating systems. The majority, however, used fireplaces, wood and coal stoves, kerosene, butane, and electric space heaters. Stoves and furnaces usually were stoked with coal, but wood and nut shells were used also. These fuels were expensive and, because they were impure or too quickly consumed, required continuous stoking operations. One American man, who was asked about his voracious furnace said, "I stoke it. My wife stokes it. The maid stokes it. Everybody stokes the furnace whenever he is cold."

Those who used butane gas or kerosene may have had to pay less attention to their heating units, but they were more dependent on periodic delivery of butane "bottles." It was not easy to keep a large supply of butane on hand, and in really cold weather when the city's stock was depleted, there often was no delivery for days or weeks. Then one would have to resort to emergency devices to keep warm: put on more clothes, spend more time under an electric blanket (if there was one), go out more to bars and cafes where the temperature was tolerable, drink.

During the winter months, then, the Americans were subject to a deprivation of warmth which delivered the *coup de grace* to any illusions they may have held about "sunny Spain." Although the temperature seldom fell below 20 degrees Fahrenheit, the cold and damp made the city an uncomfortable place for Americans in the winter. One physical consequence of the winter climate and the inadequate heating may have been an increased susceptibility to respiratory illness. Even as the hosts, Americans began to sniffle, sneeze, and cough. A theater-goer in winter had to strain to hear the actors over the coughing and sneezing audience. It is not possible to say whether Americans in the city suffered more respiratory illness than at home. However, the danger of contracting a serious disease such as tuberculosis seems to have been somewhat greater.[14]

Americans' problems with heating were similar to all the other problems they encountered in building a nest. Coming from a country with a high level of technology, comfort, and sanitation into a foreign setting where lower standards prevailed, they usually attempted to establish an American-style habitation. Some of them brought American furniture and machines to help them do this. Others tried unsuccessfully to make foreign people and machines work in the American pattern. Because they were not sufficiently powerful or skilled they could not do this. As a result, after more or less serious troubles some compromise in domestic life-style was worked out. It is of course inevitable that even the most powerful imperialists will have to make compromises in the foreign setting. In large American military enclaves abroad the average individual has to make fewer compromises because he is screened from the foreign environment. Because this was not the case in Ciudad Condal, the burden of adaptation fell on the individual or family, especially on the domestic scene, where the advance of modern ways seems to have been least rapid. The domestic style of life which resulted from Americans' compromises with their hosts will be examined in the next chapter.

4

THE
DOMESTIC SIDE OF A
FOREIGN EXISTENCE

> Her compact and crowded little chambers (in
> the Quartier Marboeuf), almost dusky, as they
> at first struck him, with accumulations, repre-
> sented a supreme general adjustment to oppor-
> tunities and conditions. . . .
>
> HENRY JAMES
> *The Ambassadors*

IT IS CUSTOMARY TO THINK OF FRONTIERSMEN AS males unencumbered with women and children. In Conrad's novels about the British overseas frontier, for example, we find a disproportionate number of unmarried men with or without native mistresses.[1] A later, more settled stage of British overseas life in which the British family is more important is depicted by Forster and Orwell.[2]

The history of the domestic side of American life abroad has yet to be written. Fragmentary information suggests that with the exception of missionaries early American overseas frontiersmen tended to conform to the customary image. We do not have the data to tell us when the American family came to occupy a signifi-cant place on the overseas stage. Louise Winfield says that "early missionaries and overseas business people took their children wher-ever they went," [3] but she cites neither evidence nor authority. Until some historian becomes convinced that the domestic side of life abroad is worthy of study, we can speak confidently only about recent history.

In the 1950's the number of American military and civilian employees of the United States abroad increased from approximately 325,000 to 645,000. In the same period their overseas dependents increased from approximately 107,000 to 506,000.[4] In this limited segment of recent history the number of overseas dependents of federal employees abroad increased at a faster rate than the employees themselves; by 1960 they were almost as numerous as the government personnel on whom they depended. At the time of the present study, American wives and children occupied a large and growing portion of the overseas stage and constituted an increasingly important factor in American adaptation abroad. By their inclusion of a chapter on the family in their survey of Americans abroad, Cleveland and his associates seem to have recognized the proper place and significance of women and children in American overseas missions.[5]

The demographic facts show that the American community in Ciudad Condal was not unusual in regard to the presence of women and children. At the time of this study there were an estimated 75 more or less complete resident American families, of which an estimated 55 had children ranging in age from infancy to late adolescence.[6] The families were for the most part unbroken; in only an estimated 8 was one parent absent. There were comparatively few mixed (international) marriages (no more than 6 between a host and an American.) In addition, there were an estimated 60 resident single adults and a few boarding children whose parents lived elsewhere. Among single adults, females outnumbered males, but marriages between Americans were rare. During the year of the study, only one such marriage took place. As a consequence of these demographic facts and a more circumscribed existence for females, the American community included a comparatively large group of lonely and unsatisfied single or divorced women.

In *From Here to Eternity,* James Jones [7] depicts the captain's wife as the kind of promiscuous woman frequently encountered on American military outposts. Castillo Puche [8] also describes a similar type in his novel about an American military enclave in Madrid. No empirical study has been conducted to evaluate the reputation for sexual promiscuity on American military and civilian outposts. Until such a study is done (and perhaps even afterwards), people will probably continue to indulge their sexual fantasies, curiosity, and suspicions about overseas communities. In Ciudad Condal some of the Americans thought that the primary mission of the anthropologist was to discover the true nature of their sex lives. Fortunately for these Americans' fears (and unfortunately for their possible aspirations), the anthropologist was not able to uncover any "sensational" sexual facts in their community. The bohemians followed their stereotyped ways with sex and drugs and the sailors of the Nth Fleet received the benefits of the prostitution mill in the Old City, but the resident Americans appeared to have no more than a low-keyed sex life structured by the canons of middle-class propriety. Even among the young, single residents, it was unusual to find love affairs or liaisons in or outside the community.

How the married Americans carried on in their own connubial beds is not known to the author, but the incidence of extra-marital sexuality seemed extremely low, if not altogether non-existent. Among the married men there was a good deal of lascivious talk at parties about the Bar Mariposa, a rendezvous frequented by more expensive prostitutes. However, visits to this bar by these or other American men were extremely rare.[9] In contrast to his counterparts among the wealthier Catalans, who often maintained mistresses and visited prostitutes as a matter of course, the American husband appeared to be a model of conjugal fidelity. There was no evidence that he became acculturated to Catalan norms in this dimension of culture during his sojourn in Ciudad Condal.

Americans abroad, particularly women, have a reputation also for succumbing to the temptations of alcohol.[10] In a place like Ciudad Condal where liquor and wine were cheap, both in the PX and at the local market, and where many Americans were wrestling with the problems of strangerhood, we might expect to find observable effects of the liberal use of alcohol. But although most resident adult Americans who gave adequate information (20 of 37) said that they were drinking more than at home, and although observation confirmed their extensive use of wine and liquor, serious disturbances by alcohol of individual functions or social relationships were rare. Here again we see that these Americans tended to conform to the norms of the sober middle class. By contrast, transient Americans, particularly the men of the Nth Fleet on leave, tended to be rambunctious in their drinking behavior and impaired the American image in the eyes of the seldom intoxicated hosts.

THE FAMILY

Most Americans in Ciudad Condal were members of resident American families. The character of these families was recognizably American, but the range of family styles extended from almost pure American middle-class, as in the military, to a sort of Americanized-Catalan middle-class in the cases of long-term sojourners and families based on mixed marriages. Here we will be concerned especially with the qualities of family life which emerged as adaptations to the foreign scene. Data about this and a number of other aspects of the American existence in the city were obtained from standardized interviews with the cross-section of adult informants mentioned in the Preface and confirmed where possible, by personal observation.

The acquisition of a home and contact with hosts such as maids, handymen, and tradespeople threatened Americans' conception of time and required concessions in the direction of the peculiar rhythm of host life. For example, some changes had to be made in meal schedules. At home, a family would have begun breakfast between 7 and 9 A.M., lunch (a small meal with father absent) at noon, and dinner between 6 and 7 P.M. The hosts maintained a different rhythm of life: breakfast began between 6 and 9 A.M., lunch (a large meal with father present) at noon,[11] and dinner (a large meal also) between 9 and 11 P.M. The response by American families to these facts usually took the form of some compromise between American and host norms. Predominantly American schedules were maintained by the military and the oil explorers. This solution was possible for them because their organizations were able to create work schedules which conformed to the American pattern.

In those families where the breadwinner was required to follow the rhythm of host life on the job, mealtimes moved closer to the host norm.

The principal obstacle to full acculturation of meal schedules was the presence of young children who ("for their health") needed to be put to bed early. American parents wanted to eat with their children, but they did not want to keep them up late. The usual result was a compromise dinner hour beginning between 7 and 8 P.M. If the parents went out to a restaurant for their evening meal, they usually could not expect to dine before 10 P.M. On such an occasion they might encounter other Americans who ate regularly in restaurants and who, in consequence, were more fully acculturated in their meal schedules.

In commenting on the American family abroad, Louise Winfield says that "frequently in a new and strange situation family members are pulled closer together." [12] Her hypothesis that the foreign experience tends to heighten family cohesiveness (i.e., the attraction of family members to each other) [13] was supported by interviews with American informants in the city. Their responses suggest that there was an increased familial involvement in the majority of families (15 of 28) for which there is adequate information. This involvement had both its positive and negative aspects. Stranger anxiety can be injected into the family and (as in several cases in Ciudad Condal) impose severe strains on family relationships. During the course of the study there were several threatened separations and one actual separation of spouses. However, in the cases of most of the informants reporting heightened involvement with their families, the positive aspects of familial commitment seemed to outweigh the negative.

A number of factors appear to have contributed to the increased cohesiveness of American families in the city. One of these was the increase in physical togetherness which occurred there.[14] The greater contact of family members with each other seems to have been related, first of all, to the distribution of American homes. Notwithstanding their concentration in certain zones of the city, it was rare for Americans to have other Americans living beside them. Only an

estimated 12 families had Americans as neighbors, the single significant exception being the 7 families living on one street near the
Hotel Cuadrado. Usually a family was surrounded by hosts who did
not speak English and who, in contrast to the American custom,[15]
were not likely to form quick friendships on the basis of propinquity. American families tended to find themselves isolated from
congenial people and forced to rely increasingly on themselves. As
an aside, we would predict that American families in a "Little
America" enclave abroad with many Americans as neighbors would
experience less centripetal pressure and, as a result, be less likely to
report an increase in family cohesiveness.

Customs related to the rhythm of work in the city also may have
heightened intra-family contact and, therefore, cohesiveness in
American families there. If an American family man worked on a
job which followed Spanish hours, he would have a lunch "break"
from 1 to 4 in the afternoon. During this time, most of the middle-
and upper-class men of the city commuted to their homes for the
mid-day meal and possibly a brief rest. The time consumed in
commuting was becoming greater because of larger and more hor-
rendous traffic jams, but the custom of commuting home for lunch
remained and was adopted by most American families. In the
United States, the father rarely is home for lunch; in Ciudad Condal
he could be together with his wife and, occasionally, his children in
the middle of the day.

Spanish *fiestas* also offered American family men greater opportunities to be together with their families. Work-oriented Americans were surprised and often exasperated by the number of days of
fiesta in the Spanish year.[16] Because it was not possible for them to
work on many of these days, they found themselves with a good
deal of unexpected leisure time on their hands. For the uninitiated,
fiesta days appeared as a surprise, but once one understood when
they would occur it became possible to plan family outings to fill
them. On these and regular vacation days, American families went
sightseeing in and around the city, skiing in the Pyrenees, or visited
the beaches, the islands off the coast, the restaurants, or another
home (usually American). In keeping with their activist tenden-

cies,[17] Americans tended to cover a good deal of ground during their Spanish sojourn. It was customary to claim that travel had important educational value for the children. It also had obvious prestige (snob) value for some of the adults.

Aside from physical togetherness, we would mention the increased need for teamwork between husband and wife as one of the causes of the greater cohesiveness in American families in the city. A State Department handbook points out that, "The role of the wife in the Foreign Service is of tremendous importance. Possibly in no other walk of life is the wife so much a part of the team. . . ."[18] In Ciudad Condal such teamwork was evident not only among those in government employ, but also among missionary couples and some business people. Indeed, when taking a vocational census, it was difficult in many cases not to list a wife as having a job. The wife's contribution to the team effort took a variety of specific forms: entertaining, mixing (at parties), participating in associational life, listening (to problems), waiting (for traveling husbands), and maintaining a home and family under more difficult conditions.

A final source of the apparent tendency of American families in the city to become more cohesive may have been the anxiety which many people experience as strangers. Such anxiety can cause people to rely increasingly on social groups as a defense. We will have more to say about stranger anxiety and group cohesiveness in Chapter 7. Meanwhile, we can note that increased involvement with one's family may have been one way of coping with the stranger anxiety experienced by some Americans in the city.

The typical American family in this foreign setting tended to follow two lines of adaptation. Though the family remained recognizably American, changes in family culture in the direction of host norms were dictated by the need to make a home, to carry out the mission of the husband-father, and to engage in transactions with others. On the other hand, changes in family structure in the direction of greater cohesiveness seem to have resulted from new situational and vocational facts of life as well as the need to defend against stranger anxiety.

THE WOMEN

What were the postures or roles which American women tended to adopt in the city? Using data from our cross-section of informants as a basis for our discussion, we again will not stress carry-overs from the United States. (Most of the American women in the city were readily identifiable as somewhat dowdy members of the American middle class.) Instead, we intend to concentrate on the new parts or roles which were learned on the foreign stage. Of these new parts, the most significant, as far as adaptation was concerned, was the role of *lady*. American women in Ciudad Condal found themselves drifting along the road to ladyship as practiced in the Spanish or Latin upper classes. According to one woman, it was not an entirely unpleasant experience. She said, "I like being spoiled and having people wait on me, having people recognize me in restaurants and move tables when I come in, getting into a taxi whenever I feel like it, being served at table, and going to a *modista* (dressmaker)."

If we assume that the term *lady* refers to a woman who can command and accept service graciously,[19] there were many opportunities for a woman of even modest means to play this role in Ciudad Condal. Having one's hair done as a matter of course was one way in which the American woman could indulge herself with service. She also could be served by maids, by a *modista* or by a famous designer of women's fashions, by people in shops, by waiters, by doormen, by the *sereno* (night watchman), by ushers, and by ball boys on the tennis courts. The women with whom she associated were probably similarly served. Thus, the American woman effortlessly entered a culture based on service. The fees and tips expected by serving people were so modest that nearly all Americans could enter this culture and, accordingly, be treated more like a lady. How well, in terms of local values, she handled this treatment was, of course, up to her.

It is difficult to conceive of a lady without a knight or troubadour. The function of the chivalrous male is to elevate the woman (lady) above the mundane.[20] In Ciudad Condal there were many men whose life seemed to be dedicated to the open admiration of even the plainest woman. If unescorted by a man on the street, a younger woman could be certain to receive more or less extravagant comments about her physical attractiveness. At first American women tended to find this attention exciting, or disturbing, or both, but as they came to realize that the glances and comments were not a prelude to further advances (they were absolutely secure on the street), they tended to relegate this kind of chivalry to the background of their experience.

Those women with a sufficiently broad acquaintance with the genre found the Catalan male a rather crude variation of the Latin type. Still, closer relations with some of these men could draw forth gestures which, to the uninitiated, were flattering enough: a woman would find her hand kissed, she would receive flowers, if she appeared to be sexually eligible she would be pursued with fervor by both married and unmarried men. But these men did not expect her to have a brain in her head nor to assert herself in their world. In short, she would be treated as an art or sex object, nothing more. If she married one of the hosts, she was likely to find herself treated as the mistress of his home, nothing more.

As we tend to think of it, ladylike behavior involves increasing doses of ritual. The lady is, after all, a species of noblewoman. In Ciudad Condal, an American's experience tended to be structured along more formal lines. The strain toward formality emanated from both diplomatic and host cultures. Diplomatic culture revolves around protocol in which women are heavily involved. As the State Department handbook points out, "The newcomer to the Foreign Service will find that accepted forms of social usage abroad are almost always more rigid than those to which they have been accustomed. . . ."[21]

Now if State Department people tend to be social leaders, as they are in many American communities abroad and as they were in Ciudad Condal, they would raise the level of formality in the culture of a community. The American women in the city, by contact with government types, came to understand that calling cards and calls, formal teas, dinners, receptions, and other social rituals could be a part of a way of life. Some denied this way of life; others accepted it; but all came to know it.

Contact with the hosts also revealed a level of formality to which an inexperienced American was not accustomed. For example, one learned that in Spanish there was a familiar form for "you" (*tu*) and that one did not use it as a matter of course. The American woman received treatment from many serving people which was accompanied by an unaccustomed veneer of formality. In the shops, her purchase, no matter how insignificant, would be extravagantly wrapped. Those Catalan women with whom she might associate never appeared in public in less than a perfectly finished condition. Indeed, many Americans remarked on the elegant looking women they saw on the street, and a few women confessed that they felt dowdy in comparison.

Ladies are expected to be charitable, and both diplomatic and host cultures encouraged charity among women of status. Government ladies were supposed to be in the forefront of charitable ventures. They provided important impetus to American participation in city-wide Red Cross and Cancer drives and support for a parochial school for poor children. Some of them were among the few American women invited to participate in private charities conducted by Catalan women. An invitation to participate in such a venture was, perhaps, the ultimate legitimation of an American woman in the city.

In general the wealthier the woman, the greater her opportunity to concentrate on the role of lady. Given sufficient means, she could leave the more mundane roles of housewife and mother to servants and focus on the things that ladies do: participate in charities, attend the opera, shop for clothes, have her hair done, entertain important and interesting people (graciously), chatter away about children and home at the club, cut an elegant figure in public, visit the "in" places on vacation—in short, do all the things that a middle class activist finds prestigious, but not really consequential.

Considering their grounding in utilitarian values, it is not surprising that most American women did not seem to this observer to be very good at this role.

It was particularly difficult for those American women who had worked or used their minds in some significant way before coming to Ciudad Condal to effect a successful adaptation there.[22] There were few opportunities to exercise one's career talent or one's mind in the city. Commenting on host women who were potential models for, and collaborators in, playing the role of lady, one dissatisfied American woman said, "The Spanish women are very boring. They can only talk about three things: their children, their family, and possibly their husbands." Another woman, ambivalent about playing the role of lady, said, "Here, I wake up each morning and feel that I really haven't anything to do today. I have more time to devote to myself here, but it is more to my vanity. Here, it is a make-believe world. I don't feel that I have my feet planted firmly on the ground. When I go back to the U. S. I will certainly go to work." For such a woman and a number of others the role of *lady* appears to have raised the specter of forbidden pleasures: narcissism and passivity. American women grappling with conflicts in these areas [23] suffered considerable anxiety. It is not surprising that several women, whose activist tendencies were most frustrated by life in the city, had turned to tranquilizers.

But if this foreign stage offered one new role which could lure one into the depths of femininity, it offered another to put a woman into a partnership with a man. Earlier, we remarked on the necessity of teamwork between husband and wife in many overseas situations. We will call the wife's part on the team the role of *helpmeet.* This role tended to occupy a more central position in the lives of married American women in the city than at home. The principal task of the *helpmeet* was the cultivation of social relationships by entertaining and being entertained. When asked what she did besides keeping house, a missionary wife said, "I run a hotel."

In the round of entertainment and counter-entertainment which occupied so much of the time of government personnel and more important business people, an American wife could combine the roles of *helpmeet* and *lady*.[24] Much of her activity involved bread-and-butter entertaining. The impressions which she created for a Captain General, a Catalan industrialist, an ambassador, an admiral of the Nth Fleet, a visiting congressman, or an important business-man could, in a cumulative way, affect her husband's career. These impressions depended not only on her own ladylike qualities, but also on the qualities of others, particularly servants. For consular women, the pressure of entertaining with occasionally unreliable servants (and scarce finances) was particularly severe. One of them said, "During all of my stay here I've had constant worry about servants. Will they be here for the party? Will the food be prepared for the party? I've never ceased worrying."

Although performance in the role of *helpmeet* depended heavily on specific social skills, it depended even more on a wife's level of adaptation. If a woman had had troubles before, and if stranger-hood had exacerbated these troubles (as it often seems to do),[25] her failure to adapt could spill over into her husband's job and affect his mission. The most notorious case of this kind in Ciudad Condal involved a government wife for whom special "protective" arrange-ments had to be made at parties (when she attended them). Her personal difficulties were so great that she had become a liability to her husband's career and a threat to the orderly work of the government mission. A case such as this one demonstrates the practical importance of selecting wives who can adapt successfully in a foreign setting.[26] By handling the problems of strangerhood successfully they may be making their most significant contribution in the role of *helpmeet.*

In Ciudad Condal American women also tended to assume new duties as *guardians of health.* Most Americans came to the city with some fears for their physical welfare in the face of what they assumed to be lower levels of sanitation and medical expertise.[27] It usually fell to the woman to guard against the real or imagined threats to her own and her family's health. At home she may have taken it for granted that various public agencies would cooperate with her in this job. In Ciudad Condal she was uncertain about the kind of cooperation she would receive. Therefore, she came to feel that she would have to perform this important task alone.

The first "requirement" of the role of *guardian of health* was to worry. (Men worried also, but they did not appear to take responsibility for it the way women did.) American women worried about tap water, food, and milk as possible sources of disease. They were unsettled by the primitive arrangements in public lavatories and the cleanliness of their maids. They felt anxiety about antisepsis and expertise in host hospitals and clinics. Concerning this, one woman said, "I'm nervous about the way they do things. I've heard some dreadful stories. They are so sloppy. When [my daughter] cut her lip and went to the hospital . . . I went into the emergency room with her. There was still blood on the table from the last patient. . . . There was a long cigarette ash hanging out of his [the doctor's] mouth. The cases of instruments were all mixed up. They probably were sterilized, but I hate to think of something going wrong there. And they are a bit cruel about things." According to a host doctor trained in the United States, most of the Americans' worries about the threat posed by the foreign setting were unjustified. Whether the dangers were real or imagined, the actions which the women took to protect themselves and their families were a very real part of their lives.

As a *guardian of health*, an American woman would buy bottled water. She would attempt to rally her maid to the cause of cleanliness. She would insist that fruits and vegetables be thoroughly washed. She would insist on pasteurized milk. She would find out the names of American-trained doctors; if she were with the government she would check on the location of the nearest military hospital. If she were a fanatic about this role she might begin to alienate the hosts who were proud of their medical facilities, their doctors, and the safe quality (if poor taste) of their tap water. By being picky in restaurants and refusing to enter any but the most antiseptic, she could, perhaps, save herself from the effects of some damaging germs, but it would be at the expense of integration into the host society.

In fairness to the American women in Ciudad Condal, they may have worried about accidents and disease, but they rarely carried their "protective" actions to the point of fanaticism. Indeed, with longer residence in the city they tended to discard some of their "protective" actions and accept lower standards of sanitation with no disastrous consequences. During the period of the study two women even went so far as to have their babies in local hospitals or clinics. Their confidence in the local facilities was such that they regarded it as a normal occurrence.

The most significant roles which American women (particularly married women) tended to acquire in Ciudad Condal were those of *lady*, of *helpmeet*, and of *guardian of health*. We have not concentrated on the roles of *housewife* or *mother* which, except for the addition of servants, were performed much the same as in the United States. Instead, we have been concerned with the new parts which a woman took on in this foreign setting.[28] The American wife and mother usually played all these roles. The nature of the performance in each which proved to be most successfully adaptive has not yet been determined.

CHILDREN

Data about American children were gathered from a group of adults who had the most intimate and widespread contact with them.[29] They were teachers and school administrators, none of whom had children in Ciudad Condal. Generalizations are based on the consensus of these informants. In cases where they did not agree, the author attempted to resolve discrepancies by contacting children and/or parents. Children were not interviewed systematically because they were of secondary importance in the overall study (which dealt primarily with the adaptation of adults), and because time did not permit the investigator to engage in the special activities which would have enabled him to penetrate their world.[30] Comments below, therefore, represent only bare beginnings in our understanding of children in this or any other overseas American community.

Up to the period of adolescence, the American children in Ciudad Condal were for the most part an unremarkable group and quite indistinguishable from middle-class children at home. According to host informants who had intimate contact with them (and who tended to adore all children), they were captivating; but they were too noisy, too assertive, and had too much power in the home. Such an observation seems to confirm that they were typically American.[31] They made and forgot friends easily and, when given the opportunity, learned and forgot host languages just as easily. It was rare for them to cause problems in school. One informant, a school administrator, said, "We have no problems with the younger children. They don't have any particular attitude about Spain. They go from one place to another and adjust very easily."

In contrast to the younger children who were largely undisturbed and disturbing, American adolescents appeared to have a disproportionate number of emotional or behavior problems. These problems tended to be concentrated among children with one or both parents absent or in families where serious parental conflict or indifference existed. These children, many of whom attended the American or Anglo-American schools in Ciudad Condal, were likely to have been problem children before coming to the city. The relatively high incidence of personal difficulties does not appear to have been brought about primarily by the encounter with this particular foreign setting.

According to the judgments of the informants, however, the bulk of Condal adolescents did not reveal significant emotional or behavior problems. They tended to be poorly prepared academically, perhaps because many had grown up in places where formal schooling was either unavailable or inadequate. Although informants from all three schools attended by American adolescents reported this deficiency in their students, one school (perhaps because it had weaker students and a less disciplined approach to studies) appeared to be making less headway than the others in improving its students' scholastic performance. In the struggle to raise their students to the level of their age-mates at home, teachers had to contend with parents who thought that their children ought to be given academic credit for overseas travel.

Since most American families had lived or traveled abroad before coming to Ciudad Condal, and since most traveled extensively while there, the children tended to be more broadly experienced than American children at home. One informant said, "They have moved around a lot in different countries. They are given to fluency in a number of languages. They show a surface sophistication." Another said, "The American girls are very mature. Most of them have lived abroad in a number of countries and they show a great facility at meeting people and with languages. They show a great deal of 'culture' as far as knowledge of places and art are concerned." The easy friendliness which this informant mentions may or may not be the result of travel. A number of scholars have mentioned it as characteristically American.

Despite the possession of apparently cosmopolitan traits, the Condal adolescents, paradoxically enough, were judged to be quite ethnocentric. They tended to think that the United States was the center of the universe and that learning about a foreign culture was a waste of time. Although most of them could speak passable Spanish and rudimentary Catalan, they resisted studying Spanish in school. One informant, whose school emphasized scholarly discipline, said, "The American girls forget that they are foreigners and that they have to make an effort to adapt to a country where the customs are very different. They have to be indoctrinated. . . ." So great was the incidence of ethnocentrism among American students that all three American (or Anglo-American) schools felt compelled to make a special effort to counteract it. The study of the Spanish language was included in their curricula, and both children and parents attended lectures on Spanish and Catalan culture.

Where did the ethnocentrism of these adolescents originate? One possible source may be the lack of special recreational facilities for teenagers in the host city; another, the failure of the schools to develop extracurricular activities which would have brought their Catalan and American students together outside of school. No "adolescent society" with its specialized facilities had yet developed in Spain. Accordingly, American teenagers tended to be turned back on themselves and their families. The family and American peer group became more potent reference groups for American adolescents in the city and contributed to an increase in their cohesiveness.[32]

In the clumping together of family members (and, possibly American adolescents) we may have found another source of adolescent ethnocentrism. It will be recalled that most American adults had a mixed or unfavorable attitude toward the city and its inhabitants. Because of increased intra-family interaction this attitude could have made a stronger impression on the children and provided reinforcement for whatever negative attitudes they themselves had acquired. A heightened valuation of America and things American, complementing the devaluation of Spain and things Spanish or Catalan, which resulted from this social process would then have been expressed by individual family members. Several informants commented that what amounts to ethnocentrism in these children was learned from the parents. We would need a longitudinal study of the kind carried out by Herman and Schild with Americans in Israel [33] to nail down this argument.

A final source of adolescent ethnocentrism may have been a process originating in the American parents' perception of what we surmise were neither irreversible nor deep-seated changes in their children. Seeing the ease with which their children, especially the younger ones, adopted languages and manners, they began to worry about their children's identity as Americans. Since many parents live vicariously through their children,[34] and since identity problems were encountered by these stranger-parents, we would suspect an element of projection in this appraisal. Worrying about their children's identity as Americans may have been an expression of a worry about their own. Their reaction, which we know took the form of ethnocentric attitudes, could have been communicated to their children and provided another basis for the ethnocentrism of adolescents—who were experiencing the usual identity problems of growing up as well as unusual ones resulting from the foreign situation.

The adaptations of American adolescents in this foreign situation were linked to those of their families and, perhaps, American peer groups. Children from breaking or broken families brought with them emotional or behavioral disorders which, presumably, impaired their function in the world around them. Most children, however, were involved in increasingly cohesive families whose ethnocentrism was fed by individual and collective opportunities and difficulties encountered in this foreign setting. These children, though apparently quite malleable, seem to have reflected their families' negative attitudes toward the host culture, which, acting through processes of interaction, tended to heighten whatever ethnocentrism they had carried with them into the city and maintained in contacts with their age-mates.

So much has been written in recent years about the supposed deleterious effects to Americans and to their country of living abroad in comparatively comfortable, all-embracing American enclaves,[35] that some American agencies have begun encouraging, or requiring, their overseasmen to live out among host peoples ("on the economy").[36] This arrangement is supposed to cause greater give-and-take with the hosts and improved cross-cultural understanding.[37] In Ciudad Condal, where no prefabricated "Little America" existed, we have had an opportunity to see how living "on the economy" actually affected the domestic side of American life.

Although American families in the Condal city needed to acquire new customs in order to establish a home and maintain it, and although seductive new opportunities for women beckoned from the host sphere, Americans tended on the whole to be reluctant to mix in the host society and culture. This lack of integration is reflected in the increased cohesiveness of American families and perhaps other groups, and in an increased valuation of American, as compared with host, culture, which may have been expressed most untactfully by American adolescents. Although the data in Chapter 8 indicate that constriction in the direction of home values tended to break down with longer residence in the city, it is not to be presumed that most of the Americans would have consented to stay on beyond the usual three- or four-year tour in this location.

5

MISSIONS

I am out here to work, mind, to hold this
wretched country by force. I'm not a missionary or a Labour Member or a vague sentimen-
tal sympathetic literary man. I'm just a servant
of the government.... We're not pleasant in
India, and we don't intend to be pleasant.
We've something more important to do.
                          RONNY HEASLOP
                       in *A Passage to India*

T HE PREOCCUPATION WITH IDENTITY WHICH OFTEN
arises among strangers was evident among Americans in
Ciudad Condal. Having lost their traditional points of
orientation, they were concerned with "sizing up" people as quickly
as possible. Their unspoken question, "Who is he?" (a correlate of
"Who am I?") often led in conversation to "What are you doing
here?" The expected response, the mention of some job, was typically American in its implications: (1) That an American ought to
be working. (2) That the kind of work a person does tells one who
he is. The reply to such a question might be: "a writer," "an
anthropologist studying the American community here," "a stockbroker," "a missionary." Sometimes a person added his organizational affiliation: "a teacher at the American School," "District
Manager of Flyaway Airways," "Director of the Cultural Institute."
Such responses meant, in effect, "The reason I am here is my job
with _____." We may refer to a person's job in Ciudad Condal as
his overseas mission.

The principal mission of the Condal Americans was business.
They were able to pursue business interests and dominate some
sectors of the Spanish scene because they possessed the capital and
technical resources required by the hosts to develop their country
rapidly. The vast majority of American business operations in Spain
were concentrated in Madrid. Though it was the second largest in

Spain, the American business establishment in Ciudad Condal included only an estimated one out of six American businesses in the Spanish theater.[1] While we intend to confine ourselves to those American or Spanish-American enterprises in which a resident American was involved, it is important to note that not all American business projects were carried on with American personnel. In Ciudad Condal those businesses which employed Americans rarely employed more than one; in Madrid most American businesses with American employees employed at least two. Being alone, or being alone on a job with a group of hosts, may have intensified the problems of adaptation.

At the time of this study, American business interests in the city and throughout Spain were growing rapidly. In order to enter the Spanish economy it was necessary that foreign businesses conform to the government's program of economic development and meet the requirements of its many bureaucracies.[2] Let us suppose that an American firm had worked out an agreement with a Spanish company to contribute capital and technique to a joint petro-chemical enterprise and had sent an American representative abroad to supervise the construction of a plant, train personnel, and build up a marketing apparatus.[3] This representative arrived in time to formalize the agreement and assist in the preparation of a proposal containing a full statement of the proposed venture to be forwarded to the Ministry of Commerce and Industry and, finally, to the Council of Ministers. The path of this proposal had been smoothed, so to speak, by one of the Spanish partners who knew the minister and had sounded him out on the acceptability of the project, and by others who had established contacts with lower-level bureaucrats. All these men reported that the proposal would be considered favorably and that there were no technical obstacles to its approval and swift passage through the necessary bureaucratic channels. The American, encouraged by the enthusiastic reports of his colleagues, obtained his residence and working permits and settled down to implement his plans.

Following the style of modern industrial enterprises, the joint project had been organized into a series of stages each of which had a deadline. These deadlines had been approved by the home office in the United States and incorporated into company schedules. *None of them would be met.* In fact, the project was delayed at the outset by problems in the Council of Ministers and then by the intricate rituals of the local bureaucracies. Repeated inquiries to various offices elicited assurances that permits would be delivered directly, but weeks and even months went by before all official documents were in the hands of the project manager. Hindrances of this kind were not unusual. One Spanish-American partnership, proposing to build much needed low income housing for workers, had secured a government subsidy and arranged *enchufe* (literally, "connections") at all bureaucratic levels; after one year it had not received all the official documents which would enable construction to begin. The American manager reported in some bewilderment that not only did he lack permits, but that he still was not completely sure what permits were needed.

There were various paths through the Spanish bureaucratic and legal labyrinths. Some American businessmen (notably those representing large and prestigious firms) sought to meet every official requirement. Others, more Latin in their style, attempted more or less daring short-cuts through the official red tape. Whatever the line taken, it was essential to employ a local lawyer to look after legal details and handle the personal transactions with officials which often decided the fate of a project in Spain. *Enchufe,* the custom of using personal connections and the bribe to further one's aims, was not as necessary as it had been before the liberalization of government policies, but experts maintained that it still might help to minimize delays and secure more favorable actions. It was difficult to discover if any American in Ciudad Condal had knowingly followed the custom of *enchufe* in his business. Americans' attitudes toward the practice varied from moral repugnance to enthusiastic acceptance. When one acculturated American was queried about it and other aspects of business expediency in the city, he replied, "What is moral? Moral is what everybody does." This attitude (which was not typical) was found more frequently among the old hands in the business community.

The deadline-conscious American businessman could not avoid frustration in Spain. Spanish officialdom was only one source of the delays which frustrated him. Suppliers did not provide, shippers did not deliver, and specialists (when available) often did not appear on schedule. Project timetables were revised and revised again to match the slower procession of Spanish events. Meanwhile, the American could either maintain his traditional inner time structure and experience accumulating frustrations, or develop a personal timetable more in keeping with Spanish reality. The latter course, though apparently more adaptive, might create difficulties with a home office which was unable to comprehend the special problems of American projects in less developed countries. If company officials at home were particularly unsympathetic, they might begin to question the qualifications of their agent and harass him with inquiries about their project's progress. At this point the American would become aware of his marginal position between two cultures and experience the conflict which such a position imposed. Because most of the American project managers in the city were employed by transculturally sophisticated companies, they were usually not subject to harassment from home. But most of them were old-fashioned frontier types with strong, driving consciences. They could not, therefore, escape harassment from within.

Delays were only one form of "sabotage" which a project originating in a highly rationalized culture could experience in Spain. In America the ideal project functions like a machine with all parts articulating perfectly in the most efficient manner, but any American who expected machine-like operations in the city would be discouraged by the less rationalized standards which prevailed there. Although most American businessmen agreed that the hosts were willing workers, they tended to find them lacking in the foresight which is necessary for making long-range plans, inclined to waste motion and energy, without the sense of perfection which is demanded in an American or modern industrial enterprise, incapable of being objective, and slow to change. Concerning his Catalan colleagues, one American project manager said, "I have been trying to keep the subjectiveness out of their lives. The incidence of subjective judgment on the part of my managers is very high. It's a matter of likes and dislikes. I've seen it elsewhere, but never to the same degree as here. . . . I have to go around with my eyes closed. The job won't be done right." Another, who maintained his sense of humor in the face of considerable difficulties, said, "There is a great deal of inefficiency. They are incapable of planning. [Q: How do you handle this?] By crying, by laughing, by threatening, by losing my hair. But everyone is so agreeable. They all say you are right. But nothing changes . . . I suppose they look at me as some kind of American nut." The American project manager faced the same kind of problem encountered by American overseas managers every-where abroad: coming to terms with the less rationalized while trying to introduce more rationalized procedures.[4]

In America, the specialization of labor is far advanced. In Ciudad Condal one could count on only a limited array of specialists. An American project manager frequently had to wear a number of hats. He might, at one time or another, be a construction engineer, production engineer, personnel manager, marketing specialist, and public relations man. In addition, because of the lower level of technology and division of labor in the host society, he usually could not count on local specialists to handle higher level technical jobs. One American explained the situation on his project as follows: "The people here don't know very much about structural steel. There are no trained personnel in advanced construction. At home you can call a millwright or a steamfitter. Here, these people don't exist. You have to hire a mechanic and supervise yourself."

Since most of the American-managed business missions in the city were related to development or discovery, it is not surprising that men with the character of frontiersmen had been "selected" to carry out many of them. In the words of one informant, they appeared to be "boy scout types." This appellation probably referred to their pursuit of challenges from the new and difficult, their desire for personal freedom and self-reliance, and their abilities as "jacks of all trades." As one of these men stated concerning his approach to his mission, "I was ready—ready for the challenge; and there certainly is a challenge here . . . of getting something off the ground, of opening horizons."

The majority of American employees of large American businesses in the Condal city were the kind of people we tend to associate with the term, Protestant Ethic, and believed that rewards ought to come to those who are successful in their work.[5] Employees of small businesses and the self-employed also were highly individualistic, but they tended to be less job-oriented, more concerned with immediate profits, and more willing to cut corners to that end. On the whole, American businessmen in Ciudad Condal tended to be individualistic entrepreneurs who, with varying styles, were seeking to realize their capitalistic ambitions on this part of the American overseas frontier. In contrast, a larger, older, and more settled American business community in the Scandinavian capital city visited by the author contained a larger proportion of men who were committed to the ways of the large organization. This situation suggests that the scope and nature of business operations in a foreign setting are related to the kind of man who is "selected" to work there.

THE AMERICAN BUSINESS MISSION

An American business is established abroad to make a profit, and its success may be measured in terms of its attainment of that end. How much profit is considered satisfactory appears to vary with the type of operation and the historical epoch. In the heyday of imperialism nothing less than sheer plunder would have been considered a fair return on an investment. With the increased power of the once exploited countries, however, present-day economic imperialists have learned to be content with a more modest profit.[6] In this sense, the American businessmen in Ciudad Condal were excellent examples of modern American economic imperialism. None of them appeared to be making a "killing," and comparatively few had hopes of doing so. Those who did have grandiose expectations soon found them inappropriate in this foreign setting.

Among the more profitable American business ventures in the city (most of which were supervised by Americans) were several small trade (export-import) enterprises, a small clothing manufacturer, a business reporting house, an airline, two steamship lines, two advertising and/or public relations agencies, a stockbroker, a pharmaceutical house, an air conditioning firm, a shoe machinery company, several motion picture distributing agencies, an auto sales office, several soft drink bottlers and/or distributors, a food products firm, and an insurance agency. Enterprises still in the state of development, but with reasonable expectations of success, included a construction firm and companies that produced plastics and plasticizers, feed and poultry, sealers for cans, and American-style bread. A large petroleum exploration outfit, which for several years had been looking for oil deposits throughout northern Spain, could not be considered a success because it had located no fields of productive capacity.

Since a capitalistic business is more or less successful according to the value of its product in a market, the list of successful enterprises in Ciudad Condal tells us something about the market potential for American business missions in the city. There was, for example, a "need" to convey travelers and tourists to and from this area (hence the air and steamship lines), for trade with the U. S. (air and steamship lines, export-import businesses), for the production and marketing of various consumer goods (advertising agencies, food products, soft drink concerns, plastics), and for serving Americans in the city and its environs (stockbroker, insurance agency). Only in oil explorations were Americans engaged in what could be called primary or basic industry. In sum, American business success in Ciudad Condal was accomplished almost entirely in secondary or tertiary areas of the economy. This situation may be contrasted with those in Madrid and the Scandinavian capital where successful American operations in the basic sector (i.e., primary industries) of the economy were in progress. It suggests that more substantial American overseas enterprises will tend to locate in or near the city which controls the economic destiny of a country. In Spain, that city was Madrid.

The historical trend toward the greater organization of American life was not reflected in the American business establishment of Ciudad Condal.[7] The absence of a powerful coordinating agency and of an interest in cooperation resulted in what was at best a loosely-knit agglomeration of individual businesses. The principal integrating association (and the seat of whatever power existed in the business community) was the local chapter of the American Chamber of Commerce in Spain, but it functioned less as a coordinating or integrating agency for American businessmen than as a bridge or transitional association between the American and host communities.[8] In general, the older (longer-term) the resident and the more prestigious his business, the greater the likelihood that he would be actively involved in the Chamber and in other associations in and outside the American community.

Although the Consulate General might seem to have been the logical agency to accomplish the integration of the American business community, it was largely ineffectual in this regard because of the lack of trust and occasional antagonism between many American businessmen and its most relevant officers. The mutual distrust between government people and businessmen and the social gap which accompanies it is characteristic of many American overseas communities. Cleveland and his associates, in speaking of this intra-community conflict, say that "at its worst, the two groups look at each other as if each were in the country solely to thwart the interests of the other." [9] The situation in Ciudad Condal was not so extreme, but it tended in this direction. In Chapter 7 we will attempt to discover the reasons for it.

The hierarchy of American businessmen in the city culminated in four men who were considered by both Americans and hosts to be the leaders of the American community.[10] All of them had occupied the presidencies of the local or national chapters of the American Chamber of Commerce in Spain. They appeared to have acquired their high status not so much by wealth or extent of industrial backing as by experience in this foreign setting. Although the prestige of one's home organization or the size of one's business operations in the city were factors in determining status, they did not seem to be as important as seniority and active involvement in local affairs. Any businessman who did not divorce himself from community life could acquire higher status simply by being on the scene longer than others. In a community with a great deal of coming and going, it is not surprising that social rewards could be derived from stability and the qualities which it implied.

Since length of residence generally was associated with acculturation and greater personal contact with the hosts, the American business leadership had become intimately associated with Catalans, particularly with those who were Americanized or American-oriented. They constituted a semi-official bridge between the American community and the host society. This fact supports the hypothesis of Nash and Schaw that top leadership in a group undergoing acculturation tends to fall to transcultural individuals who function as go-betweens.[11] We would add that the more powerful a group in the contact situation and the less the pressure on it to acculturate, the less likelihood there is that its leaders will be transcultural people. For example, in an enclave of powerful imperialists the leaders ought to exemplify traditional rather than transcultural values.

In general the American business leaders were more sympathetic toward the Consulate General and more cooperative with its officers than were most of their colleagues. They also provided a bridge between the American business community and the government people. It would not be correct, however, to adopt Mills' model of the "Power Elite" in order to depict the structure of power within the American community in Ciudad Condal.[12] In the first place, the Mills model includes the military among the top leadership of the United States; in the city, the military were not among the leaders. Second, although government and business leaders in the city did cooperate, there was considerable conflict between them. Finally, neither government nor business leaders held a great deal of power over their "followers." The leadership situation, then, was in contrast to that at the fictitious British outpost described by Forster (in *A Passage to India*)[13] in which an authoritative, military-style hierarchy was headed by a single British official.

THE GOVERNMENT MISSION

The missions of the American government in the city were carried out by the Consulate General, the Cultural Institute, and the army transportation unit at the docks. Each operated at the end of a separate chain of command from home, but the Consulate General constituted the hub of local operations.

Stated in the broadest possible terms, the mission of the American Consulate General was to promote and serve all legitimate American interests in the consular district, which included all of northeast Spain and the nearby offshore islands. The performance of this mission required many social transactions with the hosts, with the missions of foreign governments, and with resident and transient Americans. The gross aspects of consulate work here were described in Chapter 1. In that brief preamble we also intimated that the mission of this government outpost was being carried on with minimal success. By examining the reasons for its failure to perform more successfully, we can obtain a fuller picture of the structure and function of this office.

Industrial sociologists usually have learned by heart the central findings of the study of the bank wiring room by Roethlisberger and Dickson.[14] This investigation demonstrated conclusively that productivity was associated with group morale or esprit. At the time of the study, the morale at the Consulate General was very low, and it probably was this factor more than any other which contributed to the unsatisfactory performance there. We hasten to add here that a job was being done, that the day-to-day business of the American government in this setting was being carried out, occasionally with distinction. However, in comparison with other diplomatic outposts observed by the author and informants in and outside this office, the overall performance of the American consuls in Ciudad Condal tended to be sub-standard. Some Americans, in complaining about the inadequacies of these people, blamed the incompetence of several key personnel. Other more charitable informants thought that a lack of experience on the local scene, dictated by a comparatively short tour of duty, was responsible for consular deficiencies. Both of these hypotheses have some merit. Several consular officers did not appear competent enough to handle their duties in the city; and tours of duty of these consuls in Ciudad Condal did not surpass the minimum three- or four-year period because no consulate officers sought or received extensions of their assignments in this location. The absence of "reenlistments," however, was in turn related to the most significant cause of consular inadequacies, poor morale. The morale of the personnel of the Consulate General did not appear to be sufficient to carry on the numerous and occasionally arduous duties of the office with genuine enthusiasm and the extra attention which marks a noteworthy performance.

The low morale in the Consulate General was indicated by the many complaints on the part of the consuls about their jobs, by the considerable intra- and extra-group hostility, and by many references to more gratifying assignments in the past. "Belief in mission," according to Cleveland and his associates, is a factor related to successful performance abroad,[15] but these consuls did not appear to be convinced of the importance of their mission in the city. From their point of view, the really important work of the American government in Spain was accomplished at the Embassy in Madrid. In Ciudad Condal, the consuls, therefore, could not feel that their heavy work load was very significant, and they tended to look elsewhere in time and place for their satisfactions. In general, bureaucrats tend to be more conscious of their relationships to other roles in their organization,[16] but in these officials this consciousness seemed to be tinged with more than the usual amount of envy.

The source of the low morale at the Consulate General was not too difficult to locate. The quality of life at a government outpost (especially a small one) is heavily dependent on its chief of mission.[17] This role in Ciudad Condal was played by the consul general in a manner which could be characterized as English-authoritarian. Among Americans the attractiveness of a group tends to increase where some semblance of the democratic process is maintained,[18] but the consul general, uncertain about his ability to handle the job, had not been able to create an atmosphere of cooperative give-and-take. He was the personification of the cautious bureaucrat who emphasizes the rules and prerogatives in order to safeguard his career, and his formal posture did little to ingratiate him with his employees or with the public. This style of leadership, which would seem to have been more appropriate to another era and another nation, was shared by his wife in playing the demanding role of consul general's lady. Since the very impressive second-in-command of the mission (the power behind the throne in this situation) also tended to adopt an unforgiving authoritarian role in relations with subordinates, an atmosphere of unrelieved severity and tension came to pervade the office. As one informant said, it was "not much fun working here."

Following the consular tradition, the Consulate General was especially concerned with the promotion of American commercial interests and the handling of personal affairs such as passport and visa applications, funeral arrangements (one to two Americans died in the consular district each week), implementing applications for permits, and helping the destitute, those who had run afoul of the law, and the sick and injured. Most foreign service officers consider duties of this kind as hackwork, but in this office they may have required more man-hours of labor than all other consulate activities put together. Harassed from below by an importunate public and from above by unrelenting authority, the consuls began to show the effects of accumulated resentments. One such effect was the loosening of group bonds and the formation of attachments outside the circle of government people—an unusual development as far as American communities abroad are concerned.[19]

In keeping with the character of its leader, the activities of the Consulate General bore the stamp of a parochial, cautious conservatism. The respectable, well-established, and well-known received favorable consideration. The untried and unknown were suspect. Unless an innovation emanated from above in the chain of command, it probably would be treated with great circumspection. Because American diplomatic posts abroad cannot possibly accede to most of the requests or demands they receive for cooperation or assistance, the people employed in them often find themselves saying "no" with monotonous regularity. In Ciudad Condal, the Consulate General had acquired an image among Americans as a nay-saying and know-nothing agency. This observation did not extend to the U.S.I.S. people who tended to be thought of (correctly, in the opinion of the author) as more approachable, more knowledgeable, and more daring and imaginative. This contrast in character (the entrepreneurial propagandists on the one hand and the bureaucrats on the other) appeared to be a source of further conflict within the government group. The leaders of the Consulate General tended to mistrust their own schemers as much as those in the business realm, and they exerted strong pressure to keep information operations safe and respectable, as illustrated by the issue of "culture" vs. propaganda in the mission of the Cultural Institute.

The U.S.I.S. representatives did not seem to doubt that their principal mission was propaganda, and they cultivated a variety of groups among the hosts. One of these groups consisted of young people who were particularly receptive to modern trends. The Cultural Institute attracted approximately 2500 hosts to its (American) English classes during the year of the study, many of them adolescents and young adults. Around its English curriculum it had created a range of extra-curricular affairs similar to those found at an American college or university. These activities, particularly the dances and parties, were attractive to the more modern youths whose parents had not forgotten the custom of chaperonage (the young people could meet, unchaperoned but in good repute, at institute "social" functions). The growth of such extra-curricular activities was viewed with some disfavor by the consular leadership. When, for example, a sports car rally was scheduled, the consul general found that it was not in keeping with the character of a cultural institute. However, because the U.S.I.S. people were not entirely subject to his orders (or opinions), they went ahead with their "less cultural" plans, thus creating further friction within the government group.

The loose alliance which existed between the leaders of the diplomatic and business missions in the city was maintained on the government side with no great enthusiasm. Though scrupulously correct in their numerous official transactions with this group, the consuls could not entirely hide their belief in the unimportance of this local elite. Such an attitude was partly the result of previous exposure to first-line American businessmen in other foreign settings (against whom the Condal Americans were compared unfavorably). This lack of respect for local businessmen and their operations tended to undermine the primary mission of this government outpost: the promotion of American commercial interests in the city.

The Consulate General was also charged with maintaining diplomatic relations with the government of the city, of the province, and other foreign government missions in the city. The consuls were required to attend a great variety of official and semi-official functions and engage in many ceremonial activities. The business side of these more glamorous operations included the gathering of information (to be reported home), the cultivation of friends or allies, and occasional negotiations. Although the consular leadership complained about the unreliability and discourtesy of the hosts, they appeared to value their diplomatic activities more highly than their consular affairs. In this regard, they appeared to be normal State Department types who had acquired the value system of an organization in which the diplomat still is accorded higher prestige.[20] It suggests the hypothesis that unless the leaders of a Consulate General deviate from this aspect of the State Department value system, they will not be able to perform their consular duties with distinction. Thayer argues that there is a consular type "who prefers the relative obscurity of a consular post to the hectic but perhaps more glamorous activity of an embassy."[21] With the increasing standardization imposed by the State Department, however, it is not likely that able men of this kind with sufficient seniority to head a Consulate General will become more frequent in the future.[22]

THE MISSION OF THE MISSIONARIES

As is customary at American outposts abroad, the missionaries in Ciudad Condal, a small but vigorous group of fundamentalist Protestants, were minimally concerned with American community affairs and deeply involved in the host society.[23] They and their Spanish and foreign colleagues published and distributed religious propaganda, made and counseled converts, built and maintained religious organizations, and conducted religious services. Very little of their missionary effort was directed toward the Americans in Ciudad Condal who were not greatly concerned with religion, particularly of the kind offered by the missionaries.

The Protestant missionary effort in Spain was not insignificant. Nearly one hundred churches were in existence, and more were being organized. In Ciudad Condal, the Protestant churches had approximately two thousand Spanish members, mostly from the working class. Since non-Catholic proselytizing was officially prohibited, the Protestant missionaries had to be both circumspect and courageous. At the time of the study, they were subject to little harassment in the city, but some of the Americans could recall the recent raid on their printing plant, the closing of some of their churches, and the arrest of people who had been distributing tracts outside the city. Officially, their mission was illegal, and it took only one denunciation to bring the powerful repressive measures of the totalitarian, church-dominated State to bear on their activities.

Although the missionaries cooperated only slightly with other Americans in the city, the function of their mission was not unrelated to those of American business and government. All three missions appeared to be contributing to the effective modernization or Americanization of Spain. In the case of the Protestant churches, both group life and religious ideology worked toward this end. On the one hand, the warm, primary group atmosphere and emphasis on salvation tended to provide a hedge against potentially disruptive forces emanating from a disaffected and dislocated working class. On the other, the more individualized and rationalized Protestant ideology reinforced those personality tendencies which are necessary for the modern industrial machine.[24] For example, in one sermon an American missionary inveighed against the iniquities of self-indulgence and gambling, and emphasized the necessity of individual decisions for God. Thus, probably unknowingly, the

Protestant missionary may have been working toward the same end as the American businessman creating an American-style project, the teacher of English at the Cultural Institute (technical treatises were often written in English), the Army transportation man imposing the American style of logistics on his employees and contractors, and the tourist insisting on modern accommodations. This imperialistic function has been performed by Western missionaries in many other foreign locations. After noting this, Palmier says, "Trade follows the flag; but equally the convert often makes a better businessman than his unconverted brother." [25]

Like other Americans, the missionary faced the problem of adapting in a society which was not wholly enthusiastic about being rationalized. Because he spoke Spanish and usually was warmly received by his fellow believers, his initial problems of strangerhood probably were minimized. Because he tended to thrive on challenges, the opposition of the Spanish government may have added zest to his work. But the missionary could not escape all the difficulties which beset American strangers in the city. One missionary couple, apparently having affronted the *dignidad* of a group of hosts, had been asked to leave. Others found the hosts "difficult to organize" and slow to accomplish. In registering such complaints, they revealed that in at least one respect they were typical Americans.

Our aim in this chapter has not been to make an exhaustive survey of American missions in Ciudad Condal, but rather to analyze the structure and function of those which were more significant for American interests in this foreign setting. We have not treated the retired and unemployed, nor the artists, teachers, and scholars, each of whom could be considered to have a personal mission which was sanctioned by the American government, and connected in some slight way with the exercise of American influence in this area. Because of inadequate data we have not dealt further with the "private" radio station which was beaming programs toward eastern Europe. It was a substantial operation employing several hundred hosts most of whom worked at the transmitter location north of the city. The leader of this mission was one of the more important Americans in the city.

In another epoch (and possibly an epoch yet to come) we would be required to consider at greater length the mission of the military in Ciudad Condal. The city had once been a home port of the Nth Fleet and a minor Air Force base of operations. A strategic decision had eliminated these missions leaving only a small Army transportation unit to represent the military there. This fact reminds us that the make-up of an American outpost abroad may be dependent on decisions and events which occur in places often far removed from it.

Those who carried out the American missions in Ciudad Condal were agents for the diffusion of American technology, social organization, religious ideology, language, art, military logistics, work and leisure styles, and patterns of consumption. On a more general level we have spoken of the contribution of these agents of American imperialism to the rationalization of the host society (i.e., greater calculation of the means and ends of action and the use of the criterion of efficiency to measure all things). For American individuals and organizations, on the other hand, these missions functioned to produce profit (or loss) for businessmen, stimulation and knowledge for artists and scholars, religious fulfillment, better (or worse) public relations, information for governmental action, a (presumably) stronger military posture, and (sometimes) advancement in a career. The importance of this last function should not be underestimated. Americans working for large organizations, for example, knew that their performance in the city could affect their future careers. In some cases, particularly among government people, this awareness seemed to be more important than belief in the mission in determining the nature of their work. For these people this foreign sojourn was not so much an event in itself as an incident in a career which was patterned and controlled by the large organization.

To what extent were the American missions in the city integrated or coordinated? Confirmed Marxists probably would not require any scientific investigation to tell them that the government mission in the city functioned to further the missions of the businessmen and the military, and that the missionaries were contributing to the modernization or Americanization of Spain. Such a conception, however, would seriously distort the facts of life in this American outpost. We have insisted on referring to multiple American missions in the city, not a single imperialistic mission. Each of the American missions we have discussed depended on a separate chain of command and pursued its goals in different sectors of the host society in a more or less autonomous fashion. We cannot assess here the degree of integration of American institutions from which the different chains of command originated. That, as we pointed out in the first chapter, remains the subject of a lively debate.[26] Viewed on the level of this American overseas community, however, the degree of cooperation between institutions was minimal. Indeed, there was evidence of considerable indifference and even conflict between, e.g., the Consulate General and the businessmen, American School, and missionaries, and between the missionaries and all other Americans. Nor were each of the missions we have discussed highly integrated agencies. Businessmen followed their separate ways. Consuls were in conflict with each other, teachers with their administration, and Fulbright scholars with Fulbright bureaucrats. It would strain the facts only a little to say that the situation in Ciudad Condal tended to resemble nineteenth-century America, while larger and more important American outposts visited by the author reflected the modern trend toward increasing cooperation between different American institutions.

But it also would be incorrect to conclude that American missions in the city had nothing in common. They were, after all, carried on by people who shared a cultural heritage and who tended to be more like one-another than like the hosts or other foreign nationals. Further, the Americans were all strangers who shared the same problems of adaptation. They were frustrated in their mission by hosts who were said to be difficult to organize, slow to accomplish, and lacking in reliability, foresight, courtesy, objectivity, specialized skills, and precision in their work. With the possible exception of the lack of courtesy (which may have been related to unreliability), all these traits point to the lower level of rationality in the host culture. The American missions in the city functioned to rationalize host culture, but in order for the missions to be successful it was necessary that American representatives first come to terms with the less rational hosts. This problem, which appears to beset American missions everywhere abroad, is made inevitable by the extremely high level of rationalization in American culture. As Cleveland and his associates point out, "Because the United States is the most 'western' nation of the West, the most highly industrialized segment of the industrialized fifth of the world . . . , its environment may represent a cultural frontier, extended beyond the limits of most other societies. If it were possible, for example, to arrange all the world's cultures along a spectrum of attitudes toward time, the United States with its glorification of promptness and dispatch would be near one end of the spectrum while the attitudes of some Oriental societies . . . would be near the other end, with the rest of the world's cultures ranged between them. . . . If this analysis is correct, it means that an American's cultural adjustment overseas would almost always be *in the same general direction*. His attitude toward time will . . . always be moving in the direction of flexibility, to a greater or lesser degree depending on the foreign country in which he finds himself." [27]

6

CIRCLES

And now I am a daily visitor to signor di Breme's box at la Scala. The company there assembled consists entirely of men of letters. . . . My contribution to the circle takes the form of news from France. . . ; and, in return, I listen to news from Italy.

STENDHAL
Rome, Naples, and Florence

L IKE THE BULL IN THE RING, THE STRANGER SELECTS OR constructs his *querencias* or home territories on the foreign stage. On the social level these "territories" take the form of social circles which extend outward from his home to friends and acquaintances in the foreign setting and beyond. Such circles, which circumscribe the stranger's existence on the foreign scene, constitute a part of the network of overlapping groups which defines the structure of the overseas community. From the point of view of the stranger's experience, these circles also range from the past, through the present, to the future. The stranger actually belongs to some, recalls connections with others, and aspires to join still others. In this chapter we will consider some of the more significant social circles of the Americans in Ciudad Condal.

Very early in his sojourn in the city, the author became aware of the term "cocktail circuit" which he erroneously took to mean a group of people who met with each other and consumed alcoholic libations at different locations. It was not until later that he realized that the term, as used by his informants, referred not so much to a group or clique as to a custom (i.e., alcoholic sociability) in which a number of groups were involved. The cocktail party or alcoholic assembly was an important form of ritualized sociability in the American community and an occasion for the convening of social circles. By examining this custom as practiced by different groups of Americans, we will be able to acquire some insight into the nature of group life in their community.

From the point of view of numbers convened, the most important form of alcoholic assembly was the working cocktail or reception which was held to further the cause of some mission. Expense accounts were regularly tapped for this purpose by all the consuls (especially the consul general and his deputy), the U.S.I.S. representatives, and business firms (the missionaries did not hold alcoholic assemblies to further their work). Because hosts and other foreigners who shared this custom usually were invited to affairs of this kind, a working cocktail could and did become an occasion for formalized transactions between societies. As in many other modern contact situations, therefore, it tended to function to facilitate intersocietal contacts. In locations and function, this custom would qualify as part of the "third culture" which the Useems and Donoghue have identified.[1]

For the Condal Americans, the alcoholic assembly was a relatively inexpensive and efficient way to handle large numbers of people. With or without PX privileges, liquor could be obtained at low cost, and a few catering firms, accustomed to handling gatherings of this kind, could be hired to prepare and serve food and drinks. Since, according to all informants, the entertainment allowances of government people tended to be inadequate, the cocktail party or reception, rather than the dinner, became the preferred form of consular and U.S.I.S. working entertainments. As carried out by the government people, such an affair was very close to the ideal-typical form of the American version of this custom in the city.

In order to convene an alcoholic assembly, there had to be an occasion or excuse. With the usual government working cocktail it would be the visit of some visting dignitary (e.g., an admiral from the Nth Fleet, the ambassador from Madrid) or the opening of an American event such as the exhibit at the Fair. (The government mission did not convene a Fourth of July party for Americans because, according to mission leaders, expense accounts were not sufficient to include gatherings for Americans only.)[2] With the occasion at hand, the government people prepared or tapped a list of potential guests and sent them engraved invitations. A fairly stable group who were *persona grata* with the government people tended to appear over and over again at these functions. These privileged ones included all the government civilian and military officers, the more important business people, officials of host and foreign governments, and some of the Catalan upper classes. In addition, a few individuals were invited to "fill out" the party in some way or to satisfy a whim of one of the government officials or their wives. For a large working cocktail as many as two hundred invitations might be sent and as many as one hundred and fifty guests might attend.

A typical consular reception was "commanded" by the wife of the consul general in an almost military fashion. Having agonized over the preparations, she now would begin to worry about the progress of the party itself. She deployed her women to receive guests, to mix with them, and to expedite the passage of food and drink. Government women have these same duties everywhere abroad, but at some posts they seem to perform them in an unobtrusive and effortless fashion. In Ciudad Condal, very few of these women had managed to acquire the smooth and sure style of the grand lady who, without seeming to, produces a social work of art out of such an assemblage. They seemed to be very conscious of the rules and very obviously working at their mission of social catalysis.

Let us suppose that an American had received a coveted invitation to a cocktail-reception at the home of the consul general, a large single-family house located in the higher reaches of the region we have called the American district.[3] He would present himself at the door at the appointed hour of 8 P.M. After a brief lookout over the city below he would find himself moved quickly through the stations of welcome into the arena of sociability. He would be relieved of his coat by a maid, greeted by a consular lady, passed along a receiving line, and debouched into the polygot throng within. If he stood alone for long he probably would be singled out by one of the consular ladies bent on her mission of promoting social intercourse. At the ideal party, guests were not to stand alone. They were to meet other agreeable guests and converse with them more and more confidently as the liquor took effect. Meanwhile, from her supervising position, the wife of the consul general would direct her subordinates to this or that point of flagging activity. The consular women, well acquainted with their roles as social catalysts, tended to carry on their work with greater enthusiasm than the men who usually had just completed a hard day at the office. It probably was largely because of these women that consular gatherings were among the least boring of all working cocktails or receptions given by Americans.

The excitement of a consulate party was not entirely confined to what happened there. It extended to the significance of receiving an invitation. Regardless of one's nationality, such an invitation tended to raise one's social standing. By associating even in the impersonal conditions of the alcoholic assembly with the consul general and his lady, one acquired, by vicarious means, some of the prestige of the United States government. Although the same function was performed by invitations to parties given by other prestigious organizations, they could not provide the aura of charisma which could be obtained at a government assembly.

The round of working cocktails among Americans was devoted in large part to inaugurations and receptions. At the Cultural Institute local champagne was provided at gatherings to welcome visiting artists and scholars and to open exhibitions. Institute events, which tended to be less select than consular gatherings, attracted a rather different clientele: mostly students, teachers, artists, and others who were interested in "culture." However an element of distinction for social climbers was added to these occasions by the atmosphere of "culture" and the presence of artists, scholars, and Catalan aristocrats affiliated with the Institute. Below these assemblies on the ladder of prestige were the cocktails or receptions sponsored by American business firms to announce the opening of some new enterprise or to welcome company officials. By common consent, these catered, male-dominated affairs were the least distinguished and most boring of all American working cocktails in the city. These gatherings were attended by the business, consular, institute, and military leaders, relevant American host and foreign businessmen, and possibly, if the event were especially significant, some high officials(s) of the local government.

Going around the working cocktail circuit, one noticed the same American faces appearing again and again. There were, indeed, Americans who were invited to nearly all these functions: the consular leadership and relevant specialists, the top businessmen, the director of the Cultural Institute, the head of the "private" radio station, and, when available, the headmaster of the American School. By examining the guest lists on the circuit, one could identify with considerable accuracy the elite Americans in Ciudad Condal.

Although the hosts at working cocktails tended to use the sociability they generated as a means of furthering some mission-oriented end, other American alcoholic assemblies were convened primarily for the purpose of social give-and-take. The difference between these two kinds of functions corresponds roughly to the distinction drawn by anthropologists between trade (a social transaction in the service of some economic interest) and gift-giving (a social transaction serving sociability only). Primarily social parties occurred as frequently as the working cocktail among Americans in the city, but they tended to be smaller, more personalized, and more directly controlled by the principle of reciprocity. There were various forms for such events, almost all involving the consumption of both alcohol and food: the cocktail, dinner, or after-dinner soirée at home; the luncheon, dinner, or after-theater snack at a restaurant; and bar, café, or night club activities. These gatherings, which tended to be more frequent during periods of *fiesta,* varied so widely in character that it would be useless to attempt further generalizations about them. Their function, however, appeared to be similar to, although narrower in scope than, the working cocktail, i.e., they tended to promote social integration or cohesion. Anthropologists are fond of talking about the integrating powers of rituals such as those found in primitive or folk societies. But the American community in Ciudad Condal was not a folk society, and its ritualistic gatherings, though possibly contributing to the solidarity or cohesiveness of sub-groups in the colony, did not appear to add much to overall community integration. In Chapter 7 we will attempt to discover why this was so.

While in the field the author made an initial impressionistic assessment of the level and kind of sociability which prevailed on both working and non-working "cocktail circuits" in the American community. His judgment that it was somewhat higher than was customary among the middle classes at home received some support from reports of Americans who had never been abroad before. Of 14 adults who gave adequate information, 7 said they were more "social" than at home, 3 said that they were less "social," and 4 reported that they were neither more nor less "social" than at home.[4] A hyperactive "social" or party life has been found in many American communities abroad. According to Cleveland and his associates, this higher level of sociability may be explained in terms of its functions for social cohesiveness, communication, vertical (status) mobility, and, possibly, anxiety reduction.[5] Until some careful comparative studies are done, it will not be possible to test their or other hypotheses. In the city, for reasons advanced more fully in Chapter 7, we would tend to discount, at least on the community level, the function of the various "social" assemblies for cohesiveness.

One hypothesis about the higher level of sociability of Americans abroad, though obvious from our data, has not yet appeared in the literature. It concerns the use of a social gathering such as a cocktail or reception as a rite of passage, i.e., to mark an arrival, an opening, or a departure. Since the rate of occurrence of such events among Americans in Ciudad Condal, and probably in most American overseas communities, was very high, and since some kind of party was the customary way of honoring such "passages," the incidence of "social" assemblies inevitably increased. Like rites of passage everywhere, these parties appeared to function to provide some sense of stability or continuity in a situation of flux. Those who complained that one of these affairs was "just like another" and that "the same people appeared over and over again" may have been overlooking the strong need for continuity and stability among the expatriates in this "Community in Limbo."

In concluding our discussion of what the Americans in the city called "the cocktail circuit," we would like to suggest another "obvious" hypothesis, this one concerning the relationship between sociability and alcohol. We have many reports of the prevalence of alcoholism on the American overseas frontier. The high incidence of this form of deviance is usually explained as the effect of personal demoralization in the stranger situation.[6] We have no quarrel with this hypothesis, but we would add that the nature of social life in an American overseas community tends to favor the selection of alcohol as a means of defense. During the time of this study in Ciudad Condal, there probably were no more than two or three bona fide alcoholics among the American residents; but as we have learned, informants who gave adequate information tended to report that they were drinking more than at home. This could have been due partly to contact with a wine-drinking culture, but it also seems to have been related to the greater incidence of "social" assemblies in which alcohol was consumed.[7] Americans, therefore, encountered what may have amounted to a cultural "prescription" for using alcohol to feel better. With different human material and more severe problems of adaptation in another overseas situation, the human implications of the alcoholic assemblies might have been more serious.

Primary Circles

In the existential novel we often find some character preoccupied with the problem of attaining genuine intimacy with another. Subject to unstable and depersonalizing social conditions, modern man is seen as a stranger who gropes, often vainly, for the communication and personal response which, in other times and places, was supposed to have been a normal part of the human condition. People who migrate to another culture often encounter what amounts to the essence of the modern social condition in extreme form. They tend, as a result, to be very much concerned with finding or creating an intimate circle. The Americans in Ciudad Condal were no exception.

Most Americans in the city had acquired circles of friends with whom they were in frequent contact. For the majority of informants about whom there was adequate information (46 of 80), these primary circles were multi-national groups composed of Americans, hosts, and/or foreign nationals. Of less statistical significance were circles composed either entirely of Americans (18 of 80) or, with the exception of the American informant, entirely of hosts (12 of 80). The dominant factor which governed the formation of these groups was the mission and the social associations which attended it. For married persons friendships of husbands formed on the job tended to extend to wives and children and to dictate patterns of family leisure-time sociability. As in most American enclaves abroad, the mission tended to subdivide the community along vocational lines.[8] The missions which appeared to have the greatest "clumping power" were those of the missionaries, the nuns at the school for girls, the artists and intellectuals, the consulate people, the oil explorers, and the propagandists. Less significant factors which appeared to dictate the choices of intimates were the level of acculturation or degree of cultural compatibility, including language fluency, age, social standing, sex, marital status, avocational interests, kinship, and propinquity. To illustrate, one easily identifiable primary circle consisted mostly of young, mixed-marrieds and kin, and another of people whose common bond was a hatred of Spain and who spent much of their time complaining about it.

In larger American outposts abroad visited by the author, differentiation into clumps, especially on vocational grounds, seems to have been more advanced than in the city. Although the Condal civilian government people were recognized as a clique, they appeared to be vocationally less exclusive in their friendships than the government employees at larger American outposts visited by the author. Were the American community in Ciudad Condal to increase in size, we would normally expect that growing forces of social differentiation would define more distinctly the boundaries of friendship circles.

This survey of factors controlling the formation of American primary groups in the city has indicated that the process of group formation operated according to different principles than in Park Forest, a typical new American suburb, where residential propinquity was the principal factor affecting friendship patterns.[9] How may we explain this difference? We believe that it may be attributed primarily to the influence of the job on the life of a community. In the usual overseas enclave, people live constantly in the shadow of their missions. In contrast to the suburban commuter at home, it is not so easy for an American overseas to leave his work behind him at the office.[10] Living in an overseas enclave is a little like having a faculty residence on a college or university campus. In such a situation it is difficult ever to "leave" the office, one's colleagues, or one's students. The overseas job usually is not radically separated from the rest of one's life. To take an extreme case from Ciudad Condal, the consuls and their wives were expected to work throughout the day and night, and their homes often were used for working entertainments. Since the mission of these people dominated so much of their lives, it also tended to influence their friendship patterns, although to a lesser extent at this post than in other locations. On the other hand, among those Americans who tended to compartmentalize their work (certain businessmen, for example) or those who had no work (such as the retired), friendships were only slightly, or not at all, under the influence of the mission.

In contrast to most overseas enclaves, the typical American suburb is primarily a residential rather than a working community. Consequently friendships increasingly tend to follow the dictates of residential requirements. In Ciudad Condal, not only was the mission especially influential in the formation of primary circles, but the possibilities of making friends on the basis of residential propinquity were, as we have seen, severely limited. Thus, for the typical American there, one problem in adaptation may have arisen from the necessity of choosing friends from more different regions of his life space than is customary in the United States.

As at home, an important factor in the formation of primary circles in the city was status aspiration. If we confine ourselves to that area of the foreign scene where social climbing was most evident, namely the female sector, we could write a number of overseas biographies almost entirely in terms of status maneuvers. Female vertical mobility had as its aim the penetration of more prestigious primary circles up to the cliques which headed the hierarchy of prestige in the American community. The two overlapping elite groups which attracted American status seekers were: (1) The civilian government women and their satellites. (2) The Catalan aristocrats and theirs. Although many American women tended to ridicule these groups, they would, according to one informant, have given "their eye teeth to belong to either of them." The principal locale for female climbing operations was the Cultural Institute.

The details of feminine maneuvers for recognition and status were mostly beyond the reach of the male anthropologist. However, this lacuna in our data about American life in the city need not impede our analysis. If we grant a range of technique to the population of American females and assume that part of this range proved more successful for vertical mobility, we simply have to establish whether the conditions for the operation of such a technique existed. What would these conditions be? We suggest that acceptance by the elite groups required an opportunity for regular, informal association with the ladies in them. This opportunity was provided by the Cultural Institute.

Both the government women and some of the Catalan aristocrats were affiliated with the Institute: the government women in their working role as leaders and supporters of American affairs, and the upper class Catalans as patrons of the arts and borrowers of American consumer patterns. Contacts at the Cultural Institute functioned for both of these groups to provide a legitimation of status and/or increment in prestige. On the one hand, the aristocrats could associate with the representatives of a powerful nation which was a trend-setter in the process of modernization. On the other, the Americans, nourished on a dream of vertical mobility, could cap their rise in status, which began for most of them with their arrival in this foreign setting, by intimate association with genuine aristocrats. And both groups could validate their roles as ladies by participating in the cultural events and charitable activities which were sponsored by the Institute. We have said that the elite groups were not mutually exclusive. Some American women belonged to both, but others maintained such a commitment to one or the other that covert inter-group conflict occasionally ensued.

The American female status seeker could direct her status operations toward either elite group or both. If she were particularly interested in acceptance by the aristocrats, she might become affiliated with the *Section Feminina,* an Institute association made up mostly of host women. If, as was more likely, her highest aspirations were directed toward the group of elite government women, she might join the American Women's Club which had only a few hosts as associate members. Her rising fortunes would be marked by requests to participate or officiate in groups or events; and her accession to the pinnacles of prestige in this setting would be confirmed by appointments to positions of leadership in charity drives ("In charge of the American Red Cross table were . . .") or invitations into elite homes ("I've been invited to tea at Contessa _____'s").

As we would expect of people who had been socialized in a country where values are placed on both superiority and equality,[11] the vertical dimension of American social life in the city excited ambivalence among the Americans themselves. Many Americans felt both gratified and guilty about being able to live, as some of them expressed it, "higher on the hog," i.e., to have prerogatives of classes above them at home. Those Americans who proclaimed openly the attributes of their higher status usually were regarded with disfavor. ("Who does he think he is?") Those Americans who were not struggling to survive financially tended to relish the signs of higher status, but only the boorish displayed them frankly and openly.

Another indication of American ambivalence about social status is provided by the attitude of Americans toward the cliques in their community. In pursuing his inquiries into the network of informal circles among Americans, the anthropologist found that direct questions were not very effective in eliciting adequate information. Informants usually admitted that there were cliques of varying prestige in the community, but they were reluctant to identify them. They seemed to think that cliques were bad and that clique members were snobs who were trying to prove their superiority by keeping others out of their circles. Further investigation tended to confirm the initial impression that there was considerable guilt and hostility connected with cliques. Although these groups were not well-developed, many Americans were preoccupied with them as with some guilty secret. In Ciudad Condal, a community small enough to be a genuine primary group under other circumstances, the facts of social differentiation were not always easy to accept, especially when accompanied by the amount of inter-group hostility evident there. Not all Americans, however, felt guilty about their cliques, and some, having experienced what to them were grander things elsewhere, regarded American status operations in the play of cliques as an insignificant comedy.

As far as the prestige dimension in the American community was concerned, one acquired higher status by being in a clique than not and the highest status by being accepted into the circles of civilian government people, Catalan upper class, or both. These two groups provided the ultimate legitimation for the typical American female's existence in Ciudad Condal. Accession to membership in the elite groups tended to validate the role of lady and the self which went with it.

COMMUNITY CIRCLES

Of the circles in the city to which the Americans gave their allegiance, the family and friendship groups were most significant. There was relatively little commitment to community-wide groups which in some other American outposts function to integrate the colony. The weakness of community associations in Ciudad Condal may be attributed in part to the lack of external (home) initiative and support. In contrast, at a typical military base abroad, the government provides resources for the development of basic institutions such as the school and the PX, and helps to organize such activities as Little Leagues, Boy and Girl Scouts, and clubs for adults. Since the departure of most of the military from the city, the Americans there received very little external support for their associational life. Even the Cultural Institute, sponsored by the U.S.I.S., was heavily dependent on local financing and initiative.

We will deal at length with the rather feeble American associational life in the city in Chapter 7. Besides the Cultural Institute, the American Women's Club, the American Chamber of Commerce in Spain, the American Men's Luncheon Club, and perhaps one of the schools, only the church existed as a potential significant focus for American commitment. Strictly speaking, there was no American church in the city, only an Anglo-American church which was an affiliate of the Church of England. Through the cooperation of the resident archdeacon and the assistance of an erstwhile seminary student from the United States, this church had become linked with the American community in a semi-official way. Besides the regular round of Anglican observances attended by British and American nationals, it provided special Thanksgiving and funeral services for Americans. It was attended regularly by a small group of Americans, mainly civilian government employees (one of whom played the organ), and on special American occasions, by some other Americans. (The missionaries were not involved with this church.) The close liaison between the American and British government missions in the city was dramatized by the active participation of both the American and English consul generals in this church. The rather sweeping absence of other Americans from its services may be attributed to their lack of interest in organized religion,[12] the formal-liturgical character of the services which alienated some Protestants, and the disproportionate numbers of Catholics in the community. The Catholics also were not keenly interested in organized religion, and had an extremely spotty record of attendance at various churches in and around the city. Thus, organized religion was not able to perform its classic function of societal integration with any effectiveness. This lack of integrating power was typical of all of the community-wide associations maintained by Americans in the city.

EXTRA-COMMUNAL CIRCLES

In the modern era of rapid communication and expanding social units, circles which frame and control behavior usually do not end at the geographic or political boundaries of a community.[13] Americans who had just arrived in the city were usually aware of this. Friendless and confused, many of them tended to emphasize communication with friends and relatives back home. As they became better adapted their need for this kind of support was likely to decline, but most of them maintained primary contacts back home or around the world. Regular leaves granted by the large organizations provided an opportunity to renew these contacts in person. The problems which were likely to occur on such occasions are discussed in Chapter 9.

In our consideration of missions, we mentioned the various chains of command which terminated in Ciudad Condal. Under certain conditions, American agents were more responsive to people in these chains than to anyone in the city.[14] The Consulate General, for example, was in daily communication with Madrid, and through Madrid, with Washington. Through this circuit, the actions of the consulate officials were controlled by the large organizations in which they played a small part. The actions of the businessmen and missionaries, to take two other examples, appeared to be less closely controlled from home. This evidence suggests the following sociological moral: The actions of most Americans abroad must be viewed as more or less determined by the organization which they represent. The more authoritarian the organization and the greater the contact it maintains with its representatives, the more important it will be as a factor in their actions overseas.

Home organizations and people also sponsored "visiting firemen" who had to be welcomed and entertained by the Americans. Unlike the Embassy in Madrid, the Consulate General in Ciudad Condal was not plagued with visiting government people (e.g., congressmen) and dignitaries (e.g., Mrs. John Kennedy). But "visiting firemen" were enough of a burden to Americans in the city to prompt a mild editorial complaint in the *Condal Courier*. Entitled "The Silly Season," it said in part, "We . . . have begun to receive those letters which begin: 'We certainly don't want to put you to any trouble but it so happens that some dear friends of ours will be visiting Spain and we have asked them to look you up. . . .' They go on to tell us that Sam and Mildred are lovely people and that they don't want us to go to any trouble on their behalf. . . . Now we've seen a lot of Sams and Mildreds in our day and they've usually turned out to be pretty nice people. They are appropriately apologetic when they call us on a Saturday or Sunday morning. They're just in from Rome and could we please fix them with a hotel room? Also would we like to join them for drinks and dinner later on? Well, we wouldn't, particularly, but we do and usually end up paying for it all as it seems that Mildred and Sam do not have any pesetas. They haven't cashed their traveler's checks. And, of course, we take them to a bullfight which we'd just have soon missed. But anyway, we go along with it all and in the end we have some new friends whether we like it or not."

In general, settled Americans in the city did not look forward to welcoming outsiders unless these visitors were known to be important to them. They were civil enough in greeting newcomers to the Amercan Men's Luncheon Club and the American Women's Club, but on the whole, in contrast to suburban Americans, they were not very hospitable to either transients or new residents. Concerning her arrival in the city, an American resident said, "We were bitter about our arrival here. The Americans were rather indifferent . . . I was here with two tiny children and needed help and nobody offered it."

A schoolteacher, who could have spoken for many of her colleagues at one of the American schools, said, "The school does not greet you or help you or introduce you around." We would explain the Americans' lack of hospitality in terms of a hypothesis advanced by Heiss.[15] In a laboratory experiment, he introduced a third party into two-person groups (dyads) and inquired into the attitudes of the dyad members toward the newcomer. He found that those partners who liked each other tended to have a more favorable view of the new arrival. But the Condal Americans often disliked their colleagues and the hosts. Thus, their comparatively unfavorable view of the people with whom they lived may (if Heiss' hypothesis can be applied to the outside world) have been "displaced" onto strangers and resulted in the rather inhospitable atmosphere which pervaded the American community in the city.

7

COMMUNITY COHESIVENESS AND ITS SOURCES

The Europeans stayed in the Club till mid-
night.... There is nothing like an earthquake
for drawing people together....
GEORGE ORWELL
Burmese Days

OBSERVERS OF PEOPLE ABROAD OFTEN HAVE REMARKED about the attraction of strangers from the same homeland to each other. How may we account for this clumping tendency? One hypothesis states that this mutual attraction originates in stranger experience, i.e., the encounter with *anomie* (meaninglessness or normlessness) in the stranger situation.[1] If we consider that anxiety accompanies such an experience, how might the stranger attempt to deal with it? One strategy would be to draw together with people from home to defend oneself against the foreign environment. The resulting enclave could then be thought to depend for its existence on its defensive properties; and its cohesiveness, i.e., its attractiveness, could be regarded as a simple function of stranger anxiety. There is considerable evidence to support this hypothesis. American soldiers new to battle have demonstrated an "irrational" tendency to bunch up for protection under fire.[2] Certain threatening laboratory conditions devised by Schachter have caused his subjects to indicate a desire to be with others.[3] Finally, Herman and Schild have observed the formation of a strongly cohesive group among sojourners in Israel.[4] There appear to be valid grounds for maintaining that people from the same home area will be attracted to each other in a foreign setting and that their mutual attraction will be directly associated with the amount of stranger anxiety they experience. Let us see how this hypothesis fares when tested in the American community in Ciudad Condal.

To begin, we should recall that this community was small and could not sustain many home-based and American-supported institutions which might act to shield people from the foreign environment, reduce *anomie* and anxiety, and provide external support for community cohesiveness. Ciudad Condal had few focal points and little outside encouragement for American association. The Americans there were alone in their attempts to build and maintain a community.

People who become strangers find themselves in a situation in which their subjective world is threatened by a lack of external confirmation. To the extent that they require such confirmation they will become uncertain and anxious about themselves and their behavior. The evidence from the cross-section of adult informants in Ciudad Condal indicates that there was much stronger anxiety among them. A majority (20 of 35) reported a decline in their general feeling of well-being since their arrival in Spain. Most (24 of 35) noted an increase in frustration or exasperation. Thirty-one of 55 had a mixed or unfavorable attitude toward their hosts. In addition to these direct and indirect indications of stranger anxiety, one might cite the constant griping about Ciudad Condal and its people which was evident at any gathering of Americans. This hostility, which is assumed to be a manifestation of stranger anxiety,[5] often pervaded American conversations. In sum, at the time of the study, stranger anxiety appears to have been part of a majority response to this particular overseas setting.

The hypothesis further predicts that a considerable incidence of stranger anxiety will result in a more cohesive overseas enclave. In Ciudad Condal, however, the evidence is to the contrary. One American, in some exasperation, said, "When are people going to learn there is no American community here?" Another stated, "I find the people here to be the most uncooperative and self-centered of any Americans I've lived with in Europe and the Far East."

If we employ a fairly narrow, standard definition of the term, i.e., the attraction to a group, including resistance to leaving it,[6] these comments suggest that there was little cohesiveness within this American community. The attitudes and behavior of resident Americans in the city confirm these informants' judgments. Most of those who gave adequate information (29 of 44) had mixed or unfavorable attitudes toward their colleagues. These data tell us that there not only was a lack of attraction but indeed a positive aversion of many Americans to each other. Contrary to expectations generated by the hypothesis, antipathy for the hosts, presumed to be associated with stranger anxiety, was not complemented by an attraction to other Americans in Ciudad Condal.[7]

The extent of the Americans' participation in community-wide organizations and activities appears to have been consistent with their attitudes. Apart from the Thanksgiving, Christmas, and occasionally Fourth of July celebrations, there were no regular community-wide get-togethers. Only three predominantly American associations existed, and one of these, the American Men's Luncheon Club, was so ephemeral that it deserved to be called an occasion rather than an association. The Cultural Institute had a membership of four hundred Americans and hosts, but attendance by Americans at its events was spotty and participation in Institute affairs did not meet the expectations of its newly-arrived American director. The American Women's Club with approximately 50 members was an official affiliate of the Institute. It constituted the most significant community association in that it sponsored more events, undertook more projects, and made greater claims on more Americans than the other two. It represented the acme of social organization among Americans in the city and the heart of their community life. We should expect to find crystallized in this association the aspects of community life we have been examining.[8]

In order to gather information about the American Women's Club, the author made use of published materials and special informants recommended to him in initial interviews with community leaders. Concerning the Women's Club, a few published materials were available in articles in the local newspaper and letters to club members. For purposes of this analysis, however, information provided by special informants is crucial. These women, all of whom had been leaders of the club and long-term residents of the city, were able to provide the kind of information which could not appear in public print. The method used to draw conclusions about the club and other specialized areas of American life is described in the Preface. Generalizations are based on the majority testimony of special informants.

At the time of the study, the American Women's Club in Ciudad Condal had been in existence for nearly ten years. It was created primarily to meet the needs of Navy wives at a time when the city had become a home port for the Nth Fleet. In its early years it met regularly at one of the large luxury hotels, but during the time of the study it was meeting at the Cultural Institute. Since military operations in the area had been largely phased out, the bulk of the club's membership was now civilian.

The club's formal purpose was to welcome newcomers and facilitate contacts between Americans and between Americans and hosts. It also assumed the major share of responsibility in community-wide social occasions and engaged in charitable ventures. Regular monthly meetings were held for new members, the entire membership, and the board. A typical meeting for all included a business session, a social period, and some form of entertainment or recreation. A closer examination of a meeting, however, revealed that the various projects, entertainments, and educational activities of the club were little more than an excuse for its primary function, pure sociability. However the members generally did not find that the club was an indispensable instrument for the satisfaction of their needs for affiliation. One of the informants said that the clubwomen "did not have the closeness and loyalty to act as a united group." According to her, "They did not seem to like one-another." Referring to an earlier time when military and non-military government people were more numerous, she said, "There was a wonderful, active group of people here."

In studies of cohesiveness it has become customary to refer not only to the attraction of people to each other but also to the tasks of the group. Accomplishment or productivity, therefore, are signs of group commitment or cohesiveness.[9] By any criterion, the American Women's Club in Ciudad Condal was not very productive. One informant said, "In comparison with clubs at home the people here are just afraid to move forward." Another, when queried about the difficulties of instituting and maintaining club activities, said, "There is a lack of interest. It is always the same group of people doing the same things and it will always be that way. I believe that the new group of leaders is beginning to find that out." With the rapid turnover in the community, there always seemed to be a fresh supply of enthusiastic souls who intended to revitalize the club, but these women quickly discovered that their new ideas and enthusiasms were no more effective than previous ideas and enthusiasms and that they were carrying the burden of club work on their backs. In one of many discussions the author had with women about the lack of interest and participation in the club, one woman said in some exasperation, "Perhaps it should be left to die."

Although the surface atmosphere of a club meeting was of cheerful good fellowship, it was not long before a visitor saw evidence of considerable anxiety. The women seemed to be very much concerned with their own and others' difficulties, particularly those around the home. In keeping with the general atmosphere of the community, there was a good deal of hostile comment about other Americans and about the native population, especially maids and handy men. One informant described the women in the club as "touchy," which suggests that they may have been struggling with the frustrations of strangerhood. This supposition is supported by the fact that those clubwomen who were interviewed were as likely to show marks of stranger anxiety as other Americans in Ciudad Condal.

In regard to cohesiveness and anxiety the American Women's Club in Ciudad Condal seemed to reflect those attributes in the community as a whole. The evidence suggests that American women were not highly attracted toward the group and its projects and that considerable anxiety pervaded club relationships and activities. Contrary to expectations derived from our hypothesis, this group showed much anxiety but little cohesiveness.

In order to make comparisons, the author studied, by the same procedures, the American Women's Club in Madrid which had approximately one thousand members and was described by all the special informants as extremely active. Although its general structure was the same, its range of activities was much wider. In addition to the regular membership meetings, charities, and bridge parties which were held in Ciudad Condal, the Madrid club sponsored a number of hobby groups and tours in and outside Spain. The informants agreed that *all* the activities of the Madrid club were well attended and that there was no problem in generating interest for these and other proposed projects. They said that the Madrid women generally thought highly of their club and liked to attend its functions. If their testimony is accepted, we must conclude that the attraction of this group, i.e., its cohesiveness, seems to have been superior to that of the American Women's Club in Ciudad Condal.

Although it was not possible to interview a broad spectrum of Americans in Madrid, those informants who were contacted gave no indication that significant stranger anxiety existed in or outside the women's club there. As one informant said, "It is a tradition for Americans to like it here." At club meetings it was customary to gripe about maids and handymen, but the pervasive hostility toward other Americans, hosts, and the host city which prevailed in Ciudad Condal was not evident in Madrid. The lack of hostility suggests that there was less stranger anxiety among Americans in Madrid than in Ciudad Condal.

To conclude, without referring to any precise absolute standard, the relative degrees of stranger anxiety and group cohesiveness in the Madrid and Condal women's clubs, as judged by the special informants, were as follows:

	Madrid	*Ciudad Condal*
STRANGER ANXIETY	Lower	Higher
GROUP COHESIVENESS	Higher	Lower

This negative association between the two variables would appear to disconfirm the hypothesis that stranger anxiety tends to generate group cohesiveness.

The above comparison is somewhat suspect, of course, because of the possibility that different standards of evaluation were used by informants in the two cities. In order to eliminate this possibility the author interviewed a Madrid clubwoman who had returned recently from a visit to the Women's Club in Ciudad Condal. She and a friend had attended a club meeting to propose and explain a project of general interest to American women's clubs abroad. According to her, she was "demoralized by the extremely negative" attitude of the Condal women. She gained the impression that they felt that no project could be successful in their club. In addition she thought that most of them disliked Ciudad Condal. Returning to Madrid, she reported that she had had a "terrible time" in the Condal city. Her testimony, based on experience in both clubs, suggests that they did differ in group cohesiveness and stranger anxiety. The negativistic attitude of the Condal women indicates that they were pessimistic about accomplishment and therefore not a very cohesive group. The antipathy toward the host city, noted by this observer, tends to confirm other reports of signs of significant stranger anxiety.

The attempt to explain the cohesiveness of Americans in Ciudad Condal as a simple function of stranger anxiety appears to have failed. The evidence from this community and from another American enclave in Spain contradicts the hypothesis that there is an inverse relationship between stranger anxiety and cohesiveness. How then, are we to explain the low cohesiveness of Americans in Ciudad Condal? A number of hypotheses, derived primarily from the literature of small groups, invite consideration. Continuing to use the Women's Club as the focus of analysis, let us see to what extent these hypotheses are confirmed by the evidence.

Several American women in Ciudad Condal, when "theorizing" about the difficulties of their club, suggested the small size of their community as a factor. The evidence concerning the relationship between group size and cohesiveness is not consistent.[10] Also, the author's investigation of the American Women's club in a Scandinavian capital city only slightly larger than that in Ciudad Condal (approximately one hundred members) provided an impression of cohesiveness close to that reported for Madrid. Informants in the Scandinavian city reported nearly as many club activities as in Madrid—regular meetings, bridge parties, charities, tours, and hobby groups. According to them, all these functions were well attended. It would seem that under appropriate conditions both small- and large-sized groups can be highly cohesive and that we can eliminate size as a contributing factor to the low cohesiveness of the American community in Ciudad Condal.

Size, however, might be thought to act indirectly on the cohesiveness of a club. If two clubs of different size require the same dues per member, the larger club, if it is realistic about costs, will have more money for club programs and will provide more varied, interesting, and prestige-giving activities which some women in Ciudad Condal felt were essential in order to increase the attraction of their club.[11] However, the argument of these women appears to be contradicted by the weak drawing power of the various entertainments and educational programs which had been tried in the Condal club. One informant said that her attempts to bring "culture" into the group had been frustrated by an obvious lack of interest. On another occasion, a special luncheon at a restaurant on the outskirts of the city collapsed because too few women wished to attend. One major effort of the club, a fashion show and bridge, was well attended, but informants reported that the women showed little interest in the fashions. In the light of this evidence it does not seem probable that more expensive and varied projects, made possible by a larger population, could have rejuvenated this club.

Is it possible that club activities did not interest the American women because the host city offered a sufficient number and variety of entertainments?[12] There are two reasons for rejecting this view. First, it is not likely that people who held such an unfavorable attitude toward their host situation would find outside activities *that* attractive. Second, there was as much or more to interest Americans in the Spanish and Scandinavian capital cities where the women were more strongly attracted to their clubs. Therefore the kind or quantity of activities in and outside the American Women's Club in

Ciudad Condal probably were not significant factors in determining its cohesiveness.

One informant attributed the difficulties in maintaining the Condal Women's Club to the rapid turnover of American residents. (The modal period of residence of those interviewed was less than one year.) The popular argument that the more you know people and places the better you will like them may be true in some cases, but it does not apply to a situation where people already are prone to dislike the situation around them. Because the interview data do not show any significant association between length of residence in the city and liking for other Americans there, we can discard this factor from further consideration.

In discussing the difficulties of the Women's Club, one informant referred to the resident Americans as "all spread out." If she meant that the population was heterogeneous, we can take this judgment as a hypothesis which agrees with the general evidence that less homogeneous groups tend to be less cohesive.[13] To what extent were the Condal Americans like one another? If we agree to use vocational identification as an index, we can obtain a rough indication of their homogeneity by noting the four largest vocational categories comprising a majority of the work force in this community: civilian government employees, employees of large businesses, small businessmen, and military men. On the other hand, the American community in Madrid was dominated statistically by the military, and the community in Scandinavia by two categories—civilian government employees and employees of large businesses. Vocationally speaking, the Americans in Ciudad Condal were the least homogeneous and, as we would expect from the hypothesis, the least cohesive; their heterogeneity therefore may have been a source of their low cohesiveness.

A number of informants mentioned the extreme "individualism" of Americans in Ciudad Condal. If the term is used to mean self-orientation, as opposed to other-orientation, it would be reasonable to expect that a population composed of such people would demonstrate a low degree of cohesiveness. The difficulties of attracting Americans to organizations like the Women's Club might have been due to the fact that there were comparatively few other-oriented organization women in the community.

Fellin and Litwak provide some precedent for the investigation of organization men as a source of group cohesiveness. Using data from American settings, they examined "the mechanisms which speed the socialization of newcomers and thereby maintain cohesion under conditions of membership turnover." [14] They found that such mechanisms were particularly evident in the type of person they labeled "bureaucrat." According to them, this kind of individual tended to integrate more rapidly and easily into new neighborhoods than did other types.[15] Their bureaucrat is, in effect, an organization man, i.e., he works for a large organization. If, as seems likely, their findings were applicable to Americans in an overseas setting, we would expect to find fewer organization men and women in Ciudad Condal. On the other hand, communities with higher cohesiveness should have had a greater proportion of this kind of person.

If those who work for large organizations are called organization men, slightly less than half of the resident adult Americans in the city fell into this category. Arranged according to size of the category, they included all kinds of government people, business people, and missionaries (who will be excluded from further consideration because they were at odds with the values of other Americans and aimed at assimilating directly into the host society). This analysis shows that the American Women's Club in Ciudad Condal drew its membership from a community in which an estimated one in three American adults was an organization man or woman, whereas in both the Spanish and Scandinavian capital cities clear majorities of the Americans were organization people. Thus there appears to be a definite possibility that the relatively weak concentration of organization men in the city was at least in part responsible for the low cohesiveness there.

If numbers of organization men have an effect on social cohesiveness, it is reasonable to expect that their location in the power structure of a community might vary this effect. If the people with power and prestige in a community were interested in building and maintaining community-wide groups and in asserting their leader-

ship in this regard, they might prove to be more capable of impress-
ing their style on the community. In American overseas enclaves,
the titular head of social life is the wife of the chief diplomat. She
and her covey of diplomatic wives usually play a key role in
community-wide associations involving women. Unfortunately for
cohesiveness in the Women's Club in the city, the morale of the
consulate women was particularly low at the time of the study, and
they were not as effective leaders as they might have been. One
American woman said, "I feel that the drive and interest in any club
of this kind comes from the representatives of the Consulate. A few
years ago the consulate people were more active. There was a
wonderful group of people then. Now the consulate people are all
strung out. They don't seem to like one another."

The boundaries between the different sub-groups of Americans in
Ciudad Condal were points of considerable conflict. The reason
appears to be the kinds of people who predominated in each area.
All the diplomatic and military people were organization men, but
this kind of person was found infrequently in the business group,
where entrepreneurial types tended to prevail. (The business people
were nearly unanimous in their negative attitude toward the diplomats.) The consular women could not have been effective leaders in
this community: Not only were they demoralized, but they tended
to be the kind of person who antagonized the many non-organiza-
tion types among the Americans.

Our inventory of possible contributing sources of low cohesiveness among Americans in Ciudad Condal would not be complete
without some mention of social status. Many studies have shown
that for Americans at home, an increase in status—no matter how
measured—is associated with increased participation in society and
culture.[16] High status people tend to belong to more groups, to read
more, to be more concerned with civic matters and current events.
Since it was not a first-line outpost for American imperialistic
interests, there was a dearth of very important people in Ciudad
Condal. The upper echelons of large American organizations who
would be expected to contribute more than their share toward

building association life were heavily represented in Madrid but largely absent from Ciudad Condal. The low cohesiveness of the American Women's Club in the city may have been in part due to its lower status, less association-minded constituency. Some other difficulties of the club also may be explained by this factor. The special informants all complained about the lack of "polish and sophistication" of club members, their lack of interest in "educational and cultural" activities, and their refusal to try something new and different. All these qualities could be attributed to lower social status.

Let us recapitulate briefly. The predicted relationship between stranger anxiety and cohesiveness among Americans in Ciudad Condal was not confirmed. If not anxiety, what factors were responsible for the low cohesiveness of this community? Using the Women's Club as the focus of our analysis, we identified the following attributes of the community's population as possible sources of the lack of attraction of these Americans to each other: (1) Heterogeneity. (2) A weak concentration of organization men. (3) Lower social status. Is it possible to decide on one or more of these factors with greater certainty? Fortunately, the memory of informants permits us to conduct a crude historical experiment on these variables.

The American Women's Club in Ciudad Condal had not always been a struggling operation. From one informant we already have learned that at an earlier time when the government women had been more numerous there had been a "wonderful, active group" in Ciudad Condal. One man, especially cognizant of association life, confirmed this judgment. Deploring the present "lack of cooperation" among Americans, he said, "For group projects it isn't the same as in other American communities abroad. When the Navy was here it was much better. The Navy people always pitched in much better. But since the military left there has been nothing at all."

Apparently the contingents of Navy and Air Force people who left when operations in this area of Spain were phased out took with them an important ingredient of club and community cohesiveness, i.e., organization people. Their departure also removed rather formidable home-based support for community associations. We may infer that the weak concentration of organization men in the community at the time of the study was indeed a source of its low cohesiveness.

Testimony of informants further indicates that during the "golden age" of the Women's Club the military made up a majority of the American population in the city, a situation analogous to that in the Spanish capital at the time of the study. The departure of this element appears to have extracted still another ingredient of community cohesiveness, homogeneity of population. The more heterogeneous population present at the time of the study may also have been a source of lower cohesiveness. Unfortunately, the historical evidence about the status of Americans in the city is not adequate to warrant a firmer decision about its effect on community cohesiveness.

It is very difficult to separate the two most likely sources of low cohesiveness in the American community. Up to this point we have been talking about homogeneity as far as organization men are concerned. The scarcity of a particular kind of person, i.e., organization men and women, appears to be the most adequate explanation we can cite for the low cohesiveness among Americans in Ciudad Condal. There is still another way in which the effect of this factor may be weighed. A glance at the other foreign communities in the city will show that none of them displayed a very great degree of cohesiveness. As one foreign informant put it: "In the American group, it is everyone for himself. The individual doesn't care about others. . . . But this applies to every foreign colony, not just the American."

The city tended to "select" a disproportionate number of individualistic entrepreneurs. In the case of the Americans, these entrepreneurs and some of their wives made up a large part of the population from which the Women's Club drew its membership. When most of the American military had been withdrawn by an administrative decision made at home, there remained an insufficient number of organization people to maintain a highly cohesive community.

If, as far as cohesiveness is concerned, the American Women's Club in Ciudad Condal is taken as representative of the American community as a whole, our analysis suggests that there was no simple relationship, if any, between stranger anxiety and the cohesiveness of the American community there. The role of stranger anxiety in the cohesiveness of the women's club and community still is not clear. It may be that stranger anxiety was too low to be a significant factor in the overseas American communities studied. There is a remote possibility, therefore, that the lack of really severe stranger anxiety as well as other association-building factors were responsible for the less cohesive community in Ciudad Condal.

One caveat is necessary. Although we might agree that the Americans in Ciudad Condal did not clump together *as a community* to defend themselves against a threatening foreign environment, we still cannot conclude that they did not resort to a social solution for their anxiety. For example, they might have shown an increased attraction to sub-groups within the community rather than to the community as a whole. Indeed we have cited evidence which indicates that American families in the city tended to be more cohesive than at home. Moreover, those married people who reported this increased involvement were slightly more likely to hold mixed or unfavorable attitudes toward other Americans than those who did not report such an increase (67 vs. 45 percent). This difference (involving very few cases) suggests that there may have been a tendency to use the family rather than the community as a mooring point in this foreign situation. We may speculate that, unlike organization men, they were not able to generate the superficial friendliness and larger loyalties which membership in large organizations requires, and that the family and, perhaps, cliques would carry the burden of adaptation for them.

A stranger may or may not experience significant anxiety as a result of his foreign encounter. If he does, the solution he adopts will be in keeping with his character and with the situational resources available to him. Clumping together with *all* one's fellow countrymen would seem to be only one of several possible lines of defense. There is, of course, no guarantee that any of these procedures will be successful for adapting to a particular foreign setting.

8

ADAPTATION
IN A SPANISH
(CATALAN) SETTING

> In my case, the effort for these years to live in
> the dress of the Arabs, and to imitate their
> mental foundation, quitted me of my English
> self, and let me look at the West and its con-
> ventions with new eyes: they destroyed it all
> for me. At the same time I could not sincerely
> take on the Arab skin: it was an affectation
> only.
>
> T. E. LAWRENCE
> *Seven Pillars of Wisdom*

SOME OF THE AMERICANS IN CIUDAD CONDAL SPECU-
lated, at times angrily, about being chosen as subjects for
an anthropological study. When told that the study was
concerned with their "adjustment" or "adaptation," conceived in the
broadest possible sense, they were not necessarily mollified. A few
of the more experienced and suspicious said, "Why do the study
here? What is there in Ciudad Condal for Americans to adjust to?
It's just an ordinary international city." That, as they say, was a good
question, but the belief that there was nothing for most Americans
in the city to adjust or adapt to was incorrect. Regardless of past
experiences, most American residents of Ciudad Condal encountered significant problems of adaptation there.

If we think of adaptation, in the evolutionary or psychiatric
sense, as measured in terms of survival or well-being, we will have
to admit that successful adaptation in a foreign setting need not
involve significant changes by the individual.[1] If one is very powerful or if he goes to a foreign land with a culture very much like his
own, he may not be required to change greatly. If he moves to a

123

large military base abroad he may find that problems of individual adaptation have been mitigated by contractual arrangements with the hosts and by using specialized go-betweens. The complete range of American institutions which is offered on a large American military base abroad makes it unnecessary for an individual to change his style of life in order to adapt in the foreign setting. On one of these bases, a person could, conceivably, be successfully adapted even though he had had very little contact with the host culture.

The Americans in Ciudad Condal had to establish residences there without the aid of the kind of total American environment which one finds on a large American military base abroad. As we have seen, the American institutions which might have provided a focus for activity and cohesion were largely absent from this situation. The number of Americans were too few and their dispersion too great to provide effective protection from the foreign environment. These people had to come to terms with the hosts and their ways in order to adapt. This chapter deals with the process of change which for some led toward successful adaptation.

The theoretical grounds for our analysis have been provided by Alfred Schutz and Georg Simmel in their writings on the stranger.[2] As Schutz points out, strangerhood poses continual, hard-to-master problems of interpretation which are not encountered at home,[3] but neither author tells us much about this process. What does it mean to the stranger to feel strange, and how does this meaning change as he moves toward adaptation? What, in short, is the ideal-typical biography of the stranger from his own point of view? Let us ask this question of our American sojourners in Ciudad Condal.[4]

Most of the Americans in the city had come directly to Spain from the United States. But all of them, presumably, even if they had not come directly had undergone an American socialization which created a subjective world, including self, more or less in keeping with their American experience. To the extent that they felt "at home" prior to their departure, their frame of reference had received adequate confirmation from some particular American milieu. Their departure from this setting took away the props which had supported this frame of reference. If they had come to depend heavily on these props they were headed for an unsettling experience.[5]

On arrival in Ciudad Condal the Americans came up against a foreign situation which offered less confirmation of their old viewpoint. They now encountered the problem of meaninglessness which Schutz has described; [6] to the extent that they were unable to extract meaning from the foreign scene or find that which was extracted compatible with previously held definitions, their experience might be called *anomic.* The degree of *anomie* experienced by a stranger would depend on situational and personal factors. Such an experience would be threatening or anxiety-provoking and would continue until the Americans found "homes" or reorganized their subjective worlds to feel "at home" in the city. Until that happy resolution they would feel strange and their unconfirmed or disconfirmed subjective worlds would be out of balance. Their problem of adaptation, therefore, would be to locate confirming circles in the foreign scene or reorganize their frames of reference to obtain confirmation. The more profound their anxiety, the more they would be preoccupied with this problem.[7]

Because they came to a foreign setting inhabited by a proud people who showed little special consideration for outsiders, and because they were not shielded from the foreign environment by an all-encompassing enclave, the Americans could not easily locate circles which confirmed their old selves. The possibility of adapting without coming to terms with the hosts and their ways was slight. In this situation the ideal-typical American had to move toward adaptation by changing and reorganizing his subjective world. When he had attained that ultimate condition in which adequate confirmation was obtained and a satisfactory internal balance was restored he would have begun to feel at home.[8] As the saying goes, "he would have found a home in Spain." But this happy ending was by no means certain and sometimes very difficult to achieve.

If we provide a happy resolution for the ideal-typical stranger biography, we see him passing from a stage of acute *anomie* (in which there is much confusion) through simple *anomie* (in which host and home values conflict) to a condition in which a new equilibrium has been established.[9] This process would involve a continual formulation and reformulation of conceptions of the world and self. If we were to "fix" these conceptions at different points in the stranger's progress, a subjective picture of the adaptive process would emerge. Though it was not possible to do a satisfactory longitudinal study of American adaptation, the author was able to identify different degrees of adaptation among Americans there by asking people to compare themselves and their existence in the city with the period immediately prior to their arrival.[10] If we take these 36 who provided adequate information and agree that those 15 who said that they felt "less at home" were least adapted, those 9 who said that they felt "just as much at home" were well-adapted, and those 12 who said that they felt "more at home" were extremely well-adapted we can offer as a hypothesis a reconstruction of the ideal-typical stranger's biography from the beginning ("less at home") stage to its ("more at home") conclusion.[11] Of course, not all Americans entered this course of adaptation at the beginning and not all managed to make their way to the end. In fact, according to the author's judgment, a substantial minority never would get out of the stage of extreme strangerhood.

To illustrate the nature of the adaptive problems of Americans in the city let us look at the story of one American whose progress was comparatively slow and painful. She had been abroad before, but to locations with complete sets of American institutions. As a result, her previous "foreign" experience had not prepared her for her sojourn in Ciudad Condal. Here is how she describes the period after her arrival: "The first year was very frustrating. It was so frustrating that I was ill. When we went home on leave I was glad to go. You can't understand these people—at least in the first three years. You can't know them. . . . The people weren't used to our way of living. The cook quit because we didn't eat enough. The maid twisted my son's arm. We had always travelled before with everything taken care of by the services. It wasn't like that here."

This woman does not tell us very much about how she managed

to adapt, but another American, who initially experienced much frustration, said, "In the U. S. when somebody doing a job for you makes a mistake you go to him and get him to pay for it. Here, when I go to a guy he will laugh and say, 'So what?' There is no hope of getting him to pay. So you have to smile. Getting mad doesn't help a bit."

If we agree that majority tendencies among our informants represent the typical American, the data indicate that this American was very much concerned about the hosts.[12] He took these extremely vital people as a reference group or point of orientation. Other significant groups were American colleagues in the city and people at home. As we know from reference group theory, groups such as these could be expected to provide norms for behavior and, what is more important here, points of reference for measuring and maintaining a self-conception.[13] Perhaps because it was in jeopardy, the self also was of special concern to the American. Regardless of his status as stranger, he tended to report a heightened self-awareness since arriving on the foreign scene. For some Americans the problem of adaptation came very close to a matter of life or death of self. In the struggle to maintain a viable self, the hosts were the principal antagonists.

How did the typical American at the height of his strangerhood, i.e., at the first stage of adaptation when he felt "less at home," conceive of the people of the city? First, he was not likely to distinguish between natives of Ciudad Condal (Catalans) and immigrants from the south of Spain. This important distinction from the host point of view might dawn on him as he moved toward successful adaptation, but the chances were that he would continue to lump all the hosts—industrialist and workman, master and servant—into the category of Spaniard, even though most of the native population thought of themselves only secondarily as Spaniards. Being American *and* a stranger, our sojourner was concerned about friendliness, courtesy, and honesty, but these qualities appeared to be in short supply in Ciudad Condal. People may have gone out of their way to direct him on the street, but his wife said that she had been overcharged in the market, and none of his neighbors or associates among the hosts had invited him or his family into their homes.

The newly-arrived American probably noted that the hosts tended to push and shove in public, and he worried about being cheated by them. How "correct" he was in his views is not for us to say, but it should be remarked that as he progressed in his adaptation he was less likely to be concerned about the honesty of the hosts and more likely to find them courteous and sociable. Then he might say, "They're hard to get to know, but once you know them they'll do anything for you." For the typical well-adapted American, the hosts provided confirmation of the friendly American self, but at a more profound level than was possible at home.

On the whole, the unadapted American probably had an unfavorable view of the hosts and their city. Any number of things might bother him about them. They had low standards of cleanliness and hygiene. ("After all, it *is* the twentieth century.") They were not very tolerant or willing to change. They might be hard workers, but they were inefficient and had no follow-through. They were not personally reliable. They did not do what they said they would do. They did not come on time. ("It is always mañana.") They had pride; but it was a mixed blessing. It was good that they had their self-respect, but what did they have to be proud of? They had nothing which could even remotely compare with the "States," particularly in material comforts and amenities. ("Have you ever tried to wash your hair in cold water?")

This list of gripes by the unadapted American indicates that the hosts tended to function for him as a negative reference group and the "States" to some extent as a positive one. His encounter with the foreign situation seems to have made him draw back and emphasize that self which had been propped up especially by the amenities of American life. As the individual came to feel more at home, however, this rejection of the hosts and exaltation of things American tended to disappear. Host standards of cleanliness and hygiene ceased to preoccupy him. The hosts seemed to be more tolerant and willing to change. ("Once you explain things they'll go along.")

They never would be thought of as efficient by the American at any stage of his adaptation, but the more adapted American was less concerned with their inefficiency. Nor was it likely that the hosts ever would be considered reliable. However, for the adapted this lack of reliability had its charming, rather than threatening, aspects. As the typical American stranger in the city progressed towards adaptation he would be more likely to say that he liked the hosts. For the successfully adapted, the hosts then constituted a positive reference group and played a positive role in the reconstitution of self.

Extreme views (pro and con) about American colleagues in the city were to be found at all stages of adaptation, but the majority had an unfavorable attitude toward their fellow countrymen.[14] The typical sojourner, whether adapted or unadapted, was likely to take his colleagues as a negative point of reference. Since few Americans were aware of the total American community, their unfavorable evaluations of their colleagues tended to focus on specific sub-groups within it. One category receiving almost blanket condemnation by the residents was bohemians and tourists. Physical withdrawal and rejection could go hand in hand; after moving out of the hotel or pension which was his initial residence in the city, the resident had little opportunity to come into direct contact with such people. Later, as he found his niche and circle of friends, he would begin to focus his rejecting operations on one or another group of American residents. If he were an entrepreneurial type, for example, he would be likely to condemn those military and civilian organizational people who worked for the government.

To sum up, the picture of the typical American's use of reference groups in the process of adaptation is this: In the early part of his sojourn, when undergoing a severely *anomic* experience, he tended to reject the hosts and emphasize his identification with home. At the same time, according to his dependence on others, he either rejected, or identified with, his fellow Americans. Progress toward successful adaptation found him de-emphasizing and even rejecting identifications with Americans and increasingly emulating the hosts. The stranger who was less fortunate in his adaptive progress tended to find some confirmation through contacts with other Americans in the city and at home; but home was far away and the Americans in Ciudad Condal did not comprise a powerful enclave. Consequently, it was not possible for such reference groups to provide much support for one's self-respect.

Man must orient himself temporally; to use a phrase by Fraisse, he must "locate himself in the universal change that carries him through life."[15] In a country like the United States where change and efficiency are emphasized, time becomes a crucial aspect of existence.[16] Many Americans will find the encounter with a different rhythm of life particularly threatening. American strangers in Ciudad Condal were so preoccupied with time that it appears legitimate to make their struggle with this aspect of experience the key to our analysis of their adaptation.

The typical American might say that the people of the city had "no conception of time." This was his interpretation of their apparently cavalier attitude toward appointments, schedules, and the rapid, methodical accomplishment of projects. The division of days, weeks, and months was perplexing and often unpredictable. An American businessman could count on the weekend as a period of rest, but he might not know of *fiesta* days until they were upon him. How should one organize daily projects when they were found to be interrupted by a three-hour lunch period or plan long-term projects when one could not be sure if there would be a "hole" in the middle of the work week? Finally how should one organize his work around the three-hour lunch period and contain one's appetite until the host dinner hour at 10 P.M.?

Faced with so many temporal incongruities, the newly-arrived American was likely to feel more frustrated or exasperated than in the United States. The paramount, though by no means only, source of his frustration was getting things done in what was for him a reasonable amount of time. Under such conditions, time—because it was being wasted—became even more valuable. If we adopt the hypothesis that time moves more rapidly according to the value of one's experience, we would expect that an American who was trying (and failing) to get a job done might find time moving very rapidly indeed.[17] On the other hand, the new arrival might not have learned to extract value from his foreign experience. Alone and bored, he might find time moving more slowly than at home. The evidence confirms our hunch; the unadapted American was as likely to experience a slower as a more rapid passage of time.[18]

Temporal difficulties encountered in the city at the height of strangerhood appear to be related to the typical American's increased feelings of uncertainty, decreased trust in others, and the onset of stranger anxiety. (The unadapted American was likely to report a decline in his feeling of general well-being.) How would we expect him to cope with this anxiety? In making a prediction we should keep in mind his situational facts of life. First, he was in an *anomic* situation where past behavior was not likely to be effective. If, for example, he "blew up" over some real or imagined slight, the hosts probably would not react in what was for him the appropriate way. The effect of his angry action lost, he would be less likely to repeat it. Second, he was not in a powerful enough position to dictate the terms of transactions with the hosts. He could not make his action "stick." An angry outburst against the hosts might stall a project until an apology was made. If the American were proud and the project important he would be likely to think twice about "blowing up" in the future. These considerations suggest that the unadapted American would not find it very profitable to attempt to solve his difficulties by outward-directed action. Accordingly, we would expect him to deal with his anxiety by inward-directed operations just as the neurotic person substitutes psychological for motor activity. Under certain circumstances, as Alexander has suggested, his inward-directed operations could lead to psychosomatic manifestations.[19] It would be possible, then, to see the stranger situation as analogous to those major life crises, e.g., bereavement, adolescence, which are supposed to "trigger" mental disturbances and to argue that a kind of "situational neurosis" develops during the period of extreme strangerhood.

Evidence from previous laboratory studies tends to confirm our supposition. Laboratory strangers who experience stranger anxiety have displayed a typical constrictive reaction which involves draw-

ing back from the new situation. They lose freedom and spontaneity
and become obsessive about certain features of their home self.[20]
Here we have seen this to be the case in our analysis of the
American's use of reference groups. There were a number of additional symptoms of the constrictive reaction in the unadapted stage.
The typical newly-arrived American saw his mental activity re-
stricted. He said that he was increasingly concerned with orderliness. He reported feeling less relaxed. Finally, he saw that he was
more likely to give way to feelings. It seems possible to surmise that
here he is referring to those memorable emotional outbursts which
broke through the stringent controls which he attempted to maintain over his inner life.

The hypothesis about psychosomatic illness tends to be confirmed
by Americans' testimony about themselves. The unadapted American was likely to find that he felt worse physically. Although we
cannot rule out such factors as physical constitution, diet, climate,
smog, and exotic germs, it does not seem unreasonable to suggest
that failing health constituted an extension of psychological constriction into the physical domain.[21] Some support for this conclusion is provided by a Spanish doctor who treated Americans. According to him, his American patients were distinguished by their
fears of illness and a tendency toward mild psychosomatic complaints. This testimony, coupled with the evidence that the typical
American found that his health improved as his adaptation progressed, suggests the hypothesis that the poorer health in the unadapted was a consequence of stranger anxiety.

Our analysis of the state of the inner life of the typical unadapted
American has shown that his frame of reference was upset and that
he experienced stranger anxiety. The very real external threat to his
internal balance led him to attempt to maintain his old outlook by
means of constriction. But it was not easy to deny the non-confirm-
ing environment nor the emotions generated by it. If the stranger
were to move towards successful adaptation he could attempt to:
(1) Find a circle of friends or acquaintances who could provide
adequate confirmation of his old self. (2) Move away from constriction toward a genuine *rapprochement* with the hosts. We have

seen that the first alternative could not easily be realized in Ciudad Condal. The second represents the typical adaptive course.

What happened to the typical American's inner life as he began to feel less strange and more at home? We might characterize the entire process as *giving up* (the attempt to maintain the old by means of constriction) and *giving in* (to host ways). As we have seen, he became increasingly directed by the host reference group. At the same time, his feelings of uncertainty declined and his trust in others increased. He was more relaxed and less concerned with orderliness. He was less likely to report an increase in frustration or exasperation. His feelings of well-being increased. He was likely to see himself as more active in his mental and social life. Since his whole experience came to have greater value, we could expect, from our hypothesis, that time would seem to pass more rapidly. The data confirm this expectation; the well-adapted American might say that time seemed to "fly by."

Finally, the trend toward the restoration of a satisfactory mental balance was accompanied by an improvement in physical health. If the American had had an ulcer condition at home, for example, he might, if well-adapted, be pleased to find that it caused him little concern in Ciudad Condal. It is unlikely that this improvement was effected by a change in oral regimen. Alcohol and tobacco are antitherapeutic for people with ulcers,[22] yet an American, regardless of his stage of adaptation, tended to drink more and, as he became better adapted, smoke more. This suggests that the ulcer sufferer may have been able to find satisfactions or confirmations in this foreign setting which were not available to him at home. Alexander refers to the passive-receptive tendencies which are associated with the development of ulcer conditions.[23] In the city it was possible to relax, to be served, to enjoy sociability, and still be of good repute. One could, in short, gratify one's passive-receptive tendencies without worrying very much about achievement. Of course, as we have seen in the cases of several women (see Chapter 4) such gratification could have deleterious consequences, a reminder that acculturative benefits sometimes carry along with them built-in liabilities.

By way of validating the successful reorganization of self in keeping with the external "requirements" of his situation in Ciudad Condal, the adapted American was likely to report greater self-confidence. He knew his way around. He gave orders in the imperative as did the hosts. He was able to push and shove with all the others, and he did not apologize for expressing his emotions. In fact, he might at first give such an impression of cocksureness that other unadapted Americans might say, "Who does he think he is?" The impression he gave was of a person who felt "at home." He had, at this point, passed beyond the condition of extreme strangerhood.

It would be a mistake to leap to the conclusion that this story of American adaptation is a clear legitimation of the old saw about doing what the Romans do when in Rome. In the first place, there is the question of whether the Romans will let you, a stranger, do it. This problem seldom arose in Ciudad Condal where the hosts appeared content to let most law-abiding foreigners alone (with the exception of anarchists, murderers, perpetrators of fraud, etc.). Secondly, is it possible for a non-Roman ever to act entirely like a Roman? Even the American who had lived for many years in the city, married into the host society, and come to feel "more at home" could not identify completely with the hosts. Leaving aside the problem of psychic inertia, it still would not be reasonable to expect people who came from a powerful nation, who worked for some prestigious American organization, and who were dependent on American money for their style of life in a foreign place to completely reject their homeland. We have not examined the bohemian group here because their problem of adaptation is a very special one. Members of this group often were loudest in their denunciation of the United States and its policies, but not even they were likely to forget their American citizenship. As one American said, "Let something happen and you see them waving their passports around pretty quickly."

Of the resident Americans, the most fully acculturated were the longest-term residents. (One American had lived almost continuously in the city since before the Civil War.) Although we probably can make it a general rule that length of residence is associated with greater acculturation, it would be a mistake to conclude that time of exposure to the host culture was the only factor involved. *All* the "old hands" in the community had what we may consider to be a predisposition to acculturation in their backgrounds: they had been raised in cultures or sub-cultures which were more compatible with this host culture. For example, one man was born in South America and another was born of Catalan parents in the United States. With more compatible experience in their backgrounds, they seem to have had a head start in the adaptive process and spent a minimum of time in the period of extreme strangerhood. At the time of the study it could be said that several of them had taken the host society as their primary reference group. Occasionally one would hear it said about one of them, "He isn't an American." We would stress, however, that an American identity and American connections continued to be important even to these "old hands."

Besides those Americans whose adaptation had put them beyond the pale, so to speak, there were a few who had acquired the characteristics of a marginal man, a person who had come to be equally at home (or not at home) in both American and host societies. These people, who usually had married into the host society, experienced more or less severe conflict as a result of being caught between two cultures. To the question designed to assess their degree of adaptation, they responded that they felt "just as much at home" in Ciudad Condal as in the United States. But such a response masks the underlying conflict associated with their marginal position. We have to conclude, therefore, that there is a fork in the adaptive road beyond which two courses of adaptation may be followed. One of these leads toward full identification with the hosts and the other leads towards marginality.

The bulk of the successfully adapted Americans had not and would not reach this fork and there would be no question about their primary identification. One of these people was likely to have friends among the hosts and to be considerably acculturated. However he retained the United States as his primary reference group, and he probably made periodic trips there to restore contacts. (Large organizations had institutionalized leaves every 2–4 years.) Having found a "circle" and seeing himself to be more active in all spheres of life, he could appraise himself as a somewhat improved version of a typically friendly and active American.[24] There was continuity, rather than discontinuity, in the typical American's adaptive progress in Ciudad Condal. His subjective reorganization at no time involved a complete conversion, but rather a gradual resynthesis of new (host) elements with the old.[25]

In conclusion, we should remember that not all Americans in Ciudad Condal followed the ideal-typical adaptive course which has been described here and that many of them would never pass beyond the state of extreme strangerhood. Indeed, we would estimate that a substantial minority of the Americans in the city never would come to feel "at home." Their "progress" would be from the unadapted stage to the status of confirmed non-adaptors where they would continue to experience stranger anxiety and show evidence of psychological and/or social constriction.[26] Such an unflattering picture of American adaptation in one foreign place raises the question of objective factors which are related to one's adaptive fate. How can we tell if an American will prove to be adaptable abroad? In the next chapter we will consider some of the situational and personal factors which appear to have been related to Americans' adaptation in Ciudad Condal.

9

KEYS TO ADAPTATION

[Finian] knew he had to do three things very
quickly. First, he had to find at least one native
Catholic who was courageous. Second, he had
to learn the language. Third, he had to learn
to eat the food. . . .
WILLIAM LEDERER and EUGENE BURDICK
The Ugly American

ACCORDING TO OUR DRAMATURGICAL ANALOGY, AN
anomic stranger's adaptation may be seen as a process
whereby he finds or creates acceptable roles on the foreign stage. If the foreign setting is not so familiar he will tend to
experience greater anxiety in consequence of greater uncertainty
about his social location and the roles appropriate to it. As we have
seen, this anxiety seems to play a part in his reactions and, therefore,
in the kind of roles he essays. These roles may be more or less
acceptable to him and/or the hosts. If the stranger is very powerful,
he need not be overly concerned about the hosts' attitude. Whether
they like the roles he plays can have little effect on his immediate
fate as a sojourner.[1] If, as in the case of the American in Ciudad
Condal, he is not so powerful, he must eventually become more
concerned with his hosts' expectations if he is to adapt successfully.

Consider the case of an American government employee on what
he considered to be an important mission in Ciudad Condal. He was
dependent on a local transport agency to complete his project
before a deadline. The shipper was supposed to deliver materials
from the dock to the site of an exhibition, but even though the
material had been at the port for several weeks, his company had
taken no action to move it to its destination. Repeated calls by the
hard-pressed American elicited the information that the material
was on the dock and that it would be picked up *mañana*. Growing
increasingly anxious and angry, this American finally decided to "go
on over there and have it out with the boss."

137

Of the roles which the angry American carried with him in his repertoire, the most acceptable, as far as he was then concerned, involved the course of action which sometimes is called "blowing up." He proceeded to tell the shipper exactly what he thought of him, his company, and Spain. He spoke in English and was unable to comprehend the stream of Catalan expletives which the host, in turn, directed at him, but he was somewhat gratified at having expressed feelings which seemed to elicit an appropriate angry response. Although the American did not secure his material, the incident up to that point might be considered profitable to him.

But the incident, as far as the host was concerned, was not yet over. Feeling that his personal *dignidad* had been offended, he called the Consulate General to demand a personal apology from the man who had offended him. A call was put through to the still empty-handed and still seething American advising him, for the sake of his project and his government, to go to the shipper and apologize. If he did so there was a *chance* that he might receive his material before the deadline. Imagine, then, the state of mind of the American as he balanced the success of this and future projects against the possibility of telling them all to "go to hell." In this not-so-fictitious case, the American decided in favor of the success of his project at a personal cost which we are not in a position to assess.

The incident just described involved a single adaptive problem of one American in Ciudad Condal. When the host company whose cooperation he needed did not perform its part, the American felt anxious and angry. He chose to "blow up" as a means of safeguarding integrity of self, but this role was not acceptable to the Catalans. Indeed, it was so unacceptable that it threatened the completion of the project. At this "Rubicon" of adaptation, the American, in order to complete his projects and confirm his achieving self, could discard the inefficacious role which he had used previously; or he could continue to maintain his traditional integrity by reiterating this role under what to him were appropriate circumstances and wreck his projects and his sense of achievement in Spain. The success of the decision between these and possibly other alternatives, as far as adaptation is concerned, would be measured in terms of its effectiveness for guaranteeing survival and furthering the stranger's sense of well-being.

Every stranger comes to the foreign stage with a repertoire of roles, some of which are particularly congenial to him. Some strangers, however, have more advance information on the lay-out of the stage and the kind of roles which the hosts find acceptable in strangers. Advance information of this kind could minimize the problem of meaninglessness and, if accurate, speed up the process of adaptation. The State Department provides such information through lectures and a continuously up-dated series of Post Reports, and the Peace Corps has incorporated intensive area studies into its training courses.[2] Both government organizations also emphasize language study not only for purposes of communication, but also for understanding hosts' points of view. In Ciudad Condal, for example, all the American civilian government officials were proficient in Spanish and had access to the relevant Post Report before their arrival.

Although a substantial minority of the Americans could speak at least rudimentary Spanish at the time of their arrival in the city, the majority had little or no previous accurate information about the nature of this foreign setting. The data will not permit the formulation of a legitimate hypothesis, but it is tempting to speculate that misinformation was worse than no information as far as overall adaptation was concerned. Because of the rapidly changing conditions in the city, almost any information acquired beforehand was bound to be inaccurate. Where the cost of living was concerned, misinformation could—and did—threaten a sojourner's continued existence in Ciudad Condal.

Though useful, advance information about life abroad or about a specific outpost may not be as important for adaptation as more general experience in the course of one's socialization. If, for example, one's repertoire includes roles which coincide with host expectations, or if one has the potential for creating such roles, the difficulties of adaptation ought to be minimized. There is a well-known hypothesis that adaptation is a function of cultural compatibility.

Japanese and Jewish immigrants to the United States, for example, are supposed to have had an adaptive advantage over other immigrants because they came from more compatible cultures.[3] A person socialized under such conditions should possess personal qualities which will enable him to play with less strain roles which the hosts find acceptable. Nash and Schaw have called this type of individual, i.e., one who possesses an emotional repertoire which bridges specific cultures, a transitional man.[4] In a sense, everyone is *potentially* a transitional man in that he possesses qualities which will tend to facilitate his adaptation on certain foreign stages, but he does not become a transitional man *in fact* until he goes abroad to take his place on these stages. Success or failure in adaptation, therefore, may hinge on the selection of the proper stage on which to perform one's part in an overseas play.

Transitional men, because they have an adaptive advantage, ought to be more heavily represented among the successfully adapted in a foreign setting. Is there any evidence that Americans who felt "more at home" in Ciudad Condal tended to come from backgrounds which could have created transitional qualities in them? Most of those 36 who provided adequate information had had previous experience in foreign cultures, and of these most had lived in an underdeveloped culture which usually was partly Iberian in origin. When compared with Americans who had never been abroad or who had been abroad to highly developed countries, e.g., Germany, those with past experience in underdeveloped cultures were more likely to report feeling "more at home" in Ciudad Condal. Concerning his initial reaction to the city, one of these Americans said, "The people somehow seemed just like yourself. This was the first time in any place we have found that. It was like going into an American city." This man had moved directly to the city from the Middle East; earlier, he had lived in Latin America. As Campbell suggests, such overseas experiences can modify one's "adaptation level" and temper one's judgment of a foreign setting.[5] Through his previous experience abroad, the American probably had acquired transitional qualities which permitted him to view

Ciudad Condal as "an American city" in which he could feel immediately at home.

The data relating previous experience abroad and adaptation are particularly interesting because they tend to support the hypothesis that previous experience in certain foreign cultures tends to prove beneficial for adaptation in certain others, but they do not confirm the value of *any* previous transcultural experience for adaptation.[6] Those Americans who had been abroad to more developed countries, such as Germany, seem to have been no better prepared to adapt in the city than those who never had been abroad before; while those who had been abroad to less developed countries, such as Turkey or the Philippines, were better prepared than either of these classes of overseasmen. Since the culture of Ciudad Condal had qualities associated with less developed areas, these data tend to support the hypothesis implicit in the concept of the transitional man: that transitional traits, however acquired, tend to facilitate adaptation.

Sub-cultural experience in the United States seems also to have been related to successful adaptation among a people who sometimes have been called "the Jews of Spain." This appellation (usually derogatory) refers to the aggressive, commercial qualities of many of the hosts. It is not surprising, therefore, that in a society dominated by aggressive businessmen, old-fashioned, entrepreneurial American Jews seemed to be among the best adapted of the American strangers. Nor is it surprising that Americans born of Catalan parents in the United States—and therefore ideal-typical examples of the transitional man in this setting—were well-adapted.[7]

Transitional qualities limit a person's adaptability abroad. They permit one to feel at home only in a limited range of foreign cultures. There are some people whose adaptability is less limited. They are flexible individuals who, like the chameleon, are capable of taking on the color of their environment. People of this kind have a capacity for change which enables them to fit easily into the plays on a variety of foreign stages. W. I. Thomas considered that a readiness for change was the key to adaptation under the rapidly changing conditions of modern society, and he identified two types of character with this capacity: the bohemian and the creative man. Both kinds of people are open to change and may require it, but the bohemian is "unformed" while the creative man is more "settled and organized."[8] It seems probable that neither of these change-prone types would be heavily committed to their home society, a tendency which Nash and Heiss, in their study of laboratory strangers, found to be associated with the onset of stranger anxiety in the "foreign" situation.[9] They would, on the contrary, show a disposition to "travel light" in the manner of one of Forster's main characters in *A Passage to India*.[10]

In Ciudad Condal, both of Thomas' adaptive types were represented. The term bohemian applied particularly to those adolescents or post-adolescents who were using this foreign setting to try out various roles and selfs for the first time, e.g., the woman with colored hair, the bullfight *aficionado*, the artist, the model, even as adolescents at home pass from fad to fad. It was difficult to identify truly creative men in the city. An example, taken from the few possibilities, was a housewife who gave the following advice: "You should enjoy the good things that this country has to offer. Try new foods. I've tried everything—even the little *angulas* (little eels). Of course, do all this in moderation."

To illustrate this woman's ability to create roles which were acceptable both to the hosts and to herself, consider the following technique which she reported: "This business of *mañana*—I think I've figured out how to solve it. If they say something will take two weeks, I'll say that I want it in a month, and if it isn't there I won't accept it. And it works." This attitude and other evidence concerning the sojourn of this woman in Ciudad Condal reveal a considerable enthusiasm for change and an ability to utilize foreign experience in her own personal development. The social ramifications of her adaptation included what may have been the optimum arrangement for Americans in the city: a greater commitment to her family and many gratifying friendships with members of the host society.

As far as adaptation is concerned, the individual's capacity to change is not an unalloyed virtue. If a man on a mission is too changeable, he may not be able to keep faith with those who sent him or maintain the consistent pattern of action which is necessary to see his project through. The bohemian type, for example, might prove to be a liability for an organization which requires loyal, methodical labor abroad. If that organization were to maintain a large bureaucratic establishment overseas, as does the American military, it might be more important that the bulk of its agents were traditional men or, to use Thomas' term, philistines.[11] However, this type of establishment did not characterize the American presence in Ciudad Condal.

In summary, adaptation in a foreign setting tends to be facilitated if people bring with them to the foreign stage personal qualities which enable them to play roles which are acceptable both to them and to the hosts. In Ciudad Condal where Americans did not possess great power or social resources, host expectations appeared to play a significant part in the adaptive process. Those Americans who possessed transitional qualities or a disposition to change in appropriate directions could meet these expectations more readily and consequently adapt with less strain.

The personal qualities which one brings with him to the foreign stage are not the only keys to adaptation. Situational factors at home or in the foreign setting may be equally important. For example, the compatibility of a culture for the approaching stranger is not only a function of his personal attributes, but of the foreign culture's attributes as well. Because some foreign cultures make one more of a transitional man than others, one's adaptation may be aided simply by selecting the right one. Furthermore, not all sectors of the foreign stage and scenes in an overseas play are equally compatible to the approaching stranger. In Ciudad Condal, for example, there were more and less modernized or Americanized hosts. If one had greater financial means, or if one represented some prestigious American organization one could gain immediate access to more compatible sectors of Catalan society and have a greater opportunity to establish congenial friendships with a minimum of psychic reorganization.

We see, then, that adaptation on a foreign stage represents the outcome of sometimes complex interrelationships between various aspects of the foreign situation as the stranger finds them and the personal and situational resources which he brings with him to play his part or to support him in playing it. The success of his adaptation would seem to depend as much on his ability to put to use whatever favorable arrangements already exist on the stage as on his transitional qualities or his capacity to change.

In order to elucidate the situational keys to the adaptation of Americans in Ciudad Condal, let us take one fact which emerged from the interviews: Americans whose most significant relationships (friendships) in the city were exclusively with other Americans were likely to feel "less at home" while those who had any significant relationships with hosts were likely to feel "more at home." Those who had not adapted had not managed to extend their range of friendships beyond a circle of Americans. Whether the cultivation of an exclusively American circle of friends ever is consistent with successful adaptation as we have defined it will require further research, particularly in "Little Americas" abroad.[12] In Ciudad Condal, where nothing like a complete American enclave existed and where the hosts were generally reluctant to Americanize themselves, it seems to have worked against adaptation.

The well-adapted Americans, then, were able to extend their social contacts into the host society and receive gratifying self-confirmation from friendships with hosts. How were they able to do this? First, they did it by pre-arrangement. A number of Americans came to the city with what amounted to a series of commitments by the hosts to be friendly to them. In some cases, these commitments were the result of arrangements between large organizations. Fulbright scholars enjoyed special access to host artists and intellectuals. Businessmen working for Spanish-American companies found not only ready-made contacts, but help in smoothing over the difficulties of establishing a home in the city. These Americans were welcomed lavishly with flowers and reception committees and taken immediately not only into the company, but also into the bosoms of the otherwise impregnable families of company people. Contractual arrangements between business firms, therefore, assured some Americans of a friendly reception and special consideration on the foreign stage. It meant that these normally friendly and outgoing people could play an acceptable role and receive confirmation of their traditional selfs from the time of their arrival.

It should be emphasized that not all pre-arranged contacts resulted in relationships which facilitated adaptation. Some Americans received only a perfunctory response upon presenting letters of introduction, and still others did not receive any response at all. A well-known American writer said, "The major resentment we've had (and it is by no means the only resentment) is the lack of cordiality. This is carried even to the point where after I had a letter of introduction by my publisher to a publisher here that publisher had never bothered to look me up. It's unthoughtful. It's ungracious. It would be unthinkable back home. If a writer from Spain were to come to New York he would immediately be invited around to parties and to see people. . . . I've been here eight to nine months and I don't have a single Spanish friend." It is probably fair to say that this writer would have had Spanish friends if he had been considered a potential source of business by the Spanish publisher. Because he was probably not so considered, he was greeted with what seemed to him brutal indifference. This lack of interest illustrates one way in which the business atmosphere of the city could repel some foreign artists.[13]

The value of a favorable reception to the stranger has been explored by Nash and Heiss in their laboratory study.[14] Though their results are somewhat equivocal in this regard, due, presumably, to artifacts of experimental design, they found some support for the hypothesis that stranger anxiety was related to accepting acts by hosts. The feeling that one is accepted as he is, therefore, seems to minimize stranger anxiety and, as a result, facilitate stranger adaptation. In Ciudad Condal, some Americans, particularly those with pre-arranged partnerships with the hosts, benefited through the operation of this principle.

For the majority of American sojourners in the city, however, the kind of acceptance they craved was not readily available either from the hosts or from other Americans. Some Americans were enthusiastic about the friendly way in which people responded to their requests for directions on the street, but most were more or less dissatisfied by their rate of acceptance, as indicated especially by invitations into host homes. One American who had had extensive dealings with local people and who was well-acquainted with the Spanish scene said, "The people here are difficult to know and get along with. . . . During my entire stay here I have only been in six Catalan homes though I know many Catalans and have had many of them to mine. Many of them talk about it, but few ever ask you into their homes."

People raised in the land of welcome wagons and "instant" friendships could not understand the reservedness of a people who accepted kinship and pseudo-kinship through business relationships as the only keys to what Americans consider to be truly friendly relationships. Of the numerous disillusionments suffered by Americans in the city, one of the most frequently reported concerned the discovery of the non-viability of their friendly role and self in day-to-day transactions with the hosts.[15] The host attitude towards foreigners tended to be indifferent rather than prejudiced, but for friendly Americans this attitude could do serious violence to one of the sacred principles of their world taken-for-granted.

Unless an American had established contacts with the hosts by prearrangement, he was likely to find himself alone or confined to an American circle in the city. Continued confinement in such a circle appears to have been related to fluency in one or both of the host languages. People who knew Spanish prior to their arrival were not as likely to experience *anomie* and stranger anxiety. People who attempted to learn Spanish from the time of their arrival tended to speed up the process of adaptation. Perfect fluency was not required in order to establish contacts among the hosts; it was important for the stranger to be willing to try and, further, to endure often pitiless comments regarding his failures. More than a little self-confidence, providing that it did not violate host values, seems to have been required for a rapid penetration of the host society. An aggressive, rather than a passive, posture seems to have been more adaptive in this setting. The lack of such a posture seems to have been at the bottom of the adaptive problems voiced by the American writer who had not made any friends among the hosts during his stay in Ciudad Condal. He did not learn Spanish, and from the information he provided, it would seem that he expected the hosts to come to him. Such a passive attitude could succeed only under extremely favorable circumstances.

It is interesting to note that many Americans seemed to be aware of what amounted to a successful technique for adaptation. When asked to give advice to a hypothetical American arriving in the city, their most frequent response concerned the necessity of learning the language and of mixing with the hosts. But how can one summon the effort to do these things if one has been ignored, pushed out of the way on the street, shoved in the subway, and treated generally in what one considers to be an uncivil manner? Here is where the personal qualities and other resources which one brings to the foreign stage enter the picture to determine one's adaptive fate. The American who would adapt in Ciudad Condal had to want to come to terms with the hosts. Although he might begin this process out of a strictly utilitarian motive, e.g., anxiety reduction, status climbing, mission building, he eventually had to find something *simpatico* in these people. So it was with one American who said, "I like them. They are reserved (so am I). They are businesslike. They respect their spoken promise more than other Spaniards. Each has his self respect no matter his station. They like Americans." Not many Americans were capable of viewing their hosts in this manner.

Cleveland and his associates say that "the American abroad is perforce more of a political animal than he needs to be at home." [16] He is immersed in political and military developments which may have a very real bearing on his survival or continued existence (and therefore his adaptation) in a foreign society. The news media bear daily witness to this. Diplomatic relations are severed. People are deported. Revolutions occur. Wars threaten. Programs are terminated. Such events are usually not of the stranger's own doing, but they can affect his presence overseas. Peace Corps English teachers

in a Peruvian university fell victim to the revolutionary ardor of
factions which were struggling for power on local and national
political scenes; [17] and American dependents in South Vietnam
found themselves on their way home in the face of an escalating
war in that country. In these and many other cases, the kind of job
being done and the nature of personal adaptation were irrelevant to
the continued existence of Americans abroad. They had been taken
off the overseas stage by political and military events beyond their
control.

The average American citizen probably knows the basic canons
of American foreign relations: there are some countries with us,
some against us, and some possibly neutral. From political events in
South Vietnam and elsewhere, he also may have learned that in
those countries with which the United States maintains relations
there are different groups manifesting various shades of support for
American interests. The United States government has to deal
officially, if it will deal at all, with established governments, but in
many cases a government is not in firm control and may be su-
perseded in a few weeks or months by another. Where revolutions
are a regular occurrence, the protection of American interests and
the survival of Americans abroad may depend on establishing the
right political ties at the right time.

Cleveland and his associates found that "a sense for politics" was
one factor related to successful performance by Americans abroad.[18]
But no matter how astute one's political sense and how extensive
one's technical resources, one's performance in political chess games
is limited and determined by one's social position. The circle in
which one comes to feel at home in the foreign situation will tend
to color one's views and commit one to a particular political posture. In situations of flux, it may mean that one's knowledge of local
developments is faulty and that political events catch one backing
the wrong horse, so to speak. To the extent that overseas Americans
adapt in certain directions in foreign societies they will tend to
commit themselves to certain factions in times of political up-
heaval; and to the extent that they affect American foreign policies,

these people's adaptive posture will play a part in the success or failure of American imperialistic interests.

Are there indications that overseas Americans tend to adapt in one direction rather than others? What evidence there is suggests that they favor association with the wealthier, more Americanized hosts who often constitute the establishment of a country.[19] Americans tend not to associate intimately with groups who are against American policies nor with the poor in city and country. In Cuba just prior to the triumph of the Castro revolution, this fact was painfully apparent to the author. The intimate contacts of Americans with Cubans were confined largely to the Cuban aristocracy, the Batista clique, and its civilian and military sympathizers. As a result, they could not gauge the discontent among certain classes of Cubans nor properly assess the possibilities of a successful revolution. American investments in Cuba were heavy, and business expediency probably dictated a commitment to the *status quo,* but serious miscalculations seem to have been made in the months prior to the victory of Castro and his followers. At a time when anyone with broad contacts with Cubans and Cuban developments knew that the days of the Batista regime were numbered, the United States government was continuing to provide military assistance for the government's use against the rebels. We would hypothesize that the United States, wishing the Batista clique to remain in power, tended to overrate its strength partly because of the adaptive posture taken by Americans in Cuba. Many American residents had found exceedingly congenial circles in which they were well-adapted, but by confining themselves to these circles, largely comprised of Americans and Americanized Cubans, they seem to have blinded themselves to the revolutionary potential in the country. The nearness of the United States and the weight of American power also may have contributed to the feeling that whatever adaptive postures Americans took were likely to be the correct ones. Thus, a certain imperialistic arrogance affected the adaptability of American policies and possibly a continued American presence in Cuba.

The political posture of Americans in Spain at the time of the study appeared to be similar to that of Americans in Cuba. Although resident Americans were officially apolitical, their assessment of the political situation and their political sympathies tended to grow out of their association with wealthier and more powerful Spaniards. The bulk of Americans in Spain lived in enclaves. If they associated with any Spaniards at all it was likely to be with people who were supporters of the Franco establishment.[20] Unlike the Batista ruling circle, the government of Franco appeared to be securely in power. At the time of the study there did not seem to be any possibility of political developments which would take an anti-American course. Still, the question of succession had not been decided, and there were some who predicted that another civil war would break out at the time of Franco's death. In this or any other eventuality, the American presence in Spain could be affected by the tendency of Americans to associate with supporters of the Franco dictatorship.

The American adaptive posture in Ciudad Condal was similar to that for the rest of Spain, but the political implications of this posture are more difficult to assess. If the American residents in the city had any intimate associations with the hosts, they were likely to be with the middle class or the aristocracy, hardly ever with the working class or with revolutionary elements. The exceptions were the missionaries who tended to deal with what we might call the "poor but honest" working people, not apparently of revolutionary temperament, and the students and artists who sometimes associated with factions which were highly critical of the Franco regime. Although few Americans were inclined to associate with subversive elements, fear probably played as great a role as lack of desire in limiting such association. The regime was extremely vigilant and harshly punitive where potential revolutionaries were concerned. An example of the way association with subversives could affect one's continued existence in Spain was provided by an American who came to the city to pick up paintings to be sold abroad for the benefit of an anarchist cause. After contacting a number of more or less subversive Spaniards, the American suddenly disappeared. Eventually it was learned that he had been imprisoned—a very bad thing to happen to one in Spain. He was, however, treated leniently: deportation followed within the space of several days. During the period of the study, no American resident of the city compromised himself in like manner and none were arrested on either political or criminal grounds.[21]

Because of their tendency to associate with the middle and upper classes in Ciudad Condal, members of the American community lacked an intimate understanding of the working class point of view. For example, members of the Consulate General, whose job it was to report on the local political situation, had cultivated few, if any, of the kind of contacts who could give them this viewpoint; and the Cultural Institute was only just beginning to extend its operations into this area. At the time of the study, the working class did not appear to be a significant political force; but whether it was significant or not, the Americans probably would not have formed many intimate associations with its members. Therefore they could have had neither knowledge about, nor sympathy with, these people and their aspirations. Americans' continued presence here could not be supported by identification with this most numerous group among the hosts.

The tendency of the Americans in Ciudad Condal to limit their intimate connections to hosts of the middle and upper classes did not mean, as in many other countries, that they identified with a single host establishment. On the contrary, in a province with a long history of separatist tendencies and hostility toward the central government in Madrid, identification with the chauvinistic Catalans was tantamount to a mild conspiracy against the Franco regime. Of those involved Americans, some favored the Catalan cause and expressed admiration for the little gestures of defiance which were a part of the local culture, e.g., dances, songs, use of the Catalan language. Others, favoring the Madrid government, sometimes cited the beneficial effects of its firm control for both Spaniards and foreigners. ("The Spaniard is a man who needs to be controlled by force.") Still other Americans were ambivalent in regard to the conflict over autonomous tendencies between the province and the central government. On the one hand they admired the defiance of authority, but on the other they liked the stabilizing effects of a strong central regime. In their public behavior, however, all Americans in the city appeared to be appropriately circumspect in regard to this issue. The head of the Cultural Institute, for example, realized that he could speed up his cultivation of the hosts by catering to Catalan pride, but he was careful to prevent his institution from becoming a public forum for local flag-wavers.[22]

To summarize, adapting Americans in Ciudad Condal tended to follow the usual American pattern of association with upper status hosts, but the political implications of such association did not appear to threaten the American presence in this setting. Those Americans who possessed keys to establishing themselves in a congenial part of this foreign play did not threaten to undermine the entire American participation in it. We should recall, however, that Americans were acting on a number of different stages in Spain and that the success of the "company" in Ciudad Condal probably was not as important for the total American enterprise as the success of the much larger American group in Madrid which dominated American operations in the Spanish theater.

The possession of appropriate keys to successful adaptation in the Condal city enabled some members of the American community to solve one adaptive problem; but the solution of this one problem often tended to raise another problem of adaptation in the future. Most of the resident Americans were in the city for a limited period of time. Among the well-adapted, for example, were people affiliated with organizations which had adopted policies of limited engagements for their overseas representatives in a particular foreign setting. At the end of their sojourn almost all these Americans would return home for a shorter or longer stay. Although the non-adapted might have suffered during their sojourn in the city, they then could look forward to the confirming benefits of "the good old U. S. A." If the findings of Nash and Wolfe in their laboratory can be applied to the outside world, the return to familiar ground could be a truly liberating experience.[23]

However, the successfully adapted in the city, by having created a new self in the foreign milieu, were guaranteeing another bout of strangership for themselves at home.[24] Some anticipation of it came in preliminary trips back to the United States. About such trips, one woman said, "Now when I go home I feel like a fish out of water. I have to put everything I have forth to live among Americans. . . . Women are uncomfortable with me. We don't speak the same language. I don't feel like a foreigner here. I feel like a foreigner there." Thomas Wolfe said that one could never go home. Perhaps the solution for this woman and others like her was to develop the qualities of the classic stranger whose natural condition is one of coming and going. On the other hand, a nation with the organizational resources of the United States could provide her with the kind of "Little Americas" abroad which would make her feel that she had never left home in the first place.

IO

ADAPTIVE STYLES

> I want to get into European society, but I want
> to get in my own way. I don't want to run
> after people; I want them to run after me. I
> guess they will some day.
>
> (Nancy Beck Headway)
> HENRY JAMES
> *The Siege of London*

WE HAVE USED THE TERM *anomie* TO DESCRIBE THE
essence of the stranger's experience. The encounter with
the foreign tends to destructure the stranger's frame of
reference and contribute overtones of anxiety. The individual version of this experience and the style adopted to cope with it, taken
together, constitute the story of the stranger's adaptation. In this
chapter we shall be concerned with the ways in which different
Americans in the city encountered the foreign and dealt with their
experience of it.

Americans who have been abroad and administrators who have
sent them often have shown concern about the difference between
male and female adaptive styles. Women sometimes are depicted as
poor overseas risks and, in the case of wives, the weaker part of the
husband-wife overseas team.[1] There are so many reports from apparently candid observers about the difficulties of American females
abroad that some sympathetic yet objective study of male and
female adaptive styles seems to be warranted.

There are sound reasons for advancing the hypothesis that American women abroad tend to adapt less successfully than men. In
countries undergoing industrialization such as Spain, modernization
or Americanization tends to affect first the productive sector in
which the principal male role is located. Therefore the American
man abroad would be likely to encounter more of his taken-for-
granted world than would the American woman. Receiving less
confirmation from the foreign situation, the woman would tend to

154

experience greater *anomie* and stranger anxiety. She also would have difficulty finding acceptable roles with which she could cope with her anxiety. The traditional role of housewife, for example, involves a liberal amount of anxiety-reducing work which might not be possible for a servant-rich American woman abroad. Unless she could create acceptable roles, the American woman, more than her male colleague, would become burdened with a sense of meaninglessness and unresolved stranger anxiety. In an extreme case, pathology might be the result.

This analysis may sound familiar to the suburban woman who has begun to experience the meaninglessness of her domestic rounds. Indeed, it is implicit in "the problem" which Betty Friedan has discussed in her book about unsatisfied American housewives.[2] Our hypothesis clearly should not refer only to American women abroad. However, it is on the overseas frontier that the American woman probably would encounter "the problem," i.e., the meaninglessness of her existence, in its most extreme form. Nor should the argument that American women experience greater stranger *anomie* than men be confined only to those who are married. The entire female sector of a foreign culture such as the Spanish continues to center on the home. The "liberated" single woman might experience even greater *anomie* than her married colleague as a result of exposure to a culture in which the principal conception of the "liberated" single woman continued to be fixed in the image of the whore.[3]

The data for American men and women, married and single, in Ciudad Condal give some support to our hypothesis. Although both men and women shared the course of adaptation discussed in Chapter 7, there were certain differences in their adaptive progress. The women were more likely than the men to report feeling more "relaxed or loose" since their arrival; and while the men tended to report an increase in their mental activity, the women were likely to report a decrease.[4] We interpret these differences to mean that for the woman exposure to this foreign situation tended to bring about a less rigidly structured, less eventful experience, we see her as a less controlled individual who, in the Latin mode, is more willing to allow both internal and external events to have their way with her. The decline in mental activity suggests that, in contrast to the man, the woman tended to find that the procession of significant events touching her world was slowing down. When some of the American women said that they were beginning to "vegetate" they probably were referring to their more relaxed, less eventful existence in the city.

Considering the high level of activity which is customary among middle-class American women at home, we would expect that the advent of the more "vegetative" mode of life in the city would be accompanied by *anomie* and stranger anxiety. If a woman's self-respect depended on many little accomplishments around the home, it was not possible for this kind of "accomplishing" self to be confirmed by activity if a maid were present. Or consider the single woman who had expectations of finding a job or a man. Unless she had previously contracted to work at the Consulate General or one of the American schools, she would find that there were hardly any full-time jobs open to her, and that there were very few acceptable men who would date or court her in the American style. In America, an active, gregarious self receives confirmation from many quarters while other selfs are suppressed or repressed. In Ciudad Condal the woman's traditional self structure was undermined, and less acceptable selfs were given an opportunity to come to the foreground of experience. As we saw earlier, the destructuring of the woman's subjective world could lead to the emergence of threatening conflicts over passive-dependency, sexuality, or death.

Because she was subject to greater *anomic* pressures than the man, we would expect the American woman to show a greater tendency to experience stranger anxiety. The data tend to confirm this hypothesis. The women were more likely than their male colleagues to report a decline in feelings of well-being since arriving in the city. It may have been due to their greater readiness to assume a passive role, their greater exposure to *anomie,* or both. Whatever the cause, the immersion of these women into this foreign situation could have unfortunate consequences. Such a course of events is dramatized brilliantly by Forster in *A Passage to India.*[5]

Much of his story revolves around the experiences of two English women who were particularly receptive to the foreign. For one of these women, the experience of what we would call *anomie* was associated with the approach of death and for the other with the terrors of sexuality. Forster's use of women to illustrate the disastrous consequences of culture contact seems to be another instance of an artist's intuition preceding a social scientific "discovery."

Drinking may have been one way in which the American woman coped with stranger anxiety. Our rather inadequate data about American women in the city suggest a sequence of events leading to this response: First, the exposure to the foreign situation filled with servants and service, the curtailment of career-type activities, the absence of traditional avocational outlets, for single women the scarcity of eligible men, the obstacles to building up a primary circle, and the apparent indolence of host women who provided a model for a style of life; concomitantly, the destructuring of the woman's frame of reference, the emergence into consciousness of threatening selfs, and the advance of anxiety; [6] then the accessibility of alcohol and its more extensive usage on the "cocktail circuit"; and finally, the application of this readily available beverage to the anxiety associated with her peculiar *anomic* condition. We may have here in very crude form a sketch of the etiology of alcoholism among American women abroad.[7]

On the basis of reports from American men and women in Ciudad Condal we have described a process which is, in effect, a distinctively female style of adaptation. Of course, both men and women shared certain modes of response to the foreign scene. The woman, for example, was no different from the man in her tendency to report feeling more "frustrated or exasperated" or to reveal a declining concern with "punctuality." What we have been at pains to emphasize here is that which she did not share with her male compatriot, i.e., the mode of adaptation which led to increased drinking. We hesitate to offer our analysis of this feminine pattern as a hypothetical explanation for the drinking problems of American women overseas. Rather, we hope that it will serve to introduce the subject of adaptive styles or roles affected by strangers on the foreign stage. We can now put the question which we raised at the beginning of this chapter: How does the stranger-American approach the foreign, and how is it used by him to further his life projects? In short, with what style does he approach and treat the *anomie* which is inherent in any stranger situation?

An adaptive style includes the approach to, and handling of, the foreign experience. Some strangers are prevented by circumstances, e.g., wealth, assistance by hosts, from encountering the most extreme form of *anomie* which a foreign setting can offer. In Ciudad Condal such people found it difficult to comprehend that any American would encounter problems of adaptation. Others, also unsympathetic to stranger problems, were psychologically incapable of perceiving, at least at the outset of their sojourn, the incongruities inherent in their encounter with the foreign. To use a term coined by Bruner and Postman, they were not "perceptually sensitized" to the foreign situation.[8] It might not be until relatively late in their overseas career, if at all, that people in this category began to experience stranger *anomie*. Situational or personal factors, therefore, may deprive one of the most intense foreign experience which an overseas setting has to offer a stranger.

There are, then, two broad categories of strangers: those who experience *anomie* and anxiety and those who do not. Since the latter group have, in effect, no encounter with the foreign, they may be discarded for the moment from our consideration of adaptive styles. Among those who do have such an encounter we will distinguish three types of adaptive action which correlate closely with the three types of character suggested by W. I. Thomas discussed in the last chapter. We will give an overseas case history to illustrate each style and then discuss the manner in which it fits into a particular category.[9]

THE BOHEMIAN STYLE OF ADAPTATION

S., a young, unmarried, Jewish man, came to Ciudad Condal three years before the study to supervise a small, family-owned business enterprise. At first he worked in a local restaurant where he acquired a working knowledge of both host languages. Later he took charge of the local operations of his family's concern. His job at the time of the study consisted of supervising manufacturing, arranging for suppliers (some in other countries), dealing with government officials, and finding suitable buildings to carry on a growing operation.

S. said that he had not amounted to much at home. He had felt inadequate and nervous while living with his parents. After a brief, unsatisfactory college experience, he dropped out and began to look around for a job. When he was offered the opportunity to work in his family's business in the city, he saw the job as a means of establishing his independence from a father who, in his words, was "quite a man." S. worked extremely hard at his job and the business prospered. He felt that he was proving to his father that he could succeed.

S. regularly had lunch with some "secret police." In the evenings during the hour of the aperitif he came to the bar in the Hotel Moderna which was frequented by some of his friends. One evening he was dressed in a dark conservative suit, continental shoes, and carried a raincoat over his arm. He greeted his friends in familiar fashion, saying, "*¿Que hay?*" to most of them; they included the bartender, some satellites of bullfighters, and an official of a business firm. S. apparently had many friends among the hosts. He did not often see Americans who, in his opinion, were "washouts." He was contemptuous of officials at the Consulate General who, according to him, did not even know that his family's business was in the city.

According to his own testimony, S. had had enormous success with women during his sojourn in the city. One of his affairs had led to the acquisition of a rare and expensive *atico* (top floor) apartment on the border of what we have called the American district. At the time of the study S. said he was planning to marry a woman he had met during a brief period at Condal University. Although she had been at home in another country for some time, S. thought that the separation would not affect their relationship. He appeared confident that it would continue to go well when she returned.

S.'s apartment was filled with French reproductions, jazz records, a few books, and memorabilia of sport, especially bullfighting. He had become an *aficionado* of the bulls and was learning some of the techniques. He said that he went to the slaughterhouse to practice killing. Like the hosts, he had extremely positive opinions about the sport. Hemingway, for example, "didn't really know bullfighting." S. was involved in an official capacity with one of the Condal football (soccer) teams, and participated in *jai alai* on the competitive level.

One could hardly believe that S. had as many friends as he reported. He took pleasure in showing off his various friendships. A Captain General took him skiing. A famous bullfighter used the familiar *tu* with him. He also liked to demonstrate what a good friend he could be. When he said in the Spanish style, "My house is yours," he meant it. In his relationships with many different classes of people he was expansive and assured. He knew many local sayings and possessed much "inside" information. He cut a fine figure in the Latin mode. Seeing him in action one could almost credit his assertion that "you can do anything you want to do in Ciudad Condal."

S. illustrates the bohemian style of adaptation to perfection. In his formulation of this type of character Thomas pointed out that he is open to "any and all influences." His personality, however, is not composed of the "stable and systematized" set of attitudes which marks the creative man.[10] In a foreign situation a bohemian would be open to, and unafraid of, the foreign. For him, the overseas stage would provide an opportunity to try out new roles and selfs somewhat in the manner in which a chameleon changes colors in a new environment. Perhaps the best example of this style of adaptation is provided by the unformed American adolescent who "tries on" various identities as a prelude to a deeper commitment to life.[11] Such a person probably would welcome the many new possibilities of the foreign setting and suffer a minimum of stranger anxiety as a result of his foreign encounter. This attitude may be the reason that many adolescents cannot comprehend the difficulties experienced by adults abroad. To them life is still a game in which irrevocable decisions, occasionally involving life and death, do not have to be made. We do not mean to imply, however, that the bohemian style of adaptation is confined to the young. It was characteristic of many young people observed by the author during his overseas sojourn, but an occasional adult also followed this adaptive pattern.

S. is obviously trying out a variety of new roles and selfs after an enthusiastic immersion into the foreign situation. For the first time he could become an *aficionado* of the bullfight, a great lover, a successful businessman, a man of affairs, and a good friend. It is not really essential to establish whether all the myriad activities which he reported did in fact take place. Whether in fantasy or behavior, he was trying on new selfs through the agency of his foreign experience. We doubt that he had succeeded in displacing his father as the dominant figure in his frame of reference. Were he to commit himself to the role of man vis-a-vis his father, his overseas life would cease to be a game and we would no longer be able to refer to his bohemian adaptive style.

To conclude we would mention the several keys to adaptation possessed by S.: First, he entered into the foreign society and established friends there, a course which was essential for successful adaptation by an American in the city. Undoubtedly, S.'s penetration of the host society was facilitated by his readiness to learn and use both of the host languages. Second, S. was a Jew who came from a sub-culture which provided him with certain transitional qualities for this particular foreign setting. Third, he was young and flexible. Fourth, he moved into an established business with which he was familiar and in which he believed. Add the stabilizing influence of kinship, and we approach the optimum conditions for successful adaptation in the city.

THE CREATIVE STYLE OF ADAPTATION

A married woman whom we have quoted several times in previous chapters came to the city with her husband and children three years before the time of the study. She and her family received an elaborate welcome from employees and officials of the joint Spanish-American firm in which her husband was project manager. The

J. family, as we will call them, found themselves almost immediately on intimate terms with the families of Mr. J.'s business
associates. For them, there was no delay in gaining entry into a
Catalan home.

Back in the United States, Mrs. J. had lived a "busy, happy, and
productive life." Besides running a large home, she had participated
in a variety of activities of a civic and social nature, and had
handled most of the social obligations connected with her husband's
business life. She looked forward to coming to Ciudad Condal to
relax.

Mrs. J. was pregnant when she arrived in the city and suffered
from side-effects of this pregnancy. She had "serious misgivings"
about the kind of treatment she would receive from local medical
people. According to her these anxieties proved to be misplaced.
Aside from what she considered to be minor lapses in antiseptic
procedures, she found herself treated very well. She and her child
were constantly surrounded by the families of business associates
who, in her words, "were wonderful to us." The doctor, who was a
relative of some of her husband's business associates, gave her every
possible consideration. Both she and the child prospered.

Mrs. J. said that she "fell in love" with the city immediately. She
was especially interested in the people. She thought that the hosts
were handsome, warm, friendly, and industrious. She noticed that
Americans were much taller. In the beginning she was "frustrated"
by host inefficiency, but she eventually concluded that "there was no
sense in this" and began either to accept it or to invent ways to deal
with it. Extremely observant, she would turn events in her foreign
life into material for humorous anecdotes or to plan strategy for
future projects. In this way her encounters with the foreign gradually were incorporated into a coherent style of life on the overseas
stage. For Mrs. J. the hosts were not enemies, but human beings
whose normal ways of living were entirely justified. Instead of
complaining about host values, as some Americans did, she tried to
understand them and turn them to her advantage.

Mrs. J.'s primary circle was composed almost entirely of host
women married to business colleagues of her husband. In the

beginning of her sojourn she had acquired some American friends, but they had since departed and no new ones had replaced them. She did not make a point of avoiding Americans, but her satisfactions came increasingly from upper-class hosts. She participated in several sports and played bridge with her hosts, other foreigners, and Americans, and went out to dinner with her husband at various restaurants.

Mrs. J. took great satisfaction from her family and her role of helpmeet. She worked hard to entertain "visiting firemen" from home. In her eyes, however, her activities were secondary in importance to her husband's very demanding mission. An observer could not entirely agree with her attempts to deprecate her part in the husband-wife team. Mrs. J. appeared to be a considerable asset to her husband's mission. Intelligent, humorous, attractive, socially adept, extremely active, gregarious, flexible, and helpful, Mrs. J. was the kind of woman personnel managers in overseas operations might dream about.[12]

Mrs. J. learned Spanish in the city and used it with confidence. Her observing eye and keen intelligence helped her penetrate the mysteries of the host culture. She was not afraid to try out local customs and was a devotee of various *fiestas*. In the matter of acculturation, however, she believed in moderation. She was not, in short, the kind of person whom Cleveland and his associates would call a "snuggler." [13] Mrs. J. hoped eventually to return to the United States, build a home, and take up the role of homemaker without any servants.

Although Mrs. J., like most other Americans, reported that she tended to be more "frustrated or exasperated" since her arrival, such experiences did not affect her general attitude toward the hosts. She liked them and their city and thought that they liked Americans. According to Mrs. J. Americans had no right to insist that Ciudad Condal be like home. Living in the city provided one with an opportunity to add something to one's life. She said, "You should enjoy the good things that this country has to offer."

The creative style of adaptation is a more stabilized version of the bohemian type. According to Thomas, the creative man has a character which is "settled and organized, but involves the possibility and even the necessity of evolution." [14] In the foreign setting, the creative man could be as open to the foreign experience as the bohemian, but he probably would be more selective about taking on new roles and selfs. Thomas says that "he remains open to such influences as will be in line with his preconceived development." [15] Having a more settled and organized character, his essays with new roles take on a more serious, less cavalier tone. A new self must fit into a more coherent, better established self-structure. Because of this, we would expect that his life line would show fewer discontinuities than that of the bohemian under the impact of the foreign experience.

Mrs. J. possessed one of several creative styles of adaptation identified by the author in the city. She was open to the foreign situation and tended to use it in advancing various life projects. Her style of life had been altered significantly by the incorporation of foreign elements. How deeply they were embedded in her character could not, of course, be determined until she left the city and began to follow her creative style elsewhere.

Mrs. J. also possessed a number of keys to successful adaptation in the city. She and her family entered an extremely accepting atmosphere provided by her husband's firm, and through the families of her husband's colleagues she established a position in the host society. She learned the language and was not afraid to use it. She was, therefore, deeply involved with the hosts from the beginning. She believed strongly in her husband and his mission and she was part of a family which provided her with a secure base of operations. Finally, Mrs. J. was a flexible woman who perceived her foreign sojourn as an opportunity to enrich her life.

THE PHILISTINE STYLE OF ADAPTATION

Before coming to Ciudad Condal with his family about a year prior to the time of the study, Mr. R. had lived in the Orient and in northern Europe. He had made a preliminary trip to the city to sound out business possibilities after his relations with a European branch of an American company had begun to sour. He indicated that at the time he broke off with this company he had no prospective job or income. His principal assets then were a house in the United States and an insurance policy. He said that he "hocked" the insurance policy to start a family business in the city. At that time he was aware that he was taking a considerable risk, but risk-taking had become a habit with him in his overseas career. Pursuing his entrepreneurial course, he had gone from place to place around the world trying out different business schemes in frontier-like atmospheres.

The business which Mr. R. founded in Ciudad Condal began to prosper. He and his family worked extremely hard at an operation which, according to some American skeptics, could not possibly succeed in the city; they took particular satisfaction at proving these skeptics wrong. R., whose business made him one of the more important men in the American community, rose to prominence in a comparatively short period of time. It was perhaps his rapid rise which excited so much hostility against him by Americans. He and his family were aware of this hostility and turned it back on the Americans whom they regarded generally as "an insipid bunch." When R.'s business fortunes eventually declined and he and his family moved to another part of the world, it could be said that neither he nor the American community mourned his departure.

The business which Mr. R. established encountered an ever-growing series of problems with the hosts and their governments, local and national. According to R., debtors would not pay their bills on time (it was customary among the hosts not to pay bills immediately), workers would not do their jobs correctly, and potential clients would not keep their appointments. The very success of his enterprise worked against him. As his business grew larger and became well-known, government agencies began to harass him. Finding one local lawyer unsatisfactory, he hired another who was often absent from the city and who advised him to disregard most of the threatening letters he received from government agencies. Without friends in high places, he found himself facing a series of crises with very little assistance. He often complained about it, saying, "How many knocks can you take and still come back for more?"

R. disliked most of the hosts. He did not speak Spanish and he did not cultivate connections or friendships with any but those who were more Americanized and given to strong criticism of their compatriots. He possessed a series of "horror" stories about his transactions with Catalans whom he found to be backward, dishonest ("thieves"), undependable, discourteous, inefficient, and incompetent. He said, "In all your dealings with them you've got to remember that they are children, nothing more." Confronted by "insipid" Americans and "childish" hosts, we might expect that R. would have had trouble building up a primary circle in the city. He and his family did, however, succeed in forming friendships with other foreign nationals. He was interested in promoting better relations between the different foreign groups and encouraging the development of a genuine "international" community such as the one he recalled from a previous sojourn in the Orient.

Mr. R. was a moralizer. He stood for honesty and courtesy in transactions between people. When citizens of the city failed to meet his standards he felt that they had committed an immoral act. It sometimes prompted him to deliver a lecture on "common decency and courtesy." For example, he had had almost a score of appointments with an important local client, but had managed to see him fewer than five times. On some occasions he had discovered the man "skulking about" even though he had been told that he was not in. Finally, he wrote him a letter in which he spoke of "the common courtesies" found in business throughout the world. There was no evidence that this letter changed the host's appointment-keeping practices.

Toward the end of his sojourn in Ciudad Condal, R. was feeling persecuted. He saw government officials "hitting him" for something, then waiting until the time was ripe and "hitting him" again. He thought that, unlike the representatives of large American firms, he was exposed and "fair game" (*pez grande?*) for official avarice. His fortunes continued to decline and he finally decided to leave the city and give up the business. Financial ambiguities attending his departure were handled by R. in characteristic fashion. He sought to correct, explain, and even apologize for problems which he felt he had created.

Mr. R. was an individualistic entrepreneur who was attracted to the city by an opportunity to try out one of his schemes. He was, perhaps, destined inevitably to fail. Although he was internationally mobile, he does not appear to have been capable of changing, and although he had interesting ideas, he does not seem to have been able to carry them through to a successful conclusion. According to his view, good ideas, hard work, honesty, and good Western manners were the ingredients for success. He was, in short, an old-fashioned, rather ethnocentric American who sought to make his subjective world prevail in a foreign setting. He had not been notably successful in this attempt.

Although Mr. R. was comparatively open at first to the foreign, he reacted to *anomie* and anxiety in a manner which we have called constrictive. It seemed that the more difficulties he encountered, the more he emphasized American values and attempted to make them prevail over the foreign. For him, success in the foreign situation was merely a matter of victory on his own traditional terms or defeat. In this case, and apparently in at least one previous sojourn abroad, it was defeat.

R. was a philistine in his adaptive style. According to Thomas, the philistine has a set of attitudes which have attained "so great a fixity that he is accessible only to those influences constituting a permanent part of his social milieu." [16] The philistine may or may not experience *anomie* in a changed situation. If he does, he reacts with perceptual defense [17] and attempts to assert his traditional subjective world. He may or may not succeed in this design. The philistine who does not experience *anomie* because he is not sensitive to the foreign also attempts to assert his traditional subjective world, but he does not share the stranger anxiety of his more sensitive colleague. It is possible that this second type of philistine may eventually succumb to *anomie,* at which time the results in personal disorganization are likely to be catastrophic.

Although philistines can adapt abroad if situational factors are

favorable, R. did not have the advantage of such factors. He had no
prior contacts among the hosts. He did not learn the language. He
made few Spanish friends. There was no one among the hosts who
felt responsible for him when his difficulties began to grow. He was
not particularly flexible. In short, he lacked almost all the keys to
adaptation. It would be interesting to watch this "rolling stone"
take further steps around the American overseas perimeter and to
speculate about the kind of situation in which his philistine style of
adaptation would prove to be effective.

We have outlined three styles of stranger adaptation, the bohemian, the creative, and the philistine.[18] As is inevitable in any
classification, individual cases sometimes do not fit easily into a
single category. A stranger could follow different styles of adaptation at different stages of his foreign sojourn, or he might display a
mixture of styles at any one time. During the period of the field
study, for example, most American adult residents of the city
probably were more philistine than creative in their adaptive styles,
but the creative elements which many of them displayed would
make it difficult to fit them comfortably into the category of
philistine.

The question of the distribution of adaptive styles in a given type
of American overseas outpost requires further investigation. What
is the optimum "mix" of adaptive styles in a large military base
abroad, a bohemian enclave, a Peace Corps unit, or a retirement
community? How do situational factors such as the relative power
of the hosts and the compatibility of cultures affect the functionality
of the different styles? In the fictitious overseas community described by Forster in *A Passage to India*,[19] most of the English
appear to be philistine in their styles of adaptation. If Forster's
description is realistic in this regard, how would we account for the
predominance of philistines in this population? Are "good" imperialists invariably "good" philistines?

II

THE WORLD VIEW OF A
STRANGER COMMUNITY

He read him a snappish little sermon, taking as
his text the five chief beatitudes of the pukka
sahib, namely:
Keeping up our prestige,
The firm hand (without the velvet glove),
We white men must hang together.
Give them an inch and they'll take an ell, and
Esprit de corps. . . .
                              GEORGE ORWELL
                              Burmese Days

MOST PEOPLE WHO HAVE GROWN UP IN A SOCIETY ARE oriented to the world in an adaptive way. They have acquired conventional means of locating themselves in space, time, society, and culture which enable them to follow those plans of action which permit them to survive in their society. Were any of these people to be sent to a mental institution they probably would be asked questions by the examining psychiatrist which were designed to evaluate their orientation in these dimensions. The assumption of such an inquiry would be that the mentally ill are prevented from functioning in an adaptive way because they have become disoriented in one or more of these spheres.

The stranger in the foreign setting also experiences disorientation. The points of reference which have become part of his inner world no longer receive the consistent confirmation from experience which he had come to take for granted at home. As a result, he may become increasingly incoherent and ineffectual in his actions. This reaction is illustrated by a series of recent experiments concerning the effects of air travel on physiological and mental functions.[1] The investigators have found that the initial inconsistency between "biological time" and local time produced by flights across time zones tends to be associated with slower reactions, greater fatigue,

and less proficiency in accomplishing tasks. Normal functioning
was restored after a period of several days when the discrepancy
between inner and outer times had disappeared. The stranger-sub-
jects in these experiments seem to have followed a process of
disorientation and reorientation which is consistent with our view of
the stranger's career.

We would expect that because the stranger cannot take his
orientation for granted he would become more preoccupied with
the problem of locating himself than at home. These problems
would come to the foreground of his experience, and his manner of
solving them would occupy a more important part of his subjective
world. The problem of orientation or disorientation, then, would
come to dominate the world view of the stranger. In order to
understand his actions, therefore, it would be necessary for us, first
of all, to find out how he had answered the questions: Where am I?
How do I fit in? What is my place here (or everywhere)?

The world view of a community of strangers such as the one we
have been considering in Ciudad Condal would in part constitute a
collective solution to the problems of orientation which beset its
individual members.[2] In a community so heterogeneous and ill-coor-
dinated as this one, it is extremely difficult to speak about a community world view. Not only did the various sub-communities look at
the world differently, but, as we have seen, people at different stages
of adaptation possessed different outlooks. Nevertheless, provided
that we take note of significant variations or exceptions, it does
seem possible to refer to a conventional outlook of Condal Americans. This way of looking at the world, developed out of a similarity
of background, shared life conditions (including strangerhood in
the same foreign setting), and social interaction, was expressed in
the *Condal Courier,* in public statements, at formal and informal
gatherings, and in interviews. For new arrivals struggling with
stranger *anomie,* it provided formulae for orientation which could
only have been acquired by individuals from longer and perhaps
more painful experience.[3] We will consider this world view in terms
of problems of orientation in space, time, society, and culture.

Spatial Orientation

We can think of an American's mental map as extending outward from his own body to areas and objects which serve him as points of reference.[4] This map would include *querencias* or home territories in which the individual has rights of possession. The central *querencia* in the mental map would be the private domain of the body, an area which may be entered by others only under special circumstances. American conceptions of the private space of the body appear to have changed considerably as a result of experiences in Ciudad Condal. The nature of this change was anticipated by E. T. Hall in his discussion of the spatial problems encountered by Americans in stranger situations. He notes that Americans in many foreign cultures find that what they consider to be their body's private space is subject to violation by the hosts. They are, for example, unprepared for the degree of physical intimacy which they encounter on the streets of a foreign city.[5]

The Condal Americans were often disconcerted by the pushing and shoving throngs which they encountered in public places. An American woman who did not want her body touched, who expected to be addressed in low, cultivated tones, and who disliked being stared at was bound to experience anxiety in the city. Reluctantly or not, she and other Americans had to accept intrusions by touch, sound, and sight into the private space which they had come to take for granted at home. The outcome for the Americans of this clash in conceptions of the body's private space was the contraction of personal boundaries accompanied, in most cases, by the inevitable consequences of frustration. One such consequence may have been the widespread sensitivity to slights or insults in the community which several informants referred to, appropriately enough, as "touchiness."

Some American difficulties with private body space could be avoided by traveling through the city in a car or taxi or by employing servants who would go into the marketplace in one's stead. The possession of financial means enabled an American to screen himself from some intrusions into his private sector, but these "screens" introduced other problems. Some of the difficulties of driving an automobile in the city probably could be traced to a clash in host and American conceptions of private automobile space. In American eyes the hosts "pushed and shoved" in or on their motor vehicles in much the same way as on foot.[6]

The bulk of Condal Americans lived in a district which, in effect, covered much of the eastern quarter of the city and environs. This area; the downtown business, shopping, and historical districts; and the connecting streets and metro constituted a wedge-shaped sector of familiar ground extending from the mountains to the waterfront which dominated the American mental map of Ciudad Condal. Most of the "fixed" American *querencias* were located in this sector —residences, two of the three American schools, the Cultural Institute, the two principal receiving hotels, a popular supermarket, the Banco Luzon,[7] the Consulate General, various American businesses, and possibly, the Anglo-American church. Almost the entire northeastern half of the city and environs and much of the southern quarter, heavily populated by the working class, was *terra incognita* to Americans. The *barracas* (hut settlements) of the very poor rarely figured in American thoughts, and the famous (or infamous) *Metro Transversal* which carried workers back and forth across the city was little more to Americans than a sign in the Plaza Central. These *lacunae* were less likely to exist in the minds of American missionaries who were affiliated with Protestant churches located in working-class areas.

Every American's mental map of the city included scattered points of interest to the sightseer, the sportsman, or devotee of culture. It also included favorite bars, restaurants, and clubs which were visited more frequently than those at home. Most of the favorite American eating and drinking establishments were located in the wedge-shaped corridor. It was the rare American map which did not include at least one such *querencia* there.

Americans' thoughts followed streets or highways which led out of the city and down the coast to the airport, to two resort communities, and possibly to the city which was once the Roman capital of the region; northeastward to the vacation coast (where a PX was located), to the eastern Pyrenees, and to the French border; and inland to the SAC base (with PX) and beyond it to Madrid and the region surrounding it. They "flew" over water to the islands off the coast, over the barren land to Madrid, and over the sea to New York. Only a comparatively small part of northeastern Spain was of concern to Americans in the city. With the exception of the Madrid region, most of the country to the south, to the west, and to the northwest was *terra incognita* to them. Only the oil explorers who were covering the entire northern part of the country in systematic fashion were oriented in terms of points extending to the Atlantic.

The area surrounding Spain was not well developed on the American mental map. Africa scarcely existed. Italy and Portugal were of little importance. France, although fairly well defined, constituted a negative point of reference. Countries such as England, Switzerland, and West Germany constituted the most significant positive reference points in Europe. None of these countries, however, rivaled the homeland and the home town as points of reference.[8] "Pictures" of places in America sometimes occurred to Americans with excruciating clarity, especially during periods of intense anxiety. For those who had lived abroad before, such periods of discontent also were likely to call forth images associated with previous foreign sojourns. Overseas careermen, particularly toward the end of their tours of duty in Ciudad Condal, tended to think ahead to possible overseas posts to which they might move with or without a return to the homeland. Since many of these people possessed what amounted to an area specialty, e.g., Hispanic culture areas, the number of future alternatives which occurred to them was quite limited.

How would we characterize the mental map of Americans in Ciudad Condal? First, it probably covered more ground than the conventional map of people in a "typical" American suburb. The horizons of Americans in the city had been extended to include a part of Europe as familiar ground. Second, though more extensive, this mental map contained a highly selective range of objects and areas which generally tended to confirm an upper-status self. Places inhabited or frequented by more modernized middle- and upper-class hosts and foreign nationals tended to predominate in these Americans' thinking about Spain. Third, as a comparatively mobile people, they thought often in terms of highways, airways, or seaways which would take them somewhere and back. For example, the air route home, the road to Madrid, and the highways leading to favorite beach or skiing resorts were well fixed in American minds. Finally, the Americans in the city tended to conceive of themselves as less isolated in space from the bodies of others. This conception, however, was not necessarily associated with greater interpersonal communion.

ORIENTATION IN TIME

In the modern Western world the man on the street tends to conceive of time as flowing either in cycles, e.g., the succession of seasons or in a linear progression, e.g., the succession of years.[9] According to the reports of those who provided adequate information, the Condal Americans tended to experience a more rapid passage of cyclical or linear time than at home.[10] They also were likely to define the events which mark time's passage in a less precise and rigid manner. They tended to report that they were less concerned with punctuality than at home.[11] As one young woman said, "The trains don't run on time and the people don't come on time, but nobody is upset by this. . . . At first I would get upset if I were late, but as long as they [the hosts] felt you could be late, it really didn't matter." The less precise manner of marking time, which usually is acquired reluctantly by Americans, seems to be the usual consequence of American exposure to host cultures at a lower level of technological development.

Most of the Americans who came to the city probably brought with them a typically American future-orientation.[12] Under the initial impact of foreign experience, this outlook usually was given up in favor of an emphasis on some past period in one's biography. Such a reaction probably constituted an attempt to find a stable, secure point of reference in a sea of *anomie*. It was likely to persist until the American began to adapt himself externally to the foreign situation. Then a new future-orientation, phrased in terms of local events, entered his outlook. It was this new orientation toward the future, with survivals of the initial emphasis on the past, which characterized the time perspective of the American community in Ciudad Condal.

The American businessmen in the city were future-oriented. They tended to think ahead toward future times when markets would be expanded, programs of industrial development completed, new American enterprises instituted, and Spain's entry into the European Common Market actually accomplished. Generally, they were not as concerned as their colleagues in Madrid with predicting government policy relative to business and industry. However, they were as anxious as everyone in Spain about the political and economic consequences of the death (hopefully deferred) of General Franco. The future demise of the leader of Spain exercised an extraordinary fascination for hosts, Americans, and other foreigners alike, many of whom feared the possible occurrence of another Civil War.

The government people also were future-oriented. They shared with the businessmen a belief in the continued expansion of the economy and calculated the political consequences of this development. Most of them believed that the surge in the Spanish economy was associated with a liberalization of the Spanish political climate. They tended to see the Spanish problem as one of evolution vs. revolution. Would the gradual liberalization of the Spanish regime be able to forestall violent upheavals which might threaten American interests in the area? Like most Americans in Spain they tended to be both publicly and privately optimistic in this regard.

The missionaries, who perhaps had a greater stake in the Spanish future than other Americans, foresaw an increasingly tolerant attitude by the Spanish regime toward other religions. They were particularly concerned with the then forthcoming Vatican Council which, in their optimistic view, probably would provide some kind of official sanction for what appeared to them to be an increasing tolerance for other religions in Spain. These Protestant Fundamentalists also anticipated a continuous expansion of their form of religion throughout Spain. They thought that the conversion of Spain might not be confined to the working class, but might include the middle and upper classes as well.[13] The missionaries tended to share, therefore, the optimism about the future expressed by their business and government colleagues—an optimism marred by the possible consequences of the approaching demise of Franco, the rising cost of living, and the problems of adaptation posed by the host culture.

It would be inaccurate to say that Americans in the city were entirely future-oriented. They also attended to the present. But they possessed no significant sense of local history to balance their present and future orientation. They were almost completely ignorant of the brief history of their own community,[14] and although they tended to be very much aware of the material evidence of great age in and around the city, they had little knowledge of past events which were the points of reference of so many host actions. Except for the artists and intellectuals, few Americans made any serious attempts to acquaint themselves with the history of Catalonia. The historical events which had molded the host culture did not enter their world. They were only marginally aware of the Civil War, for example, and almost completely ignorant of the great events associated with the sacred mountain to the west of the city.

In a more tradition-directed Europe, the failure to grasp local history was often a serious obstacle to the adaptation of American strangers. Indeed, some of the excruciating problems of Christopher Newman, one of Henry James' Americans in Europe,[15] were of this nature. However an awareness of the local past is not as necessary for adaptation in a Europe which has given itself over to the pursuit of the American Dream. The ethnocentric American who insists that everything be measured in terms of American consumer values receives some support for his belief from the growing Americanization of European culture. Americans in the city, for example, could not help feeling more advanced on noticing the enthusiasm of the hosts for American things which they had either taken for granted or discarded. Television programs, e.g.,

Bonanza, movies, e.g., *West Side Story,* cake mixes, automobiles, computers, and electrical appliances were some of the American items which excited admiration by the hosts during the period of the study. Seeing this reaction, an American might register surprise, then amusement touched perhaps with a little contempt. In writing about modern-day Americans in Europe, Thomas Sterling refers to the Americans' encounter with diffused American culture as follows: ". . . The mature American living in Europe has a distinct impression that he has lived this life before. It's not simply a question of seeing supermarkets and motels and laundromats spring up where Caesar and Napoleon once ruled; the very conversations one overhears—though in other languages—are hauntingly reminiscent of one's youth . . . Europeans . . . are undergoing the socioeconomic revolution that hit our lives with the first administration of Roosevelt." [16]

Americans in the city were oriented not only in terms of events which formed a linear progression toward more desirable goals, but also to periodic events such as the daily round, the seasons, tours of duty, and gatherings, celebrations, and holidays. In the last category the most significant recurring events in the American calendar were the monthly meetings of the American Men's Luncheon Club and American Women's Club, the Thanksgiving celebration, the Fourth of July outing, the June Chamber of Commerce gathering, the Theater Guild play, the long Christmas-New Year's-Epiphany *fiesta* (including a communal Christmas party), and the extended Easter *fiesta*. Of these, the most important communal events were the Thanksgiving celebration and the Chamber of Commerce gathering.

The Thanksgiving celebration of the Condal Americans was traditionally American in character. It began on Thursday morning with a special religious service at the Anglo-American church. The service was marked by Thanksgiving decorations, at least one traditional Thanksgiving hymn ("Come Ye Thankful People"), and an absence of Anglican liturgy. It was followed by a "Dutch Treat" luncheon at the Cultural Institute. Two days later (Saturday), a

Thanksgiving dinner-dance was held at one of the city's larger, more luxurious hotels. The dinner usually included turkey which had been obtained from an American commissary or PX.

The Chamber of Commerce gathering coincided with the Condal Fair and the American exhibition there. It included a business meeting of Chamber members and a banquet. Although the gathering was attended by Spanish and American businessmen from all over Spain, members of the home chapter usually outnumbered all the rest. During the year of the study the gathering was clouded by a struggle for power between the local and Madrid chapters of the Chamber. Nevertheless the banquet was a glittering occasion graced by the presence of the highest ranking American and Spanish dignitaries. All the ceremonies so dear to the heart of the Spaniard and the acculturated American were evident—ritual entrances and exits by distinguished guests, high-sounding speeches containing sentiments of optimism and solidarity—and an elaborate dinner contributed to the evident satisfaction of the estimated three hundred Spanish and American men who were present.

A stranger community is located in cultural space somewhere between the home and the host society. Its position and its degree of acculturation will depend on a number of factors, among them the presence or absence of externally supported institutions, the nature of its missions, its relative power vis-a-vis the hosts, and the kind and distribution of adaptive types in its population. The communal events discussed above constituted two of the reference points which served to orient the Condal Americans in the cultural space extending from the lifeways of the American middle class to those of the Spanish middle and upper classes. By referring themselves to these and other communal events they were in fact acquiring or expressing conventions for locating themselves in cultural space. How would we characterize their location? The culture of the American community tended to range from the norms of the American middle class to those of the more Americanized or modernized sectors of the host middle and upper classes. It was a "Third Culture," but one leaning distinctly toward the American side. The two communal events cited above, one traditionally American and the other Spanish-American, appear to symbolize the boundaries of cultural space occupied by this "Community in Limbo."

In the minds of most Americans the Condal year was divided into two seasons: the hot, tourist summer and the cold, non-tourist winter. Fall and spring, though recognized, played an insignificant part in the orientation of the American community. The reason may be that these periods of the year were difficult to distinguish climatically. It is not clear, however, that climate was the major differentiating factor between summer and winter as perceived by these strangers. In this tourist-oriented setting, the ebb and flow of foreign visitors, which was viewed with mixed feelings by Americans and other "natives" of the city, appeared to be as important a factor as climate in marking the seasons.

According to many American residents American tourists were among the more barbarous of these invaders and association with them was thought to undermine one's status with colleagues and hosts. As the tourist wave receded the Americans began to be concerned with the advance of cold weather, which was not severe in absolute terms (rarely falling below 15 degrees Fahrenheit), but was oppressive enough for a people accustomed to central heating. Most of those residents who provided adequate information said that they were more preoccupied with the cold than they had been at home.[17] Mainly because of the inadequacies of local indoor heating arrangements, the Condal winter was a time when most of the strangers were physically uncomfortable. The struggle with the cold was evident during many of the interviews which took place during the winter. A sneezing and coughing informant might interrupt the interview to stoke the fire or adjust a space heater. Then he and the numbed anthropologist would attempt to get on with his story. As the end of winter approached one no longer had to stoke the stoves, supply the butane and kerosene heaters, or build and maintain fireplace fires. At this time one might plan a trip to the beach before the main invasion of tourists.

If there was anything like an official working day for Americans in the city, it probably was indicated by the hours of the Consulate General and the Cultural Institute, which corresponded closely to those of the hosts. Unless he were connected with the oil exploring outfit or the army transportation unit, a working American would follow a daily round lasting until 7 P.M., with a three-hour lunch break. The later local dinner hour posed special problems for families with children, and the longer lunch period created problems for businessmen who did not like being interrupted once a task was begun. Most of the Americans were more or less dissatisfied with the local daily schedule and some of the more thoughtful felt that it would be changed. They thought that some recent changeovers by Spanish concerns were indicative of a trend in the direction of the "superior" American system of organizing the day. Because different daily time schedules prevailed in the American community, and because those Americans who followed local time were not entirely committed to it, we must conclude that these strangers' orientation in terms of the daily round was not as clear as in terms of the seasons.

In an overseas community dominated by organization men, the tour of duty becomes an extremely significant temporal point of reference.[18] The tour of duty, which may or may not include a scheduled leave, establishes a definite beginning and end to one's sojourn in a foreign setting. People in such a community take it for granted that they and their colleagues will be departing after a certain number of months or years. In a war zone or at a "hardship post" the tour of duty may become the paramount temporal reference point.[19]

The government people were oriented in terms of a three- or four-year period of residence in the city. Most of the other Americans were counting on limited sojourns, but were not certain of the exact time of their departure. Only a few business people, some of the retired, the missionaries, and one or two others contemplated remaining in the city indefinitely or until death. Although scheduled departures had not become such a routine matter as in a community dominated by organization men, the outlook of the Condal Americans included some definite—fixed or unfixed—date of departure for home or some other place in the world.[20] In the case of the careerists, the tour of duty in the city was considered to be only one of a series of temporal events which marked a person's vocational progress. The fact that most of the Americans intended to remain in the city for a limited duration probably served to arrest acculturation and therefore limit the extension of this overseas community in cultural space.

In this brief discussion we have not attempted to include all the temporal points of reference of the American community in Ciudad Condal, but only those which were most significant for its orientation as a stranger community in this particular foreign setting. The temporal outlook of the Americans in the city tended to be slanted ahead toward a generally better future. Time for them appeared to flow more rapidly and to be marked by less discrete events of a non-periodic and periodic nature. The most significant events in these strangers' view of the world were the tour of duty, which placed definite temporal limits on this particular foreign sojourn and enabled an American to locate himself in terms of the beginning and end of his time in the city, the season cycle associated with the ebb and flow of tourists and cold weather, the yearly round of communal gatherings and Spanish and American celebrations, of which the Thanksgiving gathering and the Chamber of Commerce meeting were of greatest communal significance, and the daily round of events which tended to correspond closely to the host timetable. The Americans were not entirely satisfied with all these points of reference, and in at least one instance, i.e., the daily round, they displayed a conflict-ridden outlook. On the whole the schedule of life in this community probably was outlined with less precision and less detail than that of an American community at home.

ORIENTATION IN SOCIAL SPACE

The quotation from Orwell which heads this chapter amounts to a statement of ideology which functioned to orient a community of English colonialists to a particular host society. It expresses the communal conception of its location in social space. It would be presumptuous to claim that the Americans in the city possessed such a well articulated ideology as is attributed by Orwell to Englishmen in Burma. Nevertheless, there existed among Condal Americans a conventional point of view concerning the question of their social status in the city. In this regard, we may distinguish two levels of communal ideology, one for public consumption and the other for private use. The public ideology could be discerned in the pages of the *Condal Courier,* propaganda statements by government people, speeches at Spanish-American banquets, and ceremonial exchanges between Americans, hosts, and other foreign nationals. The private ideology emerged in gatherings of Americans, of Americans and Americanized hosts, or of Americans and some foreign nationals.

The public ideology of the American community proclaimed the dependent status of Americans in the city. They were guests among other guests. As guests, it was natural for them to be on good terms with their hosts and other foreign nationals, to take a sympathetic interest in their cultures, to support civic enterprises and economic progress, to observe local laws and taboos, to keep out of politics, and generally to disport themselves as would somewhat diffident visitors in someone else's home. The *Condal Courier* expressed some of this outlook by printing, in addition to its American content, articles about the local scene, reports on events of cross-cultural significance, legal advice for foreign residents, discussions of the history and culture of Catalonia, stories about other countries with outposts in the city, and profiles of distinguished hosts and other foreign nationals.

On the public level, Americans rarely criticised the hosts. In the pages of the *Condal Courier* one encountered only occasional criticisms. If the hosts were criticised, the criticism was of the kind which would receive a favorable reception in the host establishment. The *Courier,* like all papers in Spain, was scrutinized regularly by government press officers, and never criticised the establishment itself and only rarely meddled in politics.[21] Crimes, misdemeanors, conflicts, rebelliousness, and disasters seldom found a place in the *Courier.* In short, the paper expressed a public outlook which emphasized the happy identification of the American community with its dependent status in the city. Public statements by the various American agencies also tended to emphasize the American posture of rapprochement with other nationalities in Ciudad Condal.

The theme of happy togetherness also applied to relations within the American community. According to the public viewpoint of the Condal Americans, which was hard-pressed by the local facts of life, good relations between Americans and others went hand in hand with excellent community morale. It was perhaps best expressed in the surface air of cooperation and good fellowship which one encountered at the American Women's Club or American Men's Luncheon Club. The Luncheon Club, for example, conformed to the traditional Rotarian pattern with an elaborate meal, liberal quantities of alcohol, and boisterous good fellowship. At the end of such a gathering most of those who had attended clearly subscribed to a belief in togetherness. Since a few Spaniards, transient Americans, and foreign nationals also attended the luncheon, the image of a circle of good fellowship was extended beyond the resident Americans. To sum up, the public ideology of the American community proclaimed that an American in the city was integrated as a cooperative, somewhat dependent guest into the local scene. He was happy —even enthusiastic—about his relations with himself, his fellow guests, and his Catalan hosts.

The private ideology of the American community, expressed in the intimacy of its primary circles, was in direct contrast with its public outlook. On the private level, the Americans maintained a belief in the right of the independent individual to pursue his own personal El Dorado. With so many individualistic entrepreneurs in the community, it is not surprising that there existed at least a tacit understanding that everyone was bent on exploiting the foreign situation for his own benefit. ("Everyone is out for himself.") The city was conceived to be a kind of frontier in which one might pursue success in its various guises or pleasure in its various forms. Unfortunately for American aspirations, this foreign setting did not turn out to be as exploitable as many of them had anticipated. Failing to realize their expectations, many of them tended to become angry with the hosts and to begrudge other Americans even modest entrepreneurial successes. This hostility tended to sour the private ideology and further undermine the credibility of the public outlook of this community of American strangers.

Although the public ideology of the Condal Americans came close to expressing a belief in the equality of the different nationalities represented in a pluralistic situation, their private outlook tended to be ethnocentric. Regardless of their degree of adaptation, their valuation of different aspects of foreign cultures, or their criticisms of American society, most members of the American community believed in the essential superiority of American culture. American businessmen in the city were convinced of the industrial and commercial supremacy of the United States, American missionaries of the superiority of at least one of its religions, American government people of its higher forms of political life, American military men of the supremacy of its war machine, and American artists and intellectuals of its (currently) more significant artistic and intellectual life. All the Americans shared the belief that no culture, especially that of the hosts, could compare with the American in level of technology, in efficiency, and in the mass provision of the material amenities of life. As representatives of a superior culture many Americans thought that they should receive some special consideration from the hosts and perhaps an open field in which to realize their overseas ambitions. But the hosts provided little explicit confirmation of American superiority and no special considerations for Americans. In fact, to many Americans it appeared that the hosts were acting as if they, not the Americans or anyone else, represented the superior culture. The chauvinism of the hosts sometimes was so disconcerting as to put the Americans on the defensive. Accordingly, the American ethnocentrism tended to acquire more of the quality of a reaction formation than of a simple expression of pride.

Put in diachronic perspective, the belief of the American community in the essential superiority of American culture took the form of an evaluation of the position of different local cultures along a line of progress leading toward the American Dream. From this point of view American culture was not only superior to, but more advanced in time than, the host or other cultures. The evident direction of change in the local situation tended to reinforce this belief and foster the conception of the United States as the culture center of the world. But the insistence of the stubborn Catalans in adhering to what, from the American point of view, were archaic customs was somewhat bewildering to Americans who, even in their most abject public moments, rarely were ready to admit that the hosts were ahead of, or superior to, the Americans in anything of real importance.[22] As a result the belief in the advanced status of American culture also acquired something of a defensive character.

It is not that the Americans in the city were especially concerned with Americanizing the hosts in the way that a missionary converts a heathen people. They were simply of the belief that it was the most natural thing in the world for others to want to acquire *voluntarily* certain aspects of American culture, to collaborate with Americans in fostering the belief in American cultural superiority, and to grant them certain privileges as a result. They were quite reluctant, therefore, to believe on the private level what they expressed in public, i.e., that they were only one of a number of equally privileged, dependent guests in the host *querencia.* This clash in the Americans' conceptions of their status in this foreign setting meant that an American could not refer himself to a communal world view to get a clear, unambiguous picture of his location in social space. It would not have been possible, for example, for an American resident of the city to brief a newcomer with the conviction of one of Forster's English expatriates who says, "You're superior to them anyway. Don't forget that you're superior to everyone in India except one or two of the Ranis, and they're on an equality." [23]

To conclude, unlike some of its larger and more powerful counterparts abroad, the American community in Ciudad Condal did not possess an entirely clear, unambiguous world view which functioned as a means of orienting its members securely in this foreign setting. Americans in the city had available to them less effective conventional conceptions for coping with stranger *anomie* and anxiety. Given our knowledge of the reactions of strangers,[24] we would surmise that as a general rule expatriates attempt to transfer from home their traditional subjective world and to make it prevail in the foreign setting. How successful a group of expatriates will be in this design will depend on a number of factors of which the most significant probably is the power or prestige of the group vis-a-vis the hosts. In Ciudad Condal, American power, as measured by the willingness of the hosts to accept traditional American definitions and to render to Americans appropriate deference, was not very great. As a result, the American community, in order to adapt externally, had to compromise the traditional outlooks of its members. Wherever possible, it appears that the less painful form of compromise had been adopted. Americans tended to orient themselves in terms of more compatible points of reference in the more Americanized middle and upper host classes. However, in order to prove effective for adaptation, the world view of these strangers had to include less compatible or consistent foreign elements, many of which offered direct challenges to the Americans' preferred conception of the world and their place in it. An American who attempted to refer himself to the conventional outlook of the American community in the city would encounter ambiguities or contradictions about orientation in space, time, and socio-cultural space. It would mean that the community might not be counted on as a point of security.

As we have maintained throughout this book, the stranger tends to be preoccupied with the problem of location or orientation. The failure of the American community in Ciudad Condal to develop a world view which functioned effectively to orient its members, and therefore reduce stranger anxiety, may have been one reason for its lack of attractiveness to Americans in the city. From contact situations involving even more incompatible cultures, prophets have arisen who have synthesized apparently incompatible cultural elements into coherent world views.[25] These views, once accepted, have proved effective in orienting whole peoples to radically changed situations. But such a compromise view by an American prophet in Ciudad Condal probably would have been rejected by a people representing such a powerful nation as the United States. Regardless of the rationality or irrationality of their intention, these Americans would have liked to see their taken-for-granted view of the world prevail in Ciudad Condal. However, they could not hope to realize this intention because American power and resources in this setting were not sufficient to permit the construction of an adaptive world view according to the pattern of the traditional world at home.

12

THE OVERSEAS
COMMUNITY AND THE
IMPERIALISTIC PROCESS

> Many and many a simple community ... will
> remember for years the strange horde ... that
> called themselves Americans, and seemed to
> imagine in some unaccountable way that they
> had a right to be proud of it.
>
> MARK TWAIN
> *The Innocents Abroad*

WHEN A NATION SUCH AS THE UNITED STATES EM-barks on an imperialistic course it adds interests in foreign lands to its national interest. In this way the United States economy becomes tied to a banana crop in Central America, the defense of the United States to the maintenance of certain governments in the Middle East, and certain American religions to the conversion of African natives. The prosecution of these overseas interests requires the imperial power to send representatives abroad to carry out its various foreign missions. The greater the extent of overseas interests and missions, the greater will be the number of agents required on the overseas frontier. When a country acquires as many interests abroad as the United States today, it must of necessity develop a formidable overseas establishment.

If we look at the contemporary American foreign establishment, we see the bulk of overseas Americans clustered in outposts or communities. It is in and through these outposts that an important part of the American imperialistic design is carried out. By observing these people in their day-to-day existence, we can witness the actual working out of the imperialistic process. We are able to ascertain, for example, that no matter how grand the plan, the Americans at a particular outpost in a guerilla war zone have been

187

frustrated in their pacification of the countryside. Or we are able to learn that a group of Peace Corpsmen, contrary to the intention of the organization they represent, are creating an unfavorable image of the United States in a particular Latin American country.

In constructing their "Gauge of Success," Cleveland and his associates show that they are aware that technical skill and strong motivation ("belief in mission") are not the only factors associated with the successful performance of an overseas mission. In citing "cultural empathy" and "a sense for politics" as desirable traits in the able overseasman, they intimate that the problem of adaptation is closely related to the performance of missions abroad.[1] If we speak then of the adaptation of Americans at a particular foreign outpost, we are referring to one element in the performance of their missions and therefore to one aspect of the imperialistic process as it is being worked out in a foreign setting. In functional terms, we may refer to the adaptive functions of individuals or of overseas communities.[2] In this book we have been concerned with both the individual and collective adaptive functions of a group of American sojourners.

We have phrased the problem of adaptation abroad in terms of the encounter with strangerhood. The essence of the stranger's experience is *anomie*. Regardless of the foreign country to which a person migrates, we surmise that he is likely to experience, first, the condition of normlessness or meaninglessness (acute *anomie*) and later, the condition of value contradiction or conflict (simple *anomie*). Depending on his sensitivity and his ability to tolerate such conditions, he will tend to experience stranger anxiety. This anxiety will then become a more or less significant motivating factor in his overseas life. It will persist until he finds or works out an acceptable role which eliminates *anomie* and enables him to feel at home in the foreign situation. Essentially, the stranger's problem is to locate himself in the foreign setting in a way which is satisfactory to him and to his hosts. To use a sea-borne analogy, he must throw out psychological anchors which position him securely in a sea of *anomie*.

Since anxiety tends to interfere with effective functioning, it would, in the case of the stranger, work against his adaptation. The stranger's adaptive progress, therefore, may be measured in terms of the amount of *anomie* and associated anxiety he experiences or, conversely, in terms of the effectiveness of efforts to avoid or eliminate these experiences and to extricate himself from the condition of strangerhood. How may it be accomplished? Before reviewing the alternatives which have been set forth especially in Chapter 9 ("Keys to Adaptation"), it would be wise to recall that we are concerned here with representatives of an imperial power, most of whom must retain their primary identification with the home society if they are to perform their missions adequately. If they are spies, for example, they ought not to be the kind of person who is psychologically mobile enough to sell himself to the highest bidder as in some recent cases of espionage.[3] The alternative available to the bona fide immigrant is not usually available to the representative of an imperial power. They cannot "go native" and stay that way. Of course there is no guarantee that people who are "sent" abroad on imperialist missions will retain a primary allegiance to their home country. If enough of them were to give up this allegiance we might no longer be able to discern any imperialistic process at all. It is our hunch, however, that the vast majority of Americans who go overseas today do not have open to them the orienting option of giving up their primary identification with the United States.

It is possible that a modern American overseasman may find himself in a fortunate foreign situation which tends to minimize his experience of *anomie*. The host culture may be very compatible, the hosts very receptive to foreigners, or the stranger's power to make his own definitions prevail very great. The American may be in West Germany with plumbing similar to that found in America, in Denmark where people provide a friendly welcome to foreigners, or in Okinawa where American power has so far overridden native objections to the American presence. In any of these situations, anxiety will be avoided and adaptation facilitated, not through any effort by him and his overseas colleagues, but simply because he has chosen—or been sent to—a particular foreign location.

As we have seen from our discussion of the transitional man, every person possesses qualities which will permit him to feel more at home in certain cultures than in others. His personal adaptation in a foreign situation, therefore, will be partly a function of the "matching" of his transitional possibilities with the foreign setting. It will also depend on his ability to find or to develop acceptable roles on the foreign stage. Since this stage is never homogeneous, it is possible for the stranger to search the situation for roles which are most compatible to him. Finally, if he is sufficiently flexible, he can change himself in such a way as to find self-confirmation in foreign eyes. The options for personal adaptation in the foreign scene, therefore, include selection (of the most compatible foreign location), searching out (the most compatible sector of the host society), and changing oneself in such a way as to feel at home abroad.

If there are colleagues from home in the foreign setting one has an adaptive option not available to the lone stranger, the clump. The overseas clump can provide a collective solution to the adaptive problem by providing a social world in which home selfs are readily confirmed and stranger anxiety (produced, perhaps, by lone ventures into the foreign world) allayed. A sojourner can seal himself off more or less effectively from foreign experience if he and his family, his friends, or community are capable of constructing congenial and adaptive clumps. As we have seen from our investigation of the Americans in Ciudad Condal, the mere presence of colleagues does not mean that a clump which reduces stranger anxiety instead of reflecting or heightening it will be formed. Where the clump exists, it must be considered as a mediating factor in the adaptive progress of the strangers who comprise it. Even as we learn to consider the personal qualities which facilitate or inhibit personal adaptation to the foreign, we must begin to investigate those which permit the stranger to join with his colleagues and those which permit the clump as a whole to survive in the foreign setting while resolving its members' problems of strangerhood. These considerations have been among the more important social-psychological questions to which we have addressed ourselves in this book.

Throughout our discussion we have maintained that an overseas representative of a powerful nation such as the United States today should be considered to represent an imperial power if his presence and actions abroad are acceptable to his home government. Even the ordinary American traveler in foreign lands carries the interests and authority of his powerful homeland with him. We think, then, that some Communists are right, although it seems to be a case of the pot calling the kettle black, in their suspicions that every overseas American is, wittingly or unwittingly, an imperialist agent. They are more likely to be wrong, however, in assuming a degree of centralization in the American foreign establishment which approaches that of one of the Communist imperialistic nations. The United States is not yet a monolithic entity either at home or abroad and American overseas interests often conflict or have little connection with each other. Nevertheless, in this summary it seems feasible to speak about the entire conglomeration of individual and organizational actions toward, or on, the overseas frontier as a unitary process even as the sociologist speaks of American society as a unitary social system. Therefore when we speak about America doing this or that abroad, we are referring to any legitimate—from the American point of view—action by Americans in this realm. And when we mention the problem of American adaptation abroad we are referring to all the various shapes and sizes of *anomie* which await Americans in all the foreign locations to which they venture. Finally, when we ask how the nation can act to solve this problem, we are concerned with all the possible actions which may be taken by those multitudinous, sometimes conflicting home organizations and individuals with interests overseas. What can an imperialistic society such as the United States do to facilitate the adaptation of its overseas agents?

Since a powerful nation with many interests in many quarters of the globe *usually* cannot allow the compatibility of foreign settings to dictate the location of its outposts, it is not able to select only those overseas locations for which its potential representatives possess transitional qualities. Large numbers of Englishmen, for example, have had to pursue missions in comparatively incompatible places such as Asia or Africa. However, each country's population includes a variety of transitional qualities which can be matched against appropriate foreign locations in order to optimize adaptive potentials. A son of an Italian immigrant to the United States may be "selected" for a mission to Italy, or a child of Catalan-American parents for a life of work in Ciudad Condal. In the United States this "matching" solution to the problem of adaptation abroad appears to be quite undeveloped. The rationalization of this procedure would involve the identification of transitional qualities for specific foreign locations in a manner similar to that used by a personnel man engaged in vocational selection. How such a rationalized procedure could be applied to individualistic, freedom-seeking American frontiersmen is difficult to conceive, but some American organizations have begun to demonstrate its application to their "captive" employees.[4]

A nation has a reservoir of more or less adaptable types in its population. There are those who have the flexibility of personality which gives them a universal adaptive potential (the bohemian, the creative man) and those whose adaptability is of a more specific kind (the transitional man). In addition, there are some (organization men, for example) who possess qualities which will enable them to clump together effectively with colleagues in a foreign setting. The supply of minimally adaptable people in a given population is the result of socialization practices and training programs for overseas assignments. Without any evidence to support our contention, we would argue that different nations have different percentages of adaptable people in their population reservoirs. It would be extremely interesting to know if and how their adaptive needs abroad are reflected in the size of these reservoirs, and consequently, in the socialization and training practices which produce them.

In the United States, expanding overseas interests of businesses, the Peace Corps, and the Department of State appear to have been related to the development of special training programs for overseas assignments.[5] Further, a number of organizations are making attempts to select adaptable people for foreign missions.[6] There even have been some attempts to identify the kind of socialization pattern which produces an adaptable person. Unfortunately, empirically based knowledge about the relationship between personality and adaptation abroad is so rudimentary that a personnel man may consider himself fortunate if he exceeds chance expectations in predicting successful adaptation. Part of the reason for the low estate of our knowledge in this area may derive from inadequate conceptualization. It may be that people up against the practical problem of predicting success overseas cannot permit themselves the luxury of thinking through the problem of adaptation systematically. In this book, no practical considerations such as these have blocked our way.

Finally, a nation can help its representatives abroad to adapt by providing the kind of support which will assist them in coping with the foreign situation. We have referred to the power and prestige which representatives of an imperial power carry with them to help make their definitions prevail in a foreign setting. Large financial resources also can "buy" adaptation, up to a point, for some overseasmen. The United States has been accused of trying to "buy" its way around the world. The prejudice against such a technique of adaptation should not be allowed to obscure its effectiveness in some situations. If, for example, a man is provided with a suitable housing allowance by his company, he may be able to acquire the comparatively modern dwelling which will permit his wife to feel at least minimally at home on her new domestic rounds. Without this financial support he might have to contend with a demoralized wife as well as his own stranger anxiety.

At home one's style of life is more or less dependent on familiar artifacts. Modern conveniences and appliances which provide points of reference on the home scene might not ordinarily be available in a foreign location. But a beneficent nation can make them available to its *anomie*-threatened representatives. Arrangements can be made to see that a particular American family has an American refrigerator filled with food and drink from a local PX in its kitchen to minimize stranger anxiety. In Ciudad Condal we saw the dependence of some families, especially some of those working for the government, on material support from home. If we may generalize this dependence to all government people abroad—a group which comprises the largest category of Americans overseas—we would be entitled to conclude that the United States might not be able to maintain more than a fraction of its present overseas force at the current level of effectiveness without providing it with large-scale material support.

Material aid may be augmented by assistance from home in building overseas organizations which can act as a focus for clumping and a screen against the foreign environment. On a large American military base overseas one encounters a complete set of prefabricated American institutions which have been established and maintained with assistance from home. Not only have the foundations for the social structure of such an overseas clump been pre-programmed at home, but the basic pattern for the transactions which are to take place between the clump and the hosts may have been explored earlier by experts and worked out rationally in higher level negotiations between governments. The position of go-between may have been developed to handle important inter-group transactions according to formulae detailed in some formal contractual agreement. The stranger who comes to such an enclave finds himself dependent on such specialists, on the prior negotiations, and on the institutional "package" sent out from home to organize his particular outpost. The costs in personal freedom which may be paid when one lives in such a standardized enclave may be more than offset for the individual by the protection against stranger *anomie* which it is able to offer.

In Ciudad Condal, the American community was provided with very little organizational support from the United States. Only the Cultural Institute, supported in part by U.S.I.S. funds, and the Consulate General, established and maintained by the Department of State, could provide home-supported foci for communal life. Although PX items were available to government people from nearby locations and although families connected with large organizations had been able to bring familiar household appliances with them at company or department expense, the amount of material support from home available to Condal Americans was insignificant when compared with that of the American community in Madrid. Some Americans in Ciudad Condal were wealthy enough to "buy" a portion of their adaptation, but others, struggling to survive financially, found themselves exposed to the starker aspects of a foreign existence. On the whole this community was not able to tap more than modest economic resources to sustain itself in the foreign setting. It could, and did, give rise to miscalculations by the hosts, who liked to think that all Americans were *millonarios,* and, consequently, additional *anomie* for the Americans.

The power and prestige which supported the American presence in a city like Madrid was much more impressive than in Ciudad Condal. We have noted that the Condal city was not a first-line American outpost and that it did not attract organizations and individuals of the highest rank. We also have remarked the reluctance of the hosts to grant the Americans (or any other foreigners) a privileged status. But some Americans in the city had more power than others. In general, a representative of an American organization carried more actual power with him into this foreign situation than an unattached individual. The higher the rank of his organization in international terms, the easier it was for an affiliated person to make his definitions prevail in his own adaptive progress. The representative of Flyaway Airways, for example, had fewer difficulties with the local government than the individualistic editor of the *Condal Courier.* Taken as a whole, however, the Condal Americans were not well-connected to sources of power and prestige. The comparatively high percentage of unattached Americans in the city, combined with the usually modest ranking of the American organizations represented there, tended to reduce the leverage of these overseasmen in their transactions with hosts who were capable of being impressed by very great power, prestige, or wealth.

The Americans in the city, in a moderately incompatible foreign setting, appeared to be receiving much less support from home than the Americans in two other overseas communities investigated by the author. The enormous resources which stood behind Americans

in Madrid and in the Scandinavian capital city were not available to
stave off stranger anxiety among the Condal Americans, who were
much more dependent on their own personal and collective resources in working out their adaptation. What were these resources
and how did they work for and against adaptation in the city?

Had a sophisticated overseas personnel man been apprised of the
fact that the majority of American adults on their way to Ciudad
Condal at the time of the study (54 of 75 who provided adequate
data) had prior overseas experience, he might have predicted a
successful adaptive fate for this American overseas community. We
know now that as far as this population was concerned he would
have been in error in assuming that *any* previous overseas experience would prove to be beneficial for adaptation in this Spanish
setting. But his prediction could have stood on other grounds. A
smaller majority of the Americans (42 of 75 reporting) had presumably cultivated transitional qualities for this foreign location by
earlier residence in less rationalized countries. (Such people, it will
be recalled, were more likely to be well-adapted, i.e., "feel more at
home," in the city.) The expert might have been only slightly less
sanguine about the adaptive fate of these Americans if he had
known that a few of those with experience in less rationalized
cultures had tended to confine themselves within the boundaries of
great American enclaves.

Besides transitional resources indicated by prior residence in less
rationalized countries, the Americans in the city could have resorted
to their own personal flexibility to assist them in their adaptation.
But this resource seems to have been in relatively short supply
among them. Our difficulty in locating examples of Thomas' two
adaptive types of personality, the bohemian and the creative man,
suggests that there was a large element of the philistine in this
overseas population. Thus, speaking of personal resources likely to
facilitate individualistic adaptation, we find that the Condal Americans appear to have been characterized more by "transitability" than
by flexibility.

A successful solution to the adaptive problem by means of the
clumping process does not appear to have been a feasible alternative for this group of American strangers. We hypothesized that

their failure to clump together cohesively as a community, and thus create a screen against stranger *anomie,* was principally the result of a heterogeneous population with a weak concentration of organization men. In addition, ineffective leadership by those organization people who usually assume the responsibility for organizing an American community abroad (those working for the government) conspired to reduce further the possibility that these Americans would form a highly adaptive clump. Instead their community tended to reflect rather than alleviate the anxieties derived from foreign experience. The complex selective process which led to the migration of this small group of Americans to this particular foreign location produced a population "mix" which, without much external support, could not serve as a basis for an adaptive clump. Beyond turning to their families and small cliques to cope with the foreign, the Condal Americans showed little indication of the kind of resources which would have permitted them to develop a collective solution to the problem of adaptation in the city.

The inability of the Condal Americans to clump together and the intra- and inter-communal difficulties attending this failure placed a heavier burden of adaptive responsibility on each individual. Among these characteristically individualistic Americans it was not difficult, especially among the businessmen, to find people who welcomed such a challenge. Such individuals tended to assume an active posture vis-a-vis the problem of adaptation. Almost without exception, they believed that it was incumbent upon them to mix in the host society and take on host ways. But there were also passive individualists who believed that it was up to the hosts or other Americans to come to them, to give them special consideration, and to help them through their adaptive difficulties. This group and a substantial portion of the organization men in the community appear to have been dependent on the initiative and support of outside agencies for handling overseas life. To use a colloquial expression which pertains especially to the military, they expected to be fed.

As we would expect, it was not the passive but the active Americans who attained positions of leadership among their colleagues in Ciudad Condal. As far as adaptive styles are concerned, these people fell into two camps. On the one hand, the more numerous entrepreneurs (businessmen) tended to favor a doctrine of individual responsibility. On the other, the organization people (from the Consulate General and Cultural Institute) tended to believe that overseas life must be pursued in and through a well organized enclave. The conflict was being won by the entrepreneurs, not only because they were more numerous and experienced, having lived longer in the city, but because the other side was so demoralized. Thus the adaptive style of this community tended to reflect the preferences of its entrepreneurial leadership, but a sizeable group of Americans were opposed to this style of adaptation. They would have preferred some organizational solution to their adaptive problems. Given more effective leadership and greater support from home, this "minority" group might have been able to make its style prevail.

In sum, this overseas community failed to perform its adaptive function more successfully because its members could not agree on an adaptive style. The old fashioned frontiersmen (active, individualistic entrepreneurs) in the community were content to leave the problems of adaptation up to the individual. But many others would have preferred external support and/or a collective solution. Unfortunately for the latter group, they were not powerful enough to make their views prevail. Without much external support and without sufficient personal resources to build an effective clump, they found themselves forced in the direction of what was for them an alien style of adaptation. We have suggested that part of the bitterness which was so evident in this community was derived from the feeling by some that they had been "let down" by their colleagues in a strange place. Not enough people felt that they were getting the kind of help they needed for the style of adaptation they wanted to follow. In the case of the frontiersmen this "help" simply may have involved being let alone.

In *The Ugly American,* Lederer and Burdick have given us a picture of the type of overseas community which they think will be able to prosecute an American imperialistic design for under-developed countries especially. In such a community there would be no

PX, no private automobiles, no luxurious living quarters, and no in-grown "social" life. The members of the community would know the local language and mix with the local population. They would be capable of enduring the hardships of a difficult foreign existence with little support from their colleagues and very little material and organizational support from home. Like the Peace Corpsmen, they would have been recruited by a stress on the challenge of an assignment overseas.[7]

The kind of people Lederer and Burdick want to man America's overseas outposts appear to conform to Thomas' description of the creative man. These overseasmen, favoring the individualistic mode of adaptation, might spend as much or more time with their hosts as with their colleagues. In our study of Americans in Ciudad Condal we found a few individuals who were cut to this pattern. People of this type may constitute a vanishing breed of American. The shadow of the large organization falls increasingly over our lives, and the pursuit of material well-being becomes of greater importance to us all. Why should the requirements associated with organization life and affluence, so important in our society at home, not extend to imperial America's outposts abroad? Even now, such values pervade the lives of the most numerous group of overseas Americans, the government people; and there is evidence to indicate that traditionally individualistic, insecure spheres of overseas life such as business, art, and scholarship are coming under their influence. The businessman is more likely now than in the past to be connected with a large, affluent, American or host company; and the erstwhile starving artist or scholar is likely to find himself working under a sizeable grant from some bureaucratized organization. More rapid communication, more rationalized controls which involve increasing integration of home and overseas operations, and the evident pursuit by many host nations of American or modern values all conspire to structure American life abroad increasingly in terms of the home pattern. Even as it does not seem possible to turn the clock back on the organization man at home, as William Whyte urges us to do,[8] it seems equally difficult to turn it back in the overseas realm at the behest of Lederer and Burdick.

For better or worse then, the future of American imperialism, as

Cleveland and his associates intimate,[9] appears to lie with the large organization and the type of person who has learned its ways. We believe that American overseas representatives will find themselves increasingly subject to bureaucratic controls which reach out directly to them from home or indirectly through the overseas enclave. As Byrnes found in his study of American technical assistants abroad, adaptation to the requirements of an often myopic American bureaucracy can become a significant problem for overseas agents.[10] In Ciudad Condal, we saw that Americans in many sectors of community life were subject to the directives of some large organization. Such controls were not entirely frustrating. We cannot forget that the large organization, by providing a stable point of reference, can fend off *anomie* and therefore contribute to the adaptation of its overseas representatives. In the future, successful adaptation overseas probably will be measured as much in terms of coping with the home bureaucracy as with the foreign environment and its bureaucracy. If this is true, bureaucratic theory, rather than stranger theory, may provide the logical taking off point for studies of Americans abroad.

The demand for organization men overseas, however, will stem not only from the growth of American bureaucratic controls on the foreign frontier. Some Americans abroad have been charged with the task of Americanizing or modernizing their hosts. A measure of success in such an undertaking is, according to Cleveland and his associates, the ability to create viable American-style organizations in the host society.[11] As we saw in Ciudad Condal, the construction of such organizations out of Spanish or Catalan human material could entail considerable frustration for an American. We believe that it would not be possible for a man to endure persistent and severe frustrations of this kind if he did not believe in the ways of the large organization. Thus the "demand" for rational structures in foreign societies will continue to require the selection of organization men to build them.

As the large organization with its various national flavors proliferates by direct or indirect Western intervention in societies where American interests obtain, more and more Americans overseas will have to cope with it. The overseas frontiers will be increasingly made up of structures which, according to Useem, are "rational, secular, open-ended, developmental, and modern-oriented." [12] Americans overseas will be required to handle not only their own bureaucracy, but help to create others for their hosts, and adapt to still others which develop out of contact with Western culture. Americans being Americans, we would expect them to create some kind of overseas division of labor to prosecute their different tasks. Perhaps creative organization men would specialize in direct transactions with hosts and philistines in attending primarily to the requirements of the American bureaucracy. Most of these people would live in more or less permeable, prefabricated, home-supported enclaves which would provide basic orientations even for satellite individualists. Where such communities would be located would depend on a number of factors, principally the power of the United States and its representatives in each foreign setting.

To say simply that Americans abroad and some of their hosts inhabit a "Third Culture" may tend to obscure the often complex transactions which lead to the positioning of an overseas community somewhere in limbo between home and host cultures. It also may convey the mistaken impression that most American overseasmen acquire a political allegiance to a "Third Culture" when, in fact, they have not given up their conscious or unconscious commitment to the United States and its overseas interests. As we saw in Ciudad Condal, overseas Americans may change their ways, but they are unlikely to give up their primary allegiance to the United States. For them and for their overseas colleagues who maintain such an allegiance, biographical fates will be increasingly tied up with the historical fate of the United States in the overseas realm. We assume that, after the fashion of other imperialisms, American imperialism will wax and wane. Our study of Americans in Ciudad Condal will permit us at some future time to look back at the imperialist process as it was being worked out by both individualistic and organizational frontiersmen in one foreign setting when the United States was, perhaps, at the height of its imperial power.

APPENDIX

I. *Schedule-Interview Given to Cross-Section of Informants in Ciudad Condal*

1. Name
2. Age
3. Marital Status and Dates
4. Kind of Dwelling and Location
5. Status, age, and present home of family members.
6. Religious Affiliation and Church Attended in Ciudal Condal.
7. Date when last in U. S.
8. Date plan next to return to U. S.
9. Foreign countries Lived and Traveled in.
10. List of Jobs, Employers, and Dates.
11. Description of Job in Ciudad Condal.
12. Knowledge of Spanish, Catalan, and When Acquired.
13. Newspapers and Magazines Read in Ciudad Condal.
14. Associational Memberships in Ciudad Condal.
15. Main Interests and Activities.
16. Shopping Places
17. Children's Schools
18. Daily Meal Schedule.
19. List of Close Friends (Nationalities, Jobs) in Ciudad Condal.
20. Activities with Close Friends.
21. Reasons for coming to Ciudad Condal ("How did you come to come here?")
22. Arrival in Ciudad Condal ("Could you tell me about your arrival here?")
23. Attitude toward Ciudad Condal ("How do you find Ciudad Condal now?")
24. Attitude towards Hosts ("How do you find the local people here?")

25. Attitude towards Americans ("How do you find the Americans here?")
26. Attitude towards the States ("How do the States look to you from here?")
27. Comparison of Self and Situation Now with that for Pre-Emigration Period ("Could you compare yourself and your life now with yourself and your life in the last stable period before you came here?")
28. Comparison of Aspects of Self and Life now with those for Pre-Emigration Period.
    a. Self Consciousness ("Are you more conscious, less conscious, or just as conscious of yourself now as before you came here?")
    b. Relaxed.
    c. Punctual.
    d. Keeping Word.
    e. Mentally Active.
    f. Quality of Work.
    g. Physical Health.
    h. Drinking.
    i. Smoking.
    j. Speed of Subjective Time.
    k. Feeling of Being at Home.
    l. Feeling of Frustration or Exasperation.
    m. Self-Confidence.
    n. Concern with Orderliness.
    o. Giving Way to Feelings.
    p. Trust in Others.
    q. "Sociability."
    r. Feelings of Uncertainty.
    s. Curiosity.
    t. Concerned about Being Cold.
    u. Involvement with Family.
    v. Busy.

II. *Self Sufficiency* (S) *and Tolerance of Ambiguity* (T)
Items Given to Cross-Section of Informants in Ciudad
Condal

(T) 1. I would prefer to have a teacher who neglects me and leaves
me to my own devices rather than one who continually
watches me and makes suggestions.
__Agree __Probably Agree __Undecided __Probably Dis-
agree __Disagree

(S) 2. I would prefer to learn by class or group discussion rather
than by reading a good book on the subject in my own time.
__Agree __Probably Agree __Undecided __Probably Dis-
agree __Disagree

(T) 3. Nobody can have feelings of love and hate towards the same
person.
__Agree __Probably Agree __Undecided __Probably Dis-
agree __Disagree

(S) 4. I often feel that I must discuss something I've read before I
will really understand or remember it.
__Agree __Probably Agree __Undecided __Probably Dis-
agree __Disagree

(T) 5. The best leaders give specific enough instructions so that
those under them have nothing to worry about.
__Agree __Probably Agree __Undecided __Probably Dis-
agree __Disagree

(S) 6. I like to do my planning alone without suggestions from or
discussions with other people.
__Agree __Probably Agree __Undecided __Probably Dis-
agree __Disagree

(T) 7. It is better to keep on with the present method of doing
things than to take a way that might lead to chaos.
__Agree __Probably Agree __Undecided __Probably Dis-
agree __Disagree

(S) 8. I usually can solve a problem better by studying it alone
rather than by discussing it with others.
__Agree __Probably Agree __Undecided __Probably Dis-
agree __Disagree

(T) 9. A man can be well informed even if there are many subjects upon which he does not have a definite opinion.

__Agree __Probably Agree __Undecided __Probably Disagree __Disagree

(S) 10. When I must make a number of decisions in a comparatively short time, I prefer to make them alone rather than with the help of others.

__Agree __Probably Agree __Undecided __Probably Disagree __Disagree

(T) 11. It is better to take a chance on being a failure than to let your life get into a rut.

__Agree __Probably Agree __Undecided __Probably Disagree __Disagree

(S) 12. I like working alone.

__Agree __Probably Agree __Undecided __Probably Disagree __Disagree

(T) 13. It is always better to have a definite course of action than to be vacillating among several possibilities.

__Agree __Probably Agree __Undecided __Probably Disagree __Disagree

(S) 14. It bothers me to have someone offer me advice when I didn't ask for it.

__Agree __Probably Agree __Undecided __Probably Disagree __Disagree

(S) 15. It helps me to discuss a problem with others before coming to a decision.

__Agree __Probably Agree __Undecided __Probably Disagree __Disagree

(S) 16. If I had to carry through some project I would prefer to work with a committee of able interested people rather than on my own with one or two assistants to follow me.

__Agree __Probably Agree __Undecided __Probably Disagree __Disagree

*17. I am always looking for new things to do or see or hear.

__Agree __Probably Agree __Undecided __Probably Disagree __Disagree

*Filler item.

NOTES

Preface

1. See, e.g., W. I. Thomas and Florian Znaniecki, *The Polish Peasant in Europe and America* (New York: Alfred Knopf, 1927); W. L. Warner and Leo Srole, *The Social Systems of American Ethnic Groups* (New Haven: Yale University Press, 1945).

2. See, e.g., Richard Centers, "Occupational Mobility of Urban Occupational Strata," *American Sociological Review*, vol. 13 (April 1948), pp. 197–203; Ely Chinoy, *Automobile Workers and the American Dream* (New York: Doubleday and Co., 1955); S. M. Lipset and N. Rogoff, *Social Mobility in an Industrial Society* (Berkeley: University of California Press, 1959).

3. Samuel Stouffer and others, *The American Soldier* (Princeton: Princeton University Press, 1949).

4. See, e.g., A. I. Hallowell, *Culture and Experience* (Philadelphia: University of Pennsylvania Press, 1955), Part IV, pp. 307–366; George Spindler, "Socio-cultural and Psychological Processes in Menomenee Acculturation," *University of California Publications in Culture and Society*, vol. 5 (Berkeley: University of California Press, 1955).

5. Anthony F. C. Wallace, *Culture and Personality* (New York: Random House, 1961).

6. Georg Simmel, in *The Sociology of Georg Simmel*, ed. Kurt Wolff (Glencoe, Ill.: The Free Press, 1950), pp. 402–406.

7. Alfred Schutz, "The Stranger: An Essay in Social Psychology," *American Journal of Sociology*, vol. 49 (May 1944), pp. 499–507.

8. S. N. Herman and E. O. Schild, "The Stranger Group in a Cross-cultural Situation," *Sociometry*, vol. 24 (August 1961), pp. 165–176; Dennison Nash and Alvin Wolfe, "The Stranger in Laboratory Culture," *American Sociological Review*, vol. 22 (August 1957), pp. 149–167; Jerold Heiss and Dennison Nash, "The Stranger in Laboratory Culture Revisited," *Human Organization*, vol. 26 (Spring/

Summer 1967), pp. 47–51; Dennison Nash and Jerold Heiss, "Sources of Anxiety in Laboratory Stranger," *Sociological Quarterly,* vol. 8 (April 1967), pp. 215–221.

9. Cuba, Puerto Rico, and Mexico.

10. We might speculate that the principal problem of individual adaptation in such communities would be related to the requirements of the American organization and enclave, not the foreign society.

11. Harlan Cleveland, Gerard Mangone, and John Adams, *The Overseas Americans* (New York: McGraw-Hill, 1960).

12. William Lederer and Eugene Burdick, *The Ugly American* (New York: W. W. Norton, 1958).

13. Described in Dennison Nash and Louis Schaw, "Personality and Adaptation in an Overseas Enclave," *Human Organization,* vol. 21 (Winter 1962–1963), pp. 252–263.

14. I had learned my lesson about institutional connections during a previous field trip when I was unable to gain the cooperation of officials in the American embassy because I represented no American organization which, presumably, could stand responsible for my actions.

15. For an analysis of the give-and-take involved in this kind of research, see Arthur Vidich, "Participant Observation and the Collection and Interpretation of Data," *American Journal of Sociology,* vol. 60 (January 1955), pp. 354–360.

16. Hortense Powdermaker includes an extensive pertinent bibliography in *Stranger and Friend: The Way of an Anthropologist* (New York: W. W. Norton, 1966), pp. 307–311.

17. Dennison Nash, "The Ethnologist as Stranger: An Essay in the Sociology of Knowledge," *Southwestern Journal of Anthropology,* vol. 19 (Summer 1963), pp. 149–167.

18. If the field worker is suffering stranger anxiety he will tend to function less effectively. The assumption here is that a person who feels at home will not experience such anxiety.

19. The gain in cultural facility over most of the Condal Americans was counteracted by my need to penetrate deeply into the host society. I probably experienced as much stranger *anomie* as did the typical American resident of Ciudad Condal.

20. The multiplication of classified or secret operations abroad will pose increasing problems for the student of Americans overseas. It is fortunate that there were no such operations in Ciudad Condal.

21. The part which travel plays as a "magic helper" is discussed in Maurice Farber, "Some Hypotheses on the Psychology of Travel," *The Psychoanalytic Review,* vol. 41 (July 1954), pp. 267–271.

1. An Outpost of American Imperialism

1. Maurice Stein, *The Eclipse of Community* (New York: Harper Torchbooks, 1964), pp. 94–113.

2. The relationship of dominance and submission (which defines the imperialistic transaction) requires, as Simmel has shown in his analysis of power, the collaboration of both parties. See Georg Simmel, in *The Sociology of Georg Simmel,* ed. Kurt Wolff (Glencoe, Ill.: The Free Press, 1950), pp. 181–186.

3. See, e.g., Nikolai Bukharin, *Imperialisms and the World Economy* (New York: International Publishers, 1929); Vladimir Lenin, *Imperialism, the Highest Stage of Capitalism* (New York: International Publishers, 1933).

4. C. Wright Mills has used the monolithic model in his analysis of power in American society. See C. Wright Mills, *The Power Elite* (New York: Oxford University Press, 1956). He opposes the "balance of forces" model used, e.g., in John K. Galbraith, *American Capitalism: The Concept of Countervailing Power* (Boston: Houghton Mifflin, 1962).

5. See A. P. Thornton, *The Imperial Idea and Its Enemies* (New York: Macmillan, 1959).

6. A longitudinal study of this tendency is reported in S. N. Herman and E. O. Schild, "The Stranger Group in Cross-Cultural Perspective," *Sociometry,* vol. 24 (1961), pp. 165–176.

7. See E. M. Forster, *Passage to India* (New York: Harcourt, Brace and World, 1924); George Orwell, *Burmese Days* (New York: Harcourt, Brace and World, 1934).

8. See, e.g., P. Mercier, "The European Community in Dakar," in *Africa,* P. Van den Berghe, ed. (San Francisco: Chandler, 1965), pp. 283–300; R. E. S. Tanner, "Conflict within Small European Communities in Tanganyika," *Human Organization,* 24 (Winter 1964), pp. 319–327.

9. *Statistical Abstract of the United States,* 1965, p. 9.

10. *Economic Almanac,* 1964, p. 480.

11. Ibid., p. 479.

12. See, e.g., Daniel Lerner, *The Passing of Traditional Society* (Glencoe, Ill.: The Free Press, 1958).

13. *Statistical Abstract of the United States*, 1964, p. 210.

14. *Newsweek*, March 8, 1965, pp. 67–73; *Survey of Current Business*, August 1963, p. 18.

15. The Lincoln Brigade, for example.

16. *Statistical Abstract of the United States*, 1964, p. 258.

17. *Overseas Business Reports*, U. S. Dept. of Commerce, Dec. 1963.

18. *Economic Almanac*, 1964, p. 478.

19. Ibid.

20. "Economic Developments in Spain," *Economic Reports*, World Trade Information Service, 1960.

21. An ecological analysis of these developments in Ciudad Condal may be found in Francisco Ivern, *Hospitalet de Lobregat*, monograficos sociologicas, seccion de sociologia del centro de estudios economicos, juridicos, y sociales del consejo superior de investigaciones cientificas (Barcelona, 1960).

22. The city is easy to identify. By using another name to refer to it we simply are trying to minimize non-scholarly preoccupations. It is sometimes referred to as Ciudad Condal or the Condal City. It is a real name, but not the usual one.

23. H. J. Chaytor, *A History of Aragon and Catalonia* (London: Methuen, 1933), p. 41.

24. See, e.g., Malcolm Cowley, *Exiles Return* (New York: Norton, 1934); Ernest Hemingway, *A Moveable Feast* (New York: Charles Scribner's Sons, 1964).

25. Chapter 4 includes a discussion of overseas family life.

26. Frederick Jackson Turner, *The Frontier in American History* (New York: Holt, Rinehart and Winston, 1920).

27. David Riesman, *The Lonely Crowd* (New Haven: Yale University Press, 1950); William Whyte, Jr., *The Organization Man* (New York: Simon and Schuster, 1956).

28. See, e.g., Semour M. Lipset, "A Changing American Character?" in *Culture and Social Character: The Work of David Riesman Reviewed*, S. Lipset and L. Lowenthal, eds. (Glencoe, Ill.: The Free Press, 1961), Chapter 3.

29. *Statistical Abstract of the United States*, 1965, p. 9.

30. In the absence of more adequate means to identify such types we are using the rather crude system of Fellin and Litwak. See Phillip

Fellin and Eugene Litwak, "Neighborhood Cohesion and Mobility," *American Sociological Review,* 28 (June 1965), pp. 364–376. We are aware that some people in large organizations, particularly the top leadership, are entrepreneurial characters.

31. William Lederer and Eugene Burdick, *The Ugly American* (New York: W. W. Norton, 1958).

32. This point is developed further in Dennison Nash, "Adaptation Abroad: Some Considerations," *Boletin,* instituto de estudios norteamericanos barcelona, 11 (primavera 1965), pp. 48–53.

33. Schlesinger points out that not all people on the frontier adapted successfully. See Arthur M. Schlesinger, "What Then Is the American, This New Man?" *American Historical Review,* 48 (January 1943), pp. 225–244.

2. Entrance of the Guests

1. The principal source for the pre-Roman and Roman periods is H. J. Chaytor, *A History of Aragon and Catalonia* (London: Methuen, 1933), pp. 1–15; see also F. J. Wiseman, *Roman Spain* (London: Bell, 1956).

2. Ibid., p. 159.

3. Information was obtained from interviews and, in the case of the anthropologist, personal experience.

4. In cases where housing may not be immediately available (as on a military base), more sophisticated organizations recommend this procedure. For example, a top executive in the overseas division of a large American corporation said, "The one way to minimize the difficulties of adaptation is for the man to go ahead of his family and make the basic arrangements for living."

5. This view of the stranger's progress is suggested in Thomas Sterling, "On Being Foreign," *Holiday,* April 1966, p. 16.

6. See Erving Goffman, *The Presentation of Self in Everyday Life* (Garden City, New York: Doubleday Anchor Book, 1959), pp. 22–30.

7. Many of the proper names, including those of these hotels, are pseudonyms.

8. Alfred Schutz, "The Stranger: An Essay in Social Psychology," *American Journal of Sociology,* 49 (May 1944), p. 502.

9. Ibid., p. 503.

10. John Gillen, "National and Regional Cultural Values in the United States," *Social Forces,* 34 (December 1955), p. 108.

11. The realization of the problem of strangerhood may be a culture-related trait. We would suggest that some cultures tend to produce more rigid, insensitive personalities who are not as quick to recognize the incompatibilities in the foreign scene.

12. The ranks of the officials were: consul general, consul, vice consul, and consular assistant. They did not belong exclusively to the consular service. With the exception of one officer in the USIS, all held career appointments in the Department of State. As Ilchman has pointed out, the effective fusion of the American diplomatic and consular services had been completed by 1939. Now it is customary for the Foreign Service Officer to receive a dual commission and serve in both embassies and consulates. See Warren Ilchman, *Professional Diplomacy in the United States 1779–1939* (Chicago: University of Chicago Press, 1961), pp. 187–243; see also Charles Thayer, *Diplomat* (New York: Harper, 1959), pp. 130–132.

13. The principal challenge to the western conception of the diplomat as a sacred personage has been offered by the United States and, possibly, the Soviet Union. The American conception makes the diplomat more open, equal, and responsible to the public and its representatives in Congress. The "sacred" conception has not, however, been eliminated from the American diplomat's public image. Until recently, a disproportionate number of American diplomatic (not consular) officials came from the American "aristocracy." Today, even though the professionalization of the service is rather complete, both "sacred" and "secular" conceptions pervade this bureaucratic role. See Thayer, pp. 64–80.

14. James Baldwin, *Nobody Knows My Name* (New York: Dell, 1961), pp. 17–23.

15. Ernest Hemingway, *Death in the Afternoon* (New York: Charles Scribner's Sons, 1932), pp. 150–154.

16. Schutz, p. 502.

17. This impression was gained from interviews with a number of Americans (including those in Ciudad Condal) who had traveled in France.

3. Nesting

1. Nash and Berger have used this term in Dennison Nash and Peter Berger, "Church Commitment in an American Suburb: An Analysis of the Decision to Join," *Archives de Sociologie des Religions,* No.

13 (1962), pp. 105–120. Perhaps the most complete description of this phenomenon is given in John Seeley, R. Sim, and E. Loosley, *Crestwood Heights* (New York: Basic Books, 1956).

2. From 1890 to 1960 the percentage of married males increased approximately 17 percent. The percentage of females who were married increased approximately 11 percent. See Clifford Kirkpatrick, *The Family as Process and Institution,* 2nd ed. (New York: Ronald Press, 1955), p. 414. The rising standard of living can be measured in terms of the increasing median income in constant dollars. See, e.g., *Statistical Abstract of the United States,* 1965, p. 342.

3. Unfortunately, we do not have satisfactory data concerning the representativeness of Americans overseas in regard to these factors.

4. Such a program had produced "blocks" of American houses at the air base inland. The construction of homes for American Military in England is discussed in Clancy Sigal, "The American G.I. in Britain," *Encounter,* February 1960, pp. 30–47.

5. Some opening payments were refunded; some were not.

6. This expression or its equivalent and associated meaning does not seem to be confined to Spanish-speaking countries. It may simply be a product of the looser conception of time in less modern societies.

7. Comments of a number of Americans who have been abroad in various parts of the world seem to indicate that the maid is a fascinating topic for American women in many overseas places.

8. See Louise Winfield, *Living Overseas* (Washington, D. C.: Public Affairs Press, 1962), pp. 41–58.

9. Ibid., p. 41.

10. Bernard Malamud has written a humorous short story about an American's endless problems with his Italian maid. See "The Maid's Shoes" in *Idiots First* (New York: Farrar, Straus, 1963), pp. 153–170.

11. We use the word here in the sense of estrangement from self, body, others, etc. Many writers have dealt with the alienated state of modern man. See, e.g., Erich Fromm, *The Sane Society* (New York: Rinehart, 1955). We are arguing here that Americans have become accustomed to their alienated state and tend to be disturbed by the less alienated life conditions found in most foreign countries.

12. J. L. Castillo Puche, *Paralelo 40* (Barcelona: Ediciones Destino, 1963), p. 13.

13. John W. Masland and Laurence I. Radway, *Soldiers and Scholars* (Princeton: Princeton University Press, 1957), p. 243.

14. This observation was made by the same physician-informant who was quoted in this chapter.

4. *The Domestic Side of a Foreign Existence*

1. See, e.g., Joseph Conrad, *Lord Jim* (Garden City, N. Y.: Doubleday, 1920).

2. E. M. Forster, *Passage to India* (New York: Harcourt, Brace and World, 1924); George Orwell, *Burmese Days* (New York: Harcourt, Brace and World, 1924).

3. Louise Winfield, *Living Overseas* (Washington, D. C.: Public Affairs Press, 1962), p. 107.

4. *Statistical Abstract of the United States,* 1965, p. 9.

5. Harlan Cleveland, Gerard Mangone, and John Adams, *The Overseas Americans* (New York: McGraw-Hill, 1960), pp. 46–63.

6. These estimates are derived from a scrutiny of all published lists of Americans in Ciudad Condal and from personal acquaintance with Americans in and around the city. They are loose estimates at best.

7. James Jones, *From Here to Eternity* (New York: Charles Scribner's Sons, 1951).

8. J. L. Castillo Puche, *Paralelo 40* (Barcelona: Ediciones Destino, 1963).

9. The anthropologist visited this bar two or three evenings a week over the course of several months and encountered no resident Americans there.

10. This conclusion was reached from conversations with a number of Americans who have lived abroad.

11. In the middle and upper classes.

12. Winfield, p. 96.

13. The phenomenon of cohesiveness is treated extensively in Chapter 7.

14. Cartwright and Zander point out that if *pleasant* interaction is heightened, cohesiveness tends to increase. See Dorwin Cartwright and Alvin Zander, *Group Dynamics* (Evanston, Ill.: Row, Peterson and Co., 1953), p. 81.

15. We take Whyte's description of Park Forest to represent the American custom. See William Whyte, Jr., *The Organization Man* (Garden City, N. Y.: Doubleday Anchor Book, 1957), pp. 310–329.

16. The longest *fiestas* occurred from before Christmas to Epiphany and during Easter week, but other *fiesta* days were liberally sprinkled throughout the year.

17. Williams points to "activity and work" as a dominant value in American culture. See Robin Williams, Jr., *American Society: A Sociological Interpretation*, 2nd rev. ed. (New York: Knopf, 1960), pp. 421-424.

18. *Social Usage in the Foreign Service*, Dept. of State (Washington, D. C., June 1957), p. 16.

19. The conception of the lady which we have in mind probably originated in the Middle Ages. See Morton M. Hunt, *The National History of Love* (New York: A Black Cat Book), 1959, pp. 131-191.

20. Ibid., pp. 132-139. See also, Denis de Rougemont, *Love in the Western World* (Garden City, N. Y.: Doubleday Anchor Book, 1957), pp. 68-69.

21. *Social Usage in the Foreign Service*, Foreword.

22. This problem is similar to the one discussed in Betty Friedan, *The Feminine Mystique* (New York: W. W. Norton, 1963).

23. A more general discussion of sex role conflict of which this is a specific case may be found in George Simpson, *People in Families* (New York: Crowell, 1960), pp. 195-197.

24. A wife also could function as a kind of *helpmeet* by holding a job of her own, but the opportunities for acceptable employment were more limited in the city than in the United States. Only a few American wives held full- or part-time jobs (as teachers).

25. See Chapter 8. See also *Working Abroad*, Report 41, Group for the Advancement of Psychiatry (New York, Dec. 1958), pp. 510-525.

26. See, e.g., Winfield, pp. 72-94.

27. Overall, these levels probably were in fact lower, but most Americans' fears were exaggerated (at least initially). A number of clinics and hospitals were entirely acceptable—even admirable—by American standards.

28. These new roles certainly were not unique to this foreign setting.

29. The principals of the three American (or Anglo-American) schools and four teachers in the largest one.

30. It would have been necessary for the author to "know" the children not only by interviewing them, but by participating in their affairs.

31. Riesman's discussion of the American other-directed child (which may not be so new a phenomenon as he suggests) is pertinent. See David Riesman, *The Lonely Crowd* (New Haven and London: Yale University Press, 1961), pp. 45–55.

32. Unfortunately, there are no relevant data for adolescent peer groups.

33. S. N. Herman and E. O. Schild, "The Stranger Group in a Cross Cultural Situation," *Sociometry,* 24 (August 1961), pp. 165–176.

34. See John Seeley, R. Sim, and E. Loosley, *Crestwood Heights* (New York: Basic Books), 1956.

35. See, e.g., William Lederer and Eugene Burdick, *The Ugly American* (New York: W. W. Norton), 1958.

36. From interviews with officials in the Department of State and Department of Defense.

37. E.g., William D. Patterson in "Agenda for Travel," *Saturday Review,* January 7, 1967, p. 24, says, "Travel is a cultural catalyst, a sort of sociological mix master. It is an instrument of education, freedom, and peace. It stirs men to appreciate human diversity and it ventilates genuine differences within that diversity."

5. *Missions*

1. This estimate is based on a listing of offices of American firms, subsidiaries, and affiliates provided by the American Chamber of Commerce in Spain.

2. This information was obtained from informants and the government pamphlet, *Foreign Capital Investments in Spain,* 2nd ed. (Madrid: Ministry of Finance, 1963).

3. This example was constructed as an ideal-typical case from data provided by several American project managers.

4. See Ted Brennen and Frank Hodgson, *Overseas Management* (New York: McGraw-Hill, 1965).

5. The term Protestant Ethic originated with Max Weber. Whyte's use of the concept to describe a (supposedly) vanishing type of American businessman is particularly relevant here. See William Whyte, Jr., *The Organization Man* (Garden City, N. Y.: Doubleday Anchor Books, 1957).

6. See Harlan Cleveland, Gerard Mangone, and John Adams, *The Overseas Americans* (New York: McGraw-Hill, 1960), pp. 98–120.

7. Mills has offered the most extreme thesis of the growing inter-
connections between larger and larger American organizations. See C.
Wright Mills, *The Power Elite* (New York: Oxford University Press,
1956); see also Robert Presthus, *The Organizational Society* (New
York: Knopf, 1962), pp. 59–92.

8. The Useems and Donoghue argue that a binational "third culture" has arisen at the intersection of societies. This in-between culture,
according to them, functions to enable the members of the different
societies to work together. See John Useem, John Donoghue, and Ruth
Hill Useem, "Men in the Middle of the Third Culture," *Human
Organization,* 22 (Fall 1963), pp. 169–179. The Chamber of Commerce appears to have been an example of such a third culture.

9. Cleveland, Mangone, and Adams, pp. 117–118.

10. In order to identify this leadership, the author asked a number
of informants to single out the "most important" men in the community. There was unanimity about these four. Three other men who were
mentioned (but not by all informants) appear to have occupied a
lower rung on the status ladder. This leadership structure was checked
by reference to the participation of these men (and their wives) in
important community affairs.

11. Dennison Nash and Louis Schaw, "Personality and Adaptation
in an Overseas Enclave," *Human Organization,* 21 (Winter
1962–1963), p. 261.

12. Mills, loc. cit.

13. E. M. Forster, *A Passage to India* (New York: Harcourt, Brace
and World, 1924).

14. F. J. Roethlisberger and W. J. Dickson, *Management and the
Worker* (Cambridge: Harvard University Press, 1939).

15. Cleveland, Mangone, and Adams, pp. 131–135.

16. Whyte has recognized this in his concept of the "Social Ethic."
See Whyte, Jr., loc. cit.

17. Mottram Torre in Harlan Cleveland and Gerard Mangone, eds.,
The Art of Overseasmanship (Syracuse, N. Y.: Syracuse University
Press, 1957), p. 88.

18. The evidence for this hypothesis is from a small group study by
Ronald Lippit and R. K. White, "The Social Climate of Children's
Groups," in R. G. Barker, J. S. Kounin, and H. F. Wright, eds., *Child
Behavior and Development* (New York: McGraw-Hill, 1943), pp.
485–508.

19. The tendency of people in a vocational group to cluster together is discussed in Cleveland, Mangone, and Adams, p. 61.

20. Though the consular service and the diplomatic service are integrated, and though most foreign service officers have dual appointments, the tradition of the unequal importance of diplomatic and consular roles remains. See Warren Ilchman, *Professional Diplomacy: In the United States 1779–1939* (Chicago: The University of Chicago Press, 1961); Charles W. Thayer, *Diplomat* (New York: Harper, 1959), pp. 130–132.

21. Thayer, p. 132.

22. Young, eager consuls would not have sufficient seniority to head a Consulate General.

23. See Cleveland, Mangone, and Adams, pp. 83–84.

24. See Benton Johnson, "Do Holiness Sects Socialize in Dominant Values?" *Social Forces,* 39 (May 1961), pp. 309–316.

25. Leslie Palmier, "Changing Outposts: The Western Communities in Southeast Asia," *Yale Review,* 47 (March 1958), p. 405.

26. We refer to the dispute between Mills and Galbraith mentioned in the first chapter, and Mills and Riesman. For an analysis of the issues between Mills and Riesman, see William Kornhauser, "Power Elite or Veto Groups," in S. M. Lipset and Leo Lowenthal, eds., *Culture and Social Character* (Glencoe, Ill.: The Free Press, 1961), pp. 252–267.

27. Cleveland, Mangone, and Adams, pp. 140–141.

6. *Circles*

1. John Useem, John Donoghue, and Ruth Hill Useem, "Men in the Middle of the Third Culture," *Human Organization,* 22 (Fall 1963), pp. 169–179.

2. The entertainment allowance was supposed to be used primarily to promote contacts with the hosts.

3. This house was rented at the time of the study; it has since been bought by the United States government.

4. This information was obtained from interviews with the cross-section of informants which was described in the Preface.

5. Harlan Cleveland, Gerard Mangone, and John Adams, *The Overseas Americans* (New York: McGraw-Hill, 1960), p. 61.

6. We are referring here to interviews and conversations with a variety of expert informants.

7. Cleveland and his associates have alluded to such a hypothesis, but they stop short at making it explicit. See Cleveland, Mangone, and Adams, p. 51.

8. According to Cleveland and his associates, p. 61, this kind of subdivision occurs "at any sizable overseas post."

9. William Whyte, Jr., *The Organization Man* (Garden City, N. Y.: Doubleday Anchor Books, 1957), pp. 365–386.

10. We do not claim that the general working culture does not leave its mark on life in the suburbs. Whyte, ibid., has demonstrated this rather conclusively. Our hypothesis refers to the degree of autonomy of home or private life (more particularly, friendship life) from the job.

11. See Robin Williams, Jr., American Society: *A Sociological Interpretation,* 2nd ed. (New York: Knopf, 1960), pp. 417–424, 436–444, 466–468.

12. Cleveland and his associates intimate that this is true for most American communities abroad. See Cleveland, Mangone, and Adams, p. 96.

13. See, e.g., Arthur Vidich and Joseph Bensman, *Small Town in Mass Society* (Princeton: Princeton University Press, 1958).

14. This suggests that under certain conditions the prescribed sociological model for analyzing actions abroad will be derived from theories of large organizations. Unlike the situation of Americans in Ciudad Condal, the foreign encounter will scarcely require consideration.

15. Jerold Heiss, "The Dyad Views the Newcomer," *Human Relations,* 16 (1953), pp. 241–248.

7. *Community Cohesiveness and Its Sources*

1. See Dennison Nash, "The Ethnologist as a Stranger: An Essay in the Sociology of Knowledge," *Southwest Journal of Anthropology,* 19 (Summer 1963), pp. 149–167; Jerold Heiss and Dennison Nash, "The Stranger in Laboratory Culture Revisited," *Human Organization,* 26, (Spring/Summer 1967), pp. 47–51; Dennison Nash and Jerold Heiss, "Sources of Anxiety in Laboratory Strangers," *Sociological Quarterly,* 8 (Spring 1967), pp. 215–221.

2. Samuel Stouffer and others, *The American Soldier,* 2 (Princeton: Princeton University Press, 1949).

3. Stanley Schachter, *The Psychology of Affiliation* (Stanford: Stanford University Press, 1949).

4. S. N. Herman and E. O. Schild, "The Stranger Group in a

Cross-Cultural Situation," *Sociometry*, 24 (August 1961), pp. 165–176.

5. The application of this standard sociological term to the stranger situation is treated in Nash and Heiss. The term "culture shock" is a loose equivalent, but because it has not been related systematically to any body of theory and research, it is not used here.

6. Dorwin Cartwright and Alvin Zander, *Group Dynamics* (Evanston, Ill.: Row, Peterson and Co., 1953), p. 76.

7. If the usual "field of forces" conception of cohesiveness is employed, a common antipathy for the host environment may constitute a positive force for group cohesiveness. This is, in fact, our hypothesis phrased in "group dynamic" terms. Ibid., p. 79.

8. A precedent for using a voluntary association of strangers to stand for, and provide the key to the analysis of, a foreign enclave may be found in Leonard Broom and J. Kituse, "The Validation of Acculturation: A Condition of Ethnic Assimilation," *American Anthropologist*, 57 (February 1955), pp. 44–48.

9. See Robert Golembiewski, *The Small Group* (Chicago: University of Chicago Press, 1962), p. 157.

10. Golembiewski, p. 170, summarizes the findings concerning size and cohesiveness as follows: "Small size may encourage high (or low) cohesiveness because of the greater intimacy (or unfavorable reaction) possible in smaller units."

11. Schachter manipulated more or less interesting tasks in one of his experiments and found cohesiveness to be associated with interesting or desired activities. Stanley Schachter, "Deviation, Rejection, and Communication," *Journal of Abnormal and Social Psychology*, 46 (Apr. 1951), pp. 190–207. The question here, however, is whether *anything* in the way of club activities could interest the women in the city.

12. The "field of forces" conception of cohesiveness considers attractions outside the group which tend to pull an individual away from it. The greater such attractions for all in the group, the lower will be its cohesiveness. See Golembiewski, pp. 153–155.

13. It is very difficult to unravel which is cause and which effect, but the evidence shows a consistent association between homogeneity and cohesiveness. For example, Festinger, Schachter and Back found that more cohesive courts in a housing project had fewer deviants. See Leon Festinger, Stanley Schachter, and Kurt Back, *Social Pressures in Informal Groups* (New York: Harper, 1950, p. 93).

We have not taken "spread out" to refer to geographic distribution because a hypothesis phrased in such terms is obviously untenable.

Americans in the Scandinavian capital were more scattered yet their club was more cohesive than that in Ciudad Condal.

14. Phillip Fellin and Eugene Litwak, "Neighborhood Cohesion and Mobility," *American Sociological Review,* 28 (June 1963), p. 364.

15. Ibid., pp. 370–376.

16. See, e.g., Murray Hausknecht, *The Joiners* (New York: The Bedminster Press, 1962).

8. Adaptation in a Spanish (Catalan) Setting

1. For a discussion of adaptation, see Dennison Nash, "Adaptation Abroad: Some Considerations," *Boletin: Instituto de Estudios Norte-americanos Barcelona,* X (otoño-invierno 1964), pp. 48–53.

2. Alfred Schutz, "The Stranger: An Essay in Social Psychology," *American Journal of Sociology,* II (May 1944), pp. 499–507; Georg Simmel, in *The Sociology of Georg Simmel* (ed. Kurt Wolff) (Glencoe, Ill.: The Free Press, 1950), pp. 402–406.

3. Ibid., p. 506.

4. The phenomenological point of view suggested by Schutz is being used here. We will be concerned primarily with how a person views himself and his world.

5. The specific point of view being used to describe the stranger's progress here is a variety of "interactionist" theory as set forth, e.g., in Tamotsu Shibutani, *Society and Personality* (Englewood Cliffs, N. J.: Prentice-Hall, 1961).

6. Schutz, loc. cit.

7. For the theoretical basis of this discussion see Dennison Nash and Jerold Heiss, "Sources of Anxiety in Laboratory Strangers," *The Sociological Quarterly,* 8 (Spring 1967), pp. 215–221. The rise and decline of anxiety among strangers is demonstrated in a longitudinal study of Peace Corps volunteers in Colombia by Stein. He reports that "The volunteers were significantly less anxious during training than . . . during their stay in Colombia. But they 'recover' shortly before they leave Colombia. . . ." See M. I. Stein, *Volunteers for Peace* (New York: Wiley, 1966), p. 212.

8. This description of a stranger's progress is similar to Wallace's analysis of the change in personality in situations of acculturation (particularly in nativistic movements). The argument here is that when a person feels "at home," i.e., not like a stranger, he would have

achieved that kind of personal equilibrium which appears to mark the beginning and end of Wallace's acculturation cycle. See Anthony Wallace, *Culture and Personality* (New York: Random House, 1961), pp. 143–163.

9. This distinction between acute and simple *anomie* is derived from Robert Merton, *Social Theory and Social Structure* (*Revised*) (Glencoe, Ill.: The Free Press, 1957), p. 163.

10. Among other things the interviewees were asked to compare themselves and their lives in the city with the last stable period prior to their arrival. Then they were asked to make the same kind of comparison (but in terms of "more," "less," or "the same") for a number of specific traits which were thought to be of special significance for adaptation in this situation. An example of the last type of question is: "Do you feel more, less, or just as much at home here as before you came?"

11. All these people were adult American residents of the city. Although they came from all walks of life they do not constitute a legitimate sample. The ideal-typical stranger biography being developed here cannot be accepted as anything more than a tentative hypothesis about the course of American adaptation in the city.

Because of Small N's it was not possible to use statistical tests for assessing the differences between groups. When we speak about the characteristics of the typical American at a given stage of adaptation we are referring to the majority tendencies in the group of people at that stage. Judgments of trends have been, necessarily, impressionistic.

12. Concerning the hosts and American colleagues, interviewees were asked, "How do the _____ here strike you?"

13. We are following Merton's discussion here, especially in regard to his application of reference group theory to data taken from *The American Soldier*. See Merton, pp. 225–280.

14. We would do well to recall here that individualistic entrepreneurs tended to predominate in the American population. Less self-sufficient organization men such as most of those who worked for large American organizations were in the minority.

15. Paul Fraisse, *The Psychology of Time,* trans. Jennifer Leith (New York: Harper and Row, 1963), p. 14.

16. Edward T. Hall, *The Silent Language* (Greenwich, Conn.: A Premier Book, 1959), p. 132.

17. Under such frustrating conditions one tends to become time-

conscious. Time becomes more valuable and seems to pass more rapidly. This view contrasts with that of Fraisse, p. 205, who says, "In cases of waiting, therefore, an immediate feeling of time being too short is never found." His hypothesis that frustrations make one aware of time and cause it to seem to pass more slowly cannot be reconciled with our own. We would argue that for time-conscious Americans temporal frustrations act in exactly the opposite way.

18. Since the unadapted condition is one of frustration, Fraisse's hypothesis is found wanting in approximately half our cases. In contrast, our hypothesis that the speed of time is a function of the value of one's experience covers *all* unadapted Americans and, as we shall see, the adapted too.

19. Franz Alexander, *Psychosomatic Medicine* (New York: W. W. Norton, 1950), pp. 64-68.

20. Dennison Nash and Alvin Wolfe, "The Stranger in Laboratory Culture," *American Sociological Review*, XXII (August 1957), pp. 400-405; Jerold Heiss and Dennison Nash, "The Stranger in Laboratory Culture Revisited," *Human Organization*, 26 (Spring/Summer 1967), pp. 47-51.

21. We are following Alexander's line of thought as cited above. However no attempt has been made to differentiate kinds of illness as Alexander has done.

22. See Lucien Smith and Andrew Rivers, *Peptic Ulcer* (New York: Appleton-Century-Crofts, 1953), p. 560.

23. Alexander, pp. 101-115.

24. These traits often have been cited as a part of American "national character," if there is such a thing. See, e.g., Mead, *And Keep Your Powder Dry* (New York: Doubleday Anchor Book, 1957).

25. This manifestation corresponds exactly to one of the two psychological mechanisms in Wallace's description of the revitalization process (the other is hysterical conversation). See Wallace, pp. 152-156.

26. We use the term social constriction to refer to the clumping processes referred to earlier (i.e., mainly with family and cliques).

9. Keys to Adaptation

1. In the current struggles for independence of former colonies we see the working out of the last act in the imperialistic transaction. The long-range effect of the imperialistic presence has been to stimulate the

desire for independence. It has caused many agents of imperialism to retire from foreign stages or remain under conditions which drastically reduce their power. See, e.g., the discussion of the "Triple Revolution" in Harlan Cleveland, Gerard Mangone, and John Adams, *The Overseas Americans* (New York: McGraw-Hill, 1960), pp. 5–6. See also P. Mercier, "The European Community in Dakar," in *Africa*, ed. P. Van den Bergh (San Francisco: Chandler, 1965), pp. 283–300.

2. See Cleveland, Mangone, and Adams, pp. 269–281; Robert Textor, ed., *Cultural Frontiers of the Peace Corps* (Cambridge: M.I.T. Press, 1966).

3. William Caudill, "Japanese American Personality and Acculturation," *Genetic Psychology Monographs*, 45 (February 1952), pp. 3–102; Fred L. Strodtbeck, "Family Interaction, Values, and Achievement," in *The Jews*, ed. Marshall Sklare (Glencoe, Ill.: The Free Press, 1958), pp. 147–165.

4. Dennison Nash and Louis Schaw, "Perrsonality and Adaptation in an Overseas Enclave," *Human Organization*, 21 (Winter 1962–63), pp. 259–263.

5. Donald Campbell, "Mutual Methodological Relevance of Anthropology and Psychology," in *Psychological Anthropology*, ed. F. L. K. Hsu (Homewood, Ill.: The Dorsey Press, 1961), p. 341.

6. Cleveland, Mangone, and Adams, pp. 176–180, argue that previous transcultural experience tends to promote cultural empathy and therefore facilitates adaptation abroad. We would be inclined to grant their hypothesis, especially where earlier socialization is concerned, but we have no data concerning this aspect of our informants' backgrounds.

7. We have not included Puerto Rican residents of the city in this discussion because, although officially Americans, they come from a culture which was radically different from that of mainland Americans. The author was not sufficiently acquainted with the Puerto Rican group to attempt any generalizations about them, but they also might qualify as transitional men in this setting.

8. W. I. Thomas, in *Social Behavior and Personality*, ed. E. Volkart (New York: Social Science Research Council, 1951), pp. 158–159.

9. Dennison Nash and Jerold Heiss, "Sources of Anxiety in Laboratory Strangers," *Sociological Quarterly*, 8 (Spring 1967), pp. 215–221.

10. The character is Fielding. See E. M. Forster, *A Passage to India* (New York: Harcourt, Brace and World, 1924).

11. The concept of traditional man is used in Nash and Schaw, p.

260. The philistine type of Thomas corresponds exactly to the concept of traditional man. See Thomas, pp. 159–161.

12. In such enclaves, the problem of adaptation to the foreign environment appears to be handled by contractual agreements between governments and the use of specialized go-betweens. The average member of such a community would not need to adapt to the hosts and their culture in order to survive.

13. It did not appear to repel those artists who either did not require intimate sociability or who were able to establish gratifying associations with the hosts.

14. Nash and Heiss, loc. cit.

15. Friendliness as a component of American national character (if there is such a thing) is emphasized in Riesman's other-directed social character. See David Riesman, *The Lonely Crowd* (New Haven: Yale University Press, 1950).

16. Cleveland, Mangone, and Adams, p. 142.

17. David Palmer, "Expulsion from a Peruvian University," in Robert Textor, pp. 243–270.

18. Cleveland, Mangone, and Adams, pp. 142–149.

19. Thurber, in his survey of Americans in several countries overseas, found this pattern of association. See C. E. Thurber, *The Problem of Training Americans for Service Abroad* (diss., Stanford Univ., 1961), pp. 80–82. Such association may occur not only because more modernized or Americanized hosts are more congenial to Americans, but also because Americans' wealth and prestige enable them to meet and form attachments with predominantly upper status people.

20. This conclusion is based on the testimony of several informants who knew the American patterns of association in three of the largest American enclaves.

21. One transient American was involved in the murder of a Catalan businessman. He and his foreign colleagues-in-murder were apprehended, tried, and sentenced to prison terms. No conspicuous anti-American sentiment was evident during the trial.

22. He encouraged the occasional use of the officially banned Catalan language and the discussion of Catalan culture.

23. Dennison Nash and Alvin Wolfe, "The Stranger in Laboratory Culture," *American Sociological Review*, 22 (Aug. 1957), pp. 400–405.

24. Alfred Schutz was the first to call attention to this phenomenon

in "The Homecomer," *American Journal of Sociology,* 50 (1945), pp. 369–376.

10. *Adaptive Styles*

1. See Harlan Cleveland, Gerard Mangone, and John Adams, *The Overseas Americans* (New York: McGraw-Hill, 1960), pp. 46–63; C. E. Thurber, *The Problem of Training Americans for Service Abroad in U.S. Government Technical Cooperation Programs* (diss., Stanford Univ., 1961), pp. 64–68; *Working Abroad,* Report 41, Group for the Advancement of Psychiatry (New York, Dec. 1958), pp. 493–494.

2. Betty Friedan, *The Feminine Mystique* (New York: W. W. Norton, 1963).

3. Single American women generally found that the city was a very difficult place in which to live, and most American women who were interviewed advised against an unattached woman coming there. The principal problem appeared to be the obstacles in establishing a "respectable" attachment to some man.

4. This and subsequent information about male-female differences was obtained from interviews with adult Americans to which we have referred previously, especially in Chapter 8. Concerning mental activity, for example, 12 males reported an increase in their mental activity since coming to this city, none reported a decrease, and 3 no change. The data for females were: increase, 6, decrease, 7, no change, 7. Although no statistical test was possible, these data appear to constitute a significant difference in male and female reactions to their overseas experience. Impressionistic judgments of significant differences also were used in the other comparisons reported here.

5. E. M. Forster, *A Passage to India* (New York: Harcourt, Brace and World, 1924).

6. Anxiety is considered as a factor in the etiology of alcoholism in John Armstrong, "The Search for the Alcoholic Personality," *The Annals,* 315 (January 1958), pp. 40–47. Those theories of alcoholism which regard increased drinking as a means of coping with alienation-anxiety received a little support from our data. Those women who drank more in the city tended to have lower self-sufficiency scores than those who drank less or showed no change in their drinking habits. The appearance of the unloved or unwanted self may have been an important psychological factor in the American woman's increased drinking.

The scores in self-sufficiency were obtained from an administration of the Saunders Self-Sufficiency Scale. See D. Saunders, *Some Preliminary Interpretive Materials for the P. R. I.,* Educational Testing Service (Princeton, October 1955).

7. Our argument is related to the conceptual scheme developed by R. F. Bales. He considered three classes of factors to be associated with the onset of alcoholism: (1) anxiety or conflict-producing factors, e.g., strangerhood, (2) culturally supportive attitudes, e.g., the cocktail circuit, and (3) an absence of anxiety-reducing alternatives. See R. F. Bales, "Cultural Differences in Rates of Alcoholism," *Quarterly Journal of Studies on Alcohol,* 6 (March 1946), pp. 400–499.

8. See Jerome Bruner and Leo Postman, "Emotional Selectivity in Perception and Reaction," *Journal of Personality,* 16 (September 1947), pp. 69–77.

9. The three types of adaptive character were developed by Thomas during his consideration of personality under changing social conditions. They reflect two basic human attitudes: "the desire for new experience" and "the desire for stability." See W. I. Thomas, in *Social Behavior and Personality,* ed. E. Volkart, Social Science Research Council (New York, 1951), pp. 162–163. Thomas' typology, which is universalistic, may be applied to any people subject to changing social conditions. We use it rather than some more particularistic scheme in order to facilitate more extensive comparisons.

The data for these histories were obtained from interviews and were supplemented in some cases by observations.

10. Ibid., p. 159.

11. Erickson, in many of his writings, points out that adolescence is a time for trying out identities. See, e.g., E. H. Erickson, "The Problem of Ego Identity," *Journal of the American Psychoanalytic Association,* 4 (January 1956), pp. 56–121.

12. If a personnel manager had given her the Tolerance of Ambiguity and Self-Sufficiency Scales which she completed for the anthropologist, he would have been able to appraise her as a creative person and to predict her successful adaptation in the city. Mrs. J., by scoring high on both scales, revealed herself as tolerant of the ambiguity inherent in any foreign encounter and able to pass through a period of loneliness or social alienation without difficulty.

The scales, which have had some predictive value in the laboratory, were applied selectively to Americans in the city. Because of the variation in situational factors affecting American strangers there, they turned out to have only a limited predictive value for adaptation. For information about these scales and their application, see Dennison Nash and Jerold Heiss, "Sources of Anxiety in Laboratory Strangers," *Sociological Quarterly,* 8 (Spring 1967).

13. Cleveland, Mangone, and Adams, pp. 28–29.

14. Thomas, p. 159.

15. Ibid.

16. Ibid., p. 158.

17. The concept of perceptual defense is explained and applied in Bruner and Postman, pp. 142–154.

18. A closely related, nearly identical, scheme of adaptive types is that of Bennett, Passin, and McKnight. Using a large battery of measuring devices, they identified three kinds of Japanese overseas scholars in America: the "Constrictor" (philistine), "Idealist" (creative man), and "Adjustor" (bohemian). See John Bennett, H. Passin, and R. McKnight, *In Search of Identity: The Japanese Overseas Scholar in America* (Minneapolis: University of Minnesota Press, 1958).

19. Forster, loc. cit.

11. *The World View of a Stranger Community*

1. See, e.g., Stanley R. Mohler, "Fatigue in Aviation Activities," *Aerospace Medicine,* 37 (July 1966), pp. 722–732.

2. We are following Redfield's usage of the term world view, i.e., "the way a people characteristically looks outward upon the universe." See Robert Redfield, *The Primitive World and Its Transformations* (Ithaca: Cornell University Press, 1953), p. 85. In our terms this is the same as a collective frame of reference or subjective world. We are not here attempting to describe the complete world view of a community, but rather only that part which is especially significant for the role of stranger.

3. In short, the expatriate community may become a reference group which provides a conventionalized outlook for the newcomer. This outlook, once acquired, serves as a mediating link between the stranger and the foreign setting. An intensive examination of the stranger group as a reference group may be found in S. N. Herman and E. O. Schild, "The Stranger Group in a Cross-Cultural Situation," *Sociometry,* 24 (March 1961), pp. 165–176.

4. This view conforms to our previous use of the term, frame of reference, and to Redfield who says, "In every world view there is an 'I' from which the view is taken." Redfield, p. 86.

5. E. T. Hall, *The Silent Language* (New York: Premier Books, 1963), p. 149. An empirical demonstration of the differences between American and Arab cultures in conceptions of private body space may be found in O. M. Watson and T. Graves, "Quantitative Research in Proxemic Behavior," *American Anthropologist,* 68 (August 1966), pp. 971–985. This difference appears to be similar to that between the American and host culture in Ciudad Condal.

6. We do not mean to claim, of course, that the hosts in the city were the only ones who, in the eyes of Americans in Europe, "pushed and shoved" either on foot or in motor vehicles.

7. The bank on the street of business which was favored by the majority of Americans in the city.

8. The importance of the home town as a point of orientation for the highly mobile Americans is emphasized in Margaret Mead, *And Keep Your Powder Dry* (New York: William Morrow, 1942), pp. 27–35.

9. Hall's discussion of the American conception of time includes the cyclical, or periodic, and the linear, or nonperiodic, concepts. See Hall, pp. 19–21, 131–132.

10. Of 35 Americans who provided adequate information, 22 said that time passed more rapidly in the city than at home.

11. None of the 37 Americans who provided adequate information said that they were more concerned with punctuality in the city; 19 said that they were less concerned; and 18 reported that there had been no change in concern since their arrival.

12. See Hall, p. 20.

13. Most of their converts had until then been from the working classes.

14. Like a primitive society, this community possessed no written cultural heritage. Its history, therefore, was no longer than the memory of its members, most of whom had been in the city for less than four years.

15. Henry James, *The American* (New York: Hall, Rinehart, and Winston, 1949).

16. Thomas Sterling, "On Being Foreign," *Holiday,* Apr. 1966, p. 18.

17. Of 35 who provided adequate information, 20 said that they were more concerned with feeling cold in the city than at home, one said that he was less concerned, and 14 reported no difference in preoccupation. (Women were more likely to report an increased preoccupation with the cold than men.)

18. The importance of the tour and of the leave in the thinking of English people abroad is suggested in R. E. S. Tanner, "Conflict Within Small European Communities in Tanganyika," *Human Organization,* 24 (Winter 1964), pp. 319–327.

19. Various newspaper accounts, for example, have suggested that the end of the tour is the most important temporal point of reference for American military men in Vietnam.

20. This outlook may be contrasted with an immigrant community which is not oriented to a time of departure for home.

21. The *Courier* was required by law to employ hosts and to submit copies to relevant departments of the local and national governments.

22. Some Americans had reservations about the direction of change in the host society. They saw in the Americanization of Spain the disappearance of some of the prerogatives they had come to value.

23. E. M. Forster, *A Passage to India* (New York: Harcourt, Brace and World, 1924), pp. 41–42.

24. See Chapter 8.

25. These prophets were religious men acting on the part of subordinate peoples. See, e.g., Anthony F. C. Wallace, "Revitalization Movements," *American Anthropologist,* 58 (April 1956), pp. 264–281. The Americans in Ciudad Condal were not very religious. Neither were they a clearly subordinate people.

12. *The Overseas Community and the Imperialistic Process*

1. Harlan Cleveland, Gerard Mangone, and John Adams, *The Overseas Americans* (New York: McGraw-Hill, 1960), pp. 123–149.

2. In Talcott Parsons' view, every social system must handle the problem of adaptation to the external world. Adaptation, therefore, may be termed one of the "functional prerequisites" of a social system. See Talcott Parsons, *The Social System* (Glencoe, Ill.: The Free Press, 1951). If we were to relate our analysis to Parsons' scheme, we would

say that the overseas community's adaptive problem is *uniquely* concerned with the encounter with the foreign and the potential experience of stranger *anomie.*

3. This problem is treated by Le Carré in several novels which, according to him, constitute a realistic treatment of the spy game as it is played today. See, e.g., John Le Carré, *The Looking Glass War* (New York: Dell, 1965).

4. See John Fayerweather, "Selecting and Training Executives for Foreign Trade," in *Dartnell International Trade Handbook,* ed. L. L. Lewis (Chicago: The Dartnell Corporation, 1965), pp. 587–605.

5. See, e.g., T. R. Brennen and F. X. Hodgson, *Overseas Management* (New York: McGraw-Hill, 1965), pp. 30–81; Thomas Maretzki, "Transition Training: A Theoretical Approach," *Human Organization,* 24 (Summer 1965), pp. 128–134.

6. See Cleveland, Mangone, and Adams, pp. 168–188; Fayerweather, loc. cit.

7. William Lederer and Eugene Burdick, *The Ugly American* (New York: W. W. Norton, 1958), pp. 223–240.

8. William Whyte, Jr., *The Organization Man* (New York: Simon and Schuster, 1956).

9. Cleveland, Mangone, and Adams, pp. 150–167.

10. Francis C. Byrnes, *Americans in Technical Assistance* (New York: Praeger, 1965), pp. 71–78.

11. Cleveland, Mangone, and Adams, pp. 157–167. The Cornell Peru Project used this criterion as an index of the effectiveness of Peace Corps volunteers. See Henry Dobyns, Paul Doughty, and Allan Holmberg, *Peace Corps Program Impact in the Peruvian Andes* (Ithaca: Cornell Peru Project, 1966), pp. 483–599.

12. John Useem, "Work Patterns of Americans in India," *The Annals,* 368 (November 1966), p. 148.